More Praise for *May I Have Your Attention, Please?*

"Give Chris Hilicki your attention and she'll give you something priceless: the ability to discover and live your true story. She not only helped me tap into the core essence of my publishing company, she helped me tap into the core essence of my personal story. My brand—and my life—are the richer for it."

—Allen Arnold, Senior Vice President and Publisher,
WestBow Press, A Division of Thomas Nelson, Inc.

"A few years ago, Chris set out to build a children's book company and created a powerful brand recognized and adored by children and parents across America. Along the way, she discovered and nurtured her own 'personal brand identity'—a feat that served to catapult her career and contribute to a high level of personal satisfaction. **Chris' 'true story' approach to branding is compelling and motivational. At last we have a unique branding strategy with insight and advice to empower us on both a personal and a professional level."**

—Yvonne Martin Kidd, Director, Marketing and
Communications, Vanderbilt Owen Graduate
School of Management

"Chris Hilicki has written a profoundly human business book that urges each of us to be aware of ourselves as brands. Whether we know it or not, we all stand for something in the eyes of others. Our 'reputations' account for only part of this, for that term too narrowly reflects the rational side of our natures. Our personal brand identities encompass reputation, but also the deeper symbols and values we embody and that frame our social personas. Chris Hilicki's enormously warm and readable book reminds us that we are the ones responsible for constructing and shaping this social persona—our personal brands. It is not just Oprah Winfrey and Bill Gates who create their own personal brands—it is each of us. In awareness of this lies unique power and freedom. **In the venerable American tradition of the motivational guide, *May I Have Your Attention, Please?* is sure to be worthwhile for readers at all stages of their careers."**

—Scott McDonald, Ph.D., Senior Vice President,
Research, Condé Nast Publications

"Me? A brand? Are you kidding? *May I Have Your Attention, Please?* makes us realize that not only do our own experiences greatly impact who we are, they create an impression in others' minds that we can call our personal 'brand.' The unique history and character of a corporate organization is the true basis for a brand, much more than just a logo. Chris Hilicki persuades us to thoughtfully take the time to analyze and rebuild our own brands. By sharing her extraordinary personal and professional experiences, **Chris reveals the secrets to what truly sets brands apart.** This book helps us all realize that shining a light on what makes us different is the essential first step to creating a powerful brand. **Read it and get started on your journey to success!**"
— Theresa Reagan, Executive Director,
 Children's Health Education Center, Wisconsin
 Children's Hospital

"After reading Hilicki's book I realize I have been studying the most powerful branders in the world—babies. Babies do just what Hilicki says a brander should do: Their stories are short, incredibly clear, unapologetically attention getting, and, most important, authentic and unique. Hilicki does something for us that babies can't do. She tells us how to discover our own story. **She gives each of us ways to discover our authentic *me* and genuinely make others a part of our story. When people experience our story they will feel thrilled to know, share, and be connected to us,** just like with babies. So, when you read this book you risk becoming a baby, but the benefit is making yourself into a unique brand."
— Ed Tronick, Chief of the Child Development Unit,
 Associate Professor of Pediatrics and Psychiatry,
 Harvard Medical School

"**Chris Hilicki has put together a great resource for every CEO and company that wants to define and improve their brand.** Each of us, whether as individuals or as organizations, has a story that must be told. Chris helps us create the chapters that immediately bring the brand to a better life."
— Kevin E. Dunn, Former USA Division President,
 McDonald's Corporation

May I Have Your Attention, Please?

Build a Better Business by Telling Your True Story

Chris Hilicki

WILEY

John Wiley & Sons, Inc.

Dedicated to Rich, for loving me just the way I am

For general information about our other products and services, please contact our
Customer Care Department within the United States at 800-762-2974, outside the
United States at 317-572-3993 or fax 317-572-4002.

Wiley also publishes its books in a variety of electronic formats. Some content that
appears in print may not be available in electronic books. For more information about
Wiley products, visit our web site at www.wiley.com.

Library of Congress Cataloging-in-Publication Data:
Hilicki, Chris.
    May I have your attention, please? : build a better business by telling your true
story / Chris Hilicki.
        p.   cm.
    ISBN 0-471-67889-9 (cloth)
    1. Success in business.   2. Self-actualization (Psychology)   I. Title.
    HF5386.H52 2005
    658.8'27—dc22
2004016913

Printed in the United States of America.

10 9 8 7 6 5 4 3 2 1

Contents

Attention for Better or Worse ■ The Relationship between
Attention and Brands ■ How to Use This Book ■ What Do
You Want to Be When You Grow Up? ■ The Time for Truth Has
Truly Come ■ True Stories Can't Be Copied ■ Unlock Your
Identity and Lock onto Your Brand ■ Branding Is All about
Stories and Storytelling ■ What Do You Call Attention? ■
Attention and Humility Can Coexist ■ A Higher Rung on the
Ladder of Success ■ What Does Sharing Your Story Mean?

Brands Matter. Brands Matter. Brands Matter. ■ To Matter You
Must Be Original. To Be Original You Must Find Yourself ■ Who

Foreword

I may still be discovering who I am as each new day passes, but this much I know for sure: I'm not normal. I never did blend in and never wanted to. But I knew I wanted to be a speaker and storyteller. So I left college to continue to be the person I knew I was. I wouldn't settle for becoming something I wasn't, even if it would have been easier.

As Chris Hilicki's book illustrates, we all have important stories that make us memorable and allow us to relate to each other. What a privilege it has been for me to tell stories. I have been blessed to author more than 10 books, including a *New York Times* bestseller, *The Traveler's Gift*, which has been translated into almost 20 languages. I was honored to have spoken at the request of four different presidents of the United States, CEOs, celebrities, dignitaries, U.S. troops fighting for our freedom, and millions of other individuals throughout the world.

Throughout my career I've done things differently. Instead of following the crowd or going along with what various managers and agents had done for others, I held on to the values and decisions that I believed would be best for me. Why? Because the experiences I'd had throughout my life developed beliefs and subsequent business strategies that were unique to me. Somehow I knew what worked for others wouldn't be best for me. It might get me into business and create some success, but not the kind I envisioned. Now, Chris Hilicki explains in her book the reasons why this is so.

What belief do Chris and I have in common? Simply this: Be yourself and you'll achieve the ultimate success. This is more than a belief—it's a profound principle. It may be harder and it may even take longer, but it will take you higher and farther than will following the paths of others. It will make a difference in your own personal success as well as in every life that you touch. And, as my book *The Lost Choice* illustrates, if you touch even one life today (or don't), you can affect millions of lives for the rest of eternity.

What I've learned and continue to learn from Chris's book is the value of authenticity. This concept resonates with one of my all-time favorite movies, *The Legend of Bagger Vance*, where the mystical golf caddy, Bagger, helps the young, spiritually lost golfer, Rannulph Junuh, rediscover his one, true, "authentic swing."

When I met Chris several years ago, she was already a respected brand builder. Dinner at her house was more than lasagna. It was a quiz on the difference between Coca-Cola and Pepsi products. Today Chris is recognized around the nation as the architect of great brands. Her recognition is based on her amazing ability to help us achieve our desired level of success through building our unique brand, based on the true stories that lie within each of us.

Chris understands the power of an individual's life stories in developing a successful brand. In my book *The Traveler's Gift*, you are taken on a journey that leads you to discovering the "seven decisions that determine success." *May I Have Your Attention, Please?* will help you realize that all the knowledge and ability to make decisions doesn't matter if you don't understand who you are and where you come from. As you read this book you will learn how to look within yourself to tap the life experiences that made you who you are today. Then you will learn how to leverage those experiences into a brand that can be the foundation for making powerful decisions. This will give you a competitive edge that can never be lost or copied.

A powerful brand is becoming increasingly important as globalization continues. The potential customer base is growing quickly, but the number of companies vying for its business is growing even faster. A powerful, unique brand brings instant recognition to your company and the product or service you provide.

Whether you are the CEO of a major corporation, a professional athlete, a graduating student about to embark on the journey of life, or the owner of a local store, a powerful brand will give you an edge over those who are competing for your clients, your recognition, your job, or your business. If you want your endeavors to make a difference, Chris's book will explain how to make it happen.

This book fulfills two functions that blend together to create a seamless adventure and achievable results plan. It teaches you how to unleash the unique stories and experiences of your past and how to recognize the values you have developed as a result of your experiences. You'll find value in your factual experiences like never before. The book also provides a hard-core, brand-building guideline that helps create immediate improvement and success in life. Taken as a whole, the book blazes a path and lays a solid foundation upon which any brand can be built and maintained.

As an author, I believe in the power of books—they provide entertainment, ideas, or inspiration. It is rare that all three elements are combined in one book, but Chris delivers the total package and more. This is a practical and proven guide that anyone can use, with no two people or companies following the same path or achieving identical results.

The measurable business success you will gain is reason enough to read these pages, but the greater purpose and message is that of unlocking the power of the unique experiences and stories within you. The results are astonishing enough, but the *journey* is the reason you should read this book. It is a pathway everyone should take who desires a successful business as well as a happy life. You will gain the resolve to never again believe that it can't be done—and from this book forward, you will forever say to yourself, "This, too, is an opportunity to add to my treasure chest of stories and success!"

Andy Andrews
Orange Beach, Alabama

Preface

How can I be sure that my influence on this world will improve my life and the lives of those around me? This is a question I ask myself every day. Every day I need to learn and to grow in my personal and professional life. As this book explains, returning to the basics of self-examination builds compelling, influential brands.

We all have a brand, whether we realize it or not. Whether you are considering your organization or yourself as an individual, your brand is what people think of you. You might be referring to your brand as your image, your reputation, or the impression you make on the world. Whatever you call it, it is the reason you attract attention and why people give you attention. With the right kind of attention you can make a powerful impact on the world. The attention I'm talking about isn't what you get for standing onstage or about thinking you're the center of the universe (or even the cocktail party or board meeting). It comes in many forms, from essential self-respect, a thoughtful word from your boss, good service at a restaurant, being chosen for the team, or a successful sales call to the obvious applause and awards some envy—and some deserve. If you go through the process discussed in this book, you will uncover the secret to your personal and professional identity that will be the cornerstone of your brand.

This book is not just a business tool. It is a plan for life fulfillment. Fulfillment comes from being authentic and genuine even though it may be uncomfortable at first. You can define success in terms of fame and wealth, but it is that and more when you follow the process I've illustrated herein. Financial, emotional, and spiritual success can be gained as soon as you begin. However you define your success, it is critical that you feel fulfilled and satisfied, or you will be chasing a dream that can't be caught.

I ask myself, "What do people think of me and what impression am I leaving?" not because I care about their approval or need it in order to feel better about myself. I ask because I care about the results that I want in life. If I want successful results then I need to see how my presence affects people. Does it bring them to action as I hope? The way my presence, or even the thought of it, makes people feel is my brand. Good brand identities don't just happen. They are built.

A competitive edge depends on getting attention, but the best strategy is to get it the right way and then use it for the best purpose. That includes returning the attention back to the world for even greater good.

Ten years ago I had been building my personal and professional brand in all the wrong ways. If you asked me then what my brand was, I would have answered, "Anything you want it to be." I was seemingly very successful in life because I was able to figure out what my business, boss, friends, and husband wanted me to be and then I could become it. I almost always got the guy, the promotions, and the attention, but not necessarily for the right reasons. I typically modeled myself after other people's success and tried to do what they did.

This strategy shaped me into a successful person or company by *their* definition—not mine. If they were successful, then I thought I could be just as successful if I did what they did, looked how they looked, and sounded how they sounded. It's not that I wanted to be them as much as I wanted what they had. But deep inside, I knew there had to be a better way.

Many people go through life trying to be like the other guy for all kinds of reasons, and sometimes without even realizing what they're doing. Some do this because they don't know who they are or, if they do, they don't like who they are. Others are afraid that the world wouldn't like them if they were their true selves, so they conform to what the world says they should be.

I came to realize that most of us just don't know how to be ourselves. When we're young we are pressured with questions and instructions about what we're going to be when we grow up. The world expects us to grow, but it doesn't teach us how to hang on to the essence of who we are. Between peer pressure, role models, and training seminars, we could turn into anything.

From the time we are little children, we are asked by good-intentioned parents, teachers, and neighbors, "Who do you want to be when you grow up?" No one ever answers, "Me." Without realizing it, we try to become just like the other guy or the other company. Even as we proclaim to love individuality, we copy and imitate each other to get what we want. Often the hardest thing to do in life is to be ourselves. I'm not opposed to using the clues that successful companies and individuals leave for us, as long as we use them to uncover what is unique about ourselves.

I have been blessed and lucky to have experienced accomplishment and achievement in my young life. I traveled around the world as a scientist turned marketing executive, and became the president of a national leading children's publisher by age 38. I was respected for my opinion and work before I turned 40. Then, sick with a complicated medical condition, including cancer and a rare autonomic dysfunction disease, I had a little time on my hands to consider my life's strategy.

I had a chance to evaluate what my success was based on and how far it could take me in this world. I grasped that there was another rung on the ladder of success. I realized that emulating other people's success could only take me so far. My boss, Mr. Harold Anderson, a role model for me, often pointed to a plaque on his desk that quoted Kipling. To paraphrase, Kipling said that people can copy all they can copy, but they can't copy your mind. I understood this to mean that the ultimate competitive advantage in life is to use your mind to be original, not to copy. Be the real thing. Stop trying to be like the other guy. Stop trying to blend in when you were meant to stand out.

I'm honored to have helped build a successful publishing company with a brand. I use branding strategies to translate the unique and powerful brands of characters into books. I know how to create a look and feel that cannot be copied by our competitors. Everything else, such as pricing strategies, distribution practices, colors, textures, and special effects, can be copied. But the true and original stories that make up a brand can't be copied. Why not apply the same strategy to myself?

Being authentic will give us a competitive advantage in life. Our authenticity is the only thing that we alone possess. It is woven through the experiences and true events (stories) of our lives. No one else has had them. When we examine them and learn how to tell them, we can translate them into a powerful brand identity that the world will relate to, remember, and be loyal to. This will create influence and move people to take the kind of action we want for the betterment of everyone's life. That's the power of a brand.

I know how hard it is to be yourself. But until you master this, your success will be fleeting, inferior, or artificial. Brands matter in life. Brands have real value in our personal and professional lives because they influence people and move them to action. And the best brands are based on the truth. Nothing makes a connection like the truth. The true experiences you and your company or organization have had are your competitive edge. This book will tell you how to use them and to obtain the results you want.

Many people and organizations have used my unique brand building process to build better businesses and lives. If, by the time you finish this book, you are excited about being your true self because you see the value and power of it, then you've done well and are on your way to standing out in a world that loves to clone.

Be your true self and be your best self, and you will have unlimited success of every kind. The test of your true self is not who you have been and what you have done. It is the belief in who you are and what you can do.

Acknowledgments

More than just acknowledging, I am grateful and indebted for these important influences in my life. This book is another chapter in the complete story of my life. Without God and these people I would not be living so happily ever after. I thank:

- God, the best brand and the ultimate original story.
- My husband, Rich Hilicki, who leaves the window open for me to fly high and fly home—my faithful companion in life and love.
- My loving parents, Mary Joanne VanCronkhite and "Van" Cronkhite, who ground me\ in who I am and help me be who I'm supposed to be.
- My dear family, Cyndie Verbeten, Tess Fries, Mary Palen, Bev Mantey-VanCronkhite, Vickie Schultz, Tammy, Jodie, and my brother Bryant VanCronkhite, and the entire VanCronkhite and Hilicki family, who love me unconditionally, never give up on me, and always root for me to win.
- Theresa Reagan, who deserves more than it is possible to suitably express—my thanks for all her love and support through the years.
- My "Impossible Journey" team: Robert Smith, Andy Andrews, Scott Jeffrey, Jared McDaniel, Chip VanCronkhite, Mike and Gail Hyatt, Misty Williams, and Adam Black—your wisdom and hard

work are what success is made of. Your love and dedication are what make success worthwhile.

- My PR guy, Dick Gersh, who believed in me as much as I believed in myself.

- My editor, Pam van Giessen, who took a chance on me and guided me patiently and brilliantly, and her assistant, Jennifer MacDonald.

- Harold Anderson, who encouraged me to be true to myself and explore a new kind of professional success.

- Everyone at Dalmatian Press and Anderson Press, past and present: my training ground for reality.

- My associates at Western Publishing who hired me, taught me, and pushed me forward, and even those who held me back and thereby strengthened me.

- Ben and Judy Fein, the greatest example of strength, compassion, intelligence, and love all married together and living happily ever after.

- My doctors, who believed in healing the whole person and who didn't give up, especially Al Andrews, Dr. Rebecca Anderson, Dr. Doug Brown, Dr. Michael Ebert, Dr. Pamela Ingram, Dr. Jim Jirjis, Dr. Rogelio Mosqueda, Dr. David Robertson, Dr. Bonnie Slovis, and Dr. Norman Solomon.

- Ernie Reynolds, who taught me how to grow everything better, including myself.

- My foundation of friends, who helped live, believe in, and respect our true stories, including John Appuhn, Kathi Atha, Jean Bauer, Janet Bernberg, Linda Bruchert, Lisa Dillman, Barb Dumke, Jerry East, Marie Egeland, Susie and Emma Garland, Jeff Germanotta, Roger Gilmore, Ira Gomberg, Megan Hyatt, Mary Kay Lee, Rbin and Suzanne Lovette and the twins, John McDowell, Paul and Chryl Sallomi, Stan and Nancy Mitchell, Charmaine Nilles, Ben and Jackie Peters, Karen Schwenke, Nancy Steingard, and Patrick Yun.

- Everyone with whom I have lived on this earth to create true stories and powerful life-changing experiences in preparation for the eternal life.

Part ONE

Believe in the Brand

Chapter ONE

Everyone Needs a Little Attention, Brands Need a Lot

*Getting people to like you is simply the
other side of liking other people.*
—Norman Vincent Peale (1898–1993)[1]

Attention for Better or Worse

From the day we are born we cry out for it. Without it our needs aren't met. We learn to make all the right faces, noises, and gestures to bring us attention and improve the quality of our life, and this continues throughout our lives. By the time we are grown up we may object to the idea that we need attention. It makes us sound so desperate, and it goes against popular advice to keep our ego in check. So we replace the word *attention* with *respect* and *recognition*. But whatever you want to call it, it's still attention. And it's okay to want it and need it because it can make your life better or worse. It's *how* we get it that's the key to life's happiness, and it's *what* we do with it that can make us successful in life.

The Relationship between Attention and Brands

We get attention because of what people think of us. Whether we are concerned about our personal image or the identity of our corporation or organization, we are talking about our brand identity. Where is your brand identity now?

This book is about building a better business based on how you share your genuine identity. Whether you are developing your personal image or your Fortune 500 corporate brand, the best strategy is the same: Build it on the truth and on your true experiences.

Whether you are a college graduate beginning to embark on a new career or a middle manager striving to improve himself and the influence he has in his company, the process starts at the same point: Be yourself. Stop trying to be like the other guy.

Whether you are just now learning the meaning of the world of branding or are charged with protecting your entire corporation's brand value, it starts here and now. Know yourself and you'll know how far you can go.

How to Use This Book

This book provides the two essential elements that everyone who invests in self-improvement understands. Part I describes the theory, philosophy, and a little psychology about brand building, and Part II outlines a practical process with steps for immediate application in your plans for success.

The chapters contain numerous examples that illustrate and analyze how other individuals and businesses have built brands. Everyone is different, which is why we are all able to build unique brands. But this means that the examples are just that—merely examples. To use this brand/image-building process, you have to get underneath these brand examples and understand this brand theory. When you follow the steps and answer the questions, if you're doing it correctly you will come up with a unique brand identity.

The basic process of building a better brand has three steps:

1. Know your own true stories, experiences, and life-changing events in your personal or professional life.
2. Determine what's important to you based on your stories. This will reveal your values and beliefs.
3. Translate these values into a corresponding look, sound, and feel that no one else can copy, because it's *your* story, not theirs. This will result in your authentic and unique brand that gives you the competitive edge in life for greater success—no matter how you define it.

The work required to examine, analyze, and define your true story and values from your experiences can be done alone or within the context of a group where responsible people help you ask and answer questions. Many of the questions you'll need are in this book. Take your time and answer them. Later on you can answer them again because your answers may be braver, more honest, or different. Enjoy the process.

The translation of your unique values and authentic identity into your brand identity can be done with the help of the many examples given herein. Follow the logic behind the case examples to your own brand conclusion. Just as a skilled musician can hear a melody and know how to perfectly rearrange it, or a surgeon can look at a body and know how to repair damage, building a better brand takes training and knowledge as well as a lot of experience and talent. Don't be discouraged if, after you've defined your true stories and values, you can't immediately translate them into your brand image. By the end of the book you'll catch on. The key is to keep asking if your brand's expression in every form is accurately conveying the true you. Enjoy the results.

What Do You Want to Be When You Grow Up?

From the time we dress up in our mother's costume jewelry or our dad's hat and big shoes, we are faced with the question, "What do you want to be when you grow up?" Nobody ever answers, "Me." I can remember teachers, neighbors, and job interviewers asking me the very question I wanted them to answer for me. Well-intentioned or just curious, they leaned over toward me and asked me what I didn't yet know: "Who do you want to be?"

From early on, we pretend and we copy. We deal with personal peer pressure, professional image-makers, and brand consultants. We create identities for ourselves and for our companies. And by doing so, we have created a world of brands.

Just being "me" is both the easiest and the hardest thing to do. For many people, it's a lot easier to be like the other guy. From the day we send our children to school, they are caught up in trying to become more like their little friends. They want to fit in, to feel comfortable, and to be liked. Some things never change: Most of us want to fit in as adults, too, even when we are meant to stand out.

These days, people are into building their images, otherwise referred to as *branding*. In today's world, where we are assaulted with world-class brands everywhere we turn, it is an easy leap to understand that people have personal brands just as businesses have corporate brands. Brands matter. Brands matter because they can get the results you want in life.

Developing your brand can help you get where you want to go in life. If you want to go on to greater professional success, fame, and fortune, then you need to improve your brand identity. But if you want to like yourself more and become more satisfied with your relationships, then you need to improve your brand identity all the more.

Current branding strategies mostly work the same, creating brands that copy other brands. This doesn't result in unique brands or authenticity. A brand must be unique and authentic to be lasting and powerful.

The Time for Truth Has Truly Come

We need a brand-new way to think about brands in our lives. The best brands aren't what you think. The best brands are based on true stories about your real-life experiences. It sounds simple, doesn't it? "Just be yourself." Well, if it is so simple why don't we do it? Could it be that we don't believe that being ourselves can result in more success, happiness, and satisfaction? A friend of mine used to say, "Whenever I feel bad about myself, I feel better if I can blame it on someone else." Is that why we look at others who seem to have it all and think, "If I'm just more like them, I'll have what they have"?

Authentic brands make a different promise. They turn the promise of an abundant life into the *practice*. The most successful people have an identity that is founded on authentic, true-life stories. These kinds of identities garner the kind of attention from others that simply makes life better. Identities that are based on authentic, actual experiences create brands that can positively influence the world. That kind of influence makes your life matter. And we all want to matter in life, don't we?

I believe that branding is ultimately all about stories and storytelling. A brand is essentially like the bare-bones plot of a longer story. The best brands are based on the true stories of our experiences, filled with the human qualities that we can all relate to and believe in. To claim a brand, you have to make the connection between yourself and your world. Whether you're an individual or a corporation, you must make this connection. And nothing connects like the truth. It is the only thing that we can all relate to and accept.

The corporate world is learning the hard way that building a false image is not the right way to create a brand. Big corporate images that were previously hot have suddenly gone up in flames. Such world-class corporate logos as Enron and WorldCom are now remembered as En-Wrong and World-Con. Organizations spent too much money rolling out images with splashy logos and seductive ad campaigns that required us to have the sleuthing powers of Columbo. And, like Columbo, we discovered that they were lying.

For years, the practice of corporate branding has been used to create a lasting image and to demonstrate power and size. Corporations and organizations create designs for hot-air balloons, parades, credit cards, and clothing. And individuals wear the sweatshirt, use the credit card, and wave the flag to become associated with the images or to try to become what they promise. But is that what branding is—logos and merchandise and new corporate profit centers?

Forget about the image. Branding is not based on mere appearance. The best brands are based on the true stories and authentic experiences that only you have had. Behold who you truly are and become what you see; that's your brand. Branding is not a logo or a musical jingle. Branding is about influence. And there is nothing more influential than the truth.

What does this have to do with you? You may not believe it yet, but you have a story of your own that is true and powerful and the foundation for your success. It's your powerful brand identity.

The concept of a brand being based on truth is an idea whose time has truly come. There is a connection between the corporate brand and the personal brand, a connection that has never been stronger, tighter, or closer. That connection is truth. When we build personal brands on our true stories, we get the best results, both personally and professionally. Best of all, we have respect for ourselves, which gives us a sense of value and importance that will affect everything we do for the rest of our lives.

True Stories Can't Be Copied

We love true stories, don't we? We can't help reading the juicy headlines while waiting in line at the store. We love to hear what Paul Harvey calls "the rest of the story." Television is filled with reality TV, where audiences tune in to see what really happens, live and unrehearsed. Biographies and autobiographies are best-sellers. We love true stories, especially when they relate experiences of uncompromised success, overcoming of obstacles, and beating the odds.

Everyone has a true story of his or her own. Our stories, which are our experiences, shape our values for life. And when you learn to put words to your unique story, you can use it and the values you've developed to define you in a way that no one can copy. When you build your brand identity on your true experiences, you will bring to the world the only thing that no one else can.

More than what you look like or what you do, or even the gifts and talents you possess, you have something that no one else can compete with or build success on. You have had experiences that no one else has had. To the extent that a brand must be unique and special to influence behavior, you've got it. You've got a brand that will be as special and influential as Oprah or Steven Spielberg. You've got a related corporate brand as promising as Harpo Productions and Dreamworks. Like them, you can build your brand on the true stories of your personal experiences that only you can share.

Too many brands start at the wrong end of the equation. They decide who or what they want to be and then set out to become just that. This is a book about building your brand by starting from the other end of that equation. In fact, at the outset, I ask you to consider that the end result of building your brand identity is the *second* thing you consider, not the first.

Take a moment and take the pressure off yourself. Trust in this process and you will discover who you are meant to become based on who has been uniquely created. Remember, only after you define who you are can you consider what you want to become. Start figuring out who you really are. When you know who you are you can figure out who you want to become. You'll know what you're made of and see what you're capable of. See. Believe. Go for it.

You have your very own individual brand identity. Whether you are 18 years old and leaving home, a middle manager seeking advancement, a retiree entering a new stage of your life, or somewhere in between, you are dependent on having a strong, powerful brand identity that gets you the right kind of attention for the right kind of results you have dreamed of.

If you are a Fortune 500 CEO and want to set yourself apart, be more memorable, and build loyalty, you need a better kind of brand in order to compete. If you are at a turning point in your life and taking stock of your life's ups and downs, you need to take control of your personal brand identity. In a world in which we wear other people's brands as easily as pulling a sweatshirt over our heads, we forget that we have our own special, unique fingerprint that creates an identity to build and value.

Unlock Your Identity and Lock onto Your Brand

Inside all of us are things that should be uncovered, polished, and refined for the world to see. And these things should not just be seen but should be shown off in a way that tells the world we are valuable. These things are our essence. They are our treasures. Let me say right now that these things are the very things that we typically hide. We keep this stuff hidden or buried. We masquerade and pretend to be what we are not, because we're afraid that if our real identity is discovered, no one will like us or we will fail. Worse yet, we're afraid we won't like ourselves.

In 1960 a high school boy named Frank Abagnale ran away from home when his parents divorced. He vowed to reunite them by regaining what his dad had lost in business. With only $25 in his checking account he became an expert at pretending to be whoever he thought would live up to his dad's expectations. Along the way he masqueraded as a pilot, a pediatrician, and an attorney. Steven Spielberg, Tom Hanks, and Leonardo DiCaprio captured this story in a 2002 blockbuster movie about a boy who wouldn't live his own life. It was called *Catch Me If You Can*. He, like many of us, lived a series of other people's lives because he was afraid that his true self wasn't adequate.

Every day we read about people who have been pretending to be someone they are not. We find out that they have falsified their college records and created diplomas on their home graphic design computer programs. Prisons are full of people who have masqueraded as medical doctors or other professionals because assuming that illegal identity seemed less risky than being who they really were meant to be. They were afraid that no one would like them or give them as much attention if they built their future on just being themselves.

In 2003 a *New York Times* reporter, Jayson Blair, resigned in shame for faking stories and quotes and plagiarizing other publications to make it appear that the stories were his. He wanted to be the reporter he thought he should be, and he copied and even fabricated stories to accomplish this goal.

It is risky to base our future or the future of our company on ourselves. If our plans don't meet our hopes and dreams, then we have no one else to hold responsible. But if we do develop and expand from our unique and rare characteristics, then we have the ultimate advantage in life. We've got a monopoly on unique resources and the natural ability to influence and shape the world. No one has access to the experiences you've had like you do. The way you show the world your true story is the way your glory is revealed.

My husband and I recently saw the smash Broadway musical *The Producers*, with Tony award winners Matthew Broderick and Nathan Lane. While we sat in our expensive orchestra seats I was captivated by the story. In the musical, we meet a frightened and risk-adverse accountant named Leo Bloom (played by Broderick). Leo is afraid of everything. He needs to have the safety of a predictable life or, he believes, he'll cease to exist.

One of his clients is a renowned but unscrupulous Broadway show producer named Max Bialystock (Nathan Lane). Max tries to get Leo to join him in a wily get-rich scheme. Leo is horrified and returns to his boring accounting office, where he realizes he is miserable in such an uninteresting and tedious routine. He sings a song we can all relate to, repeating the words, "I wanna be . . ." He soon rushes back to Max and shouts, "I'll do it. I'll join you in this scheme. I want to be a producer, too!" This comes as a complete surprise to the audience, as well as to Max, who exclaims, "Leo, there's more to you than there is to you!"

What does that mean? It is simple. Despite what we all look like on the outside, there is more to us on the inside waiting to come out. When our whole self is summed up and brought into focus, we realize that "There is more to me than there is to me." This means that what we are on the inside should be drawn out and be seen, heard, and felt. All that we are, deep inside, should surface in such a way that it is incorporated through our entire existence. I can say this because I believe that deep down inside we are all created good and pure and worthy of sharing. I agree with Stan Mitchell, minister and national speaker extraordinaire, who spoke and counseled us with these wise words: "There exists the worst in the best of us and the best in the worst of us, and we're better off not trying to figure out who's in which group."[2] The whole of you is indeed greater than the value of all your individual parts. In the case of *you*, parts are not just parts.

Lest we have too much pride in ourselves, who we are now and who we become in the future is merely an inevitable extension of who we have always been. Whether we believe in God, a higher power, and evolution, we can acknowledge that we didn't start from nothing! We had nothing to do with our own original creation. We are each inherently unique from the outset because each of us is a one-and-only, genuine, original creation. There are no duplicates. Everything else on this earth can be copied and imitated, even cloned. You are the only one who has experienced your life and can share the values you've formed. There is only one *you*. Don't forget it.

> *You desire truth in the inward parts, and in the hidden part*
> *You will make me to know wisdom.*
> —Psalm 51:6 (New King James Version)

Branding Is All about Stories and Storytelling

As I just said, branding is all about stories and storytelling. I'm sharing my story, which is the basis for my personal and professional brand, because I want to stir up your memories of your own life. As you read about how I grew up, how I got through school, and the various jobs I worked at, I want you to think about the same stages in your life.

As you read about some of the difficulties in my life and the wonderful times I've had, I want you to think about similar events you've been through. Follow along and compare your experiences with mine. Think about your hopes and values as you read along. Because as you do, you'll lay the foundation for developing your personal brand identity and improving the quality of your life.

Once upon a time a small girl grew up with many sisters and two loving parents. She became very successful in the eyes of the world, with professional position, status, and the associated power, money, prestige. A scientist, publisher, founder of one of America's best children's book companies, author, model, and television personality, with awards and acclaim, she had reached the top. Described by the media as "a real live wonder woman,"[3] Chris Hilicki had a great life and a great personal brand. Or so it seemed.

As with most people and organizations, what the world sees is usually not the whole story. And the first lesson in building brands is that how we seem on the outside is often very different than who we are on the inside.

To a publisher, the word *story* is an important word. My story, like yours, has taken a lot of turns and twists. The plot has been complicated and it has gone from fairy tale to horror novel to action adventure. My story may not sound too different from yours, yet stories are all different, and that is what enables us all to build better, distinct, and authentic brands.

I share my story here as an example of how to use your story as the foundation of your brand that can never be copied. Follow along and think about your true story. Ask yourself as you read:

- What were the life-changing events in my life?
- What are some things in my life that occur over and over?
- What are the most important values in my life, and where did they come from?

I was raised in a middle class family in the conservative midwestern United States. My father worked for Ford Motor Company and was considered to be a bit of a charming con artist out of New York City. Brilliant, hardworking, and likeable, he made things happen for himself and those he loved. My mother was a homemaker who raised three children, born right in a row. As a woman of the 1960s Mom volunteered for everything: the PTA, the book fair, and field trips. She was homeroom mother and Girl Scout Leader, and she drove the car pool. She did this all for no pay, no bonus plan, and no commission.

Where were you born and raised? Did your mother work inside or outside of the home? Did they call it work back then?

I remember going to the Children's Day carnival every summer near my grandfather's Wisconsin home on Lake Winnebago. The best part of the carnival was the parade. At the parade, we all dressed up to march around in a circle, to the delight of cheering parents and grandparents. Back then, little boys arrived as firemen, astronauts, and football players. Little girls dressed up as ballerinas, fairy princesses, and nurses. I desperately wanted to be a fairy princess, too. But my mom had something special in mind for her three little girls. She wanted to pay respect to our grandparents, who were known as the best gardeners around. So my mom dressed us up as a vegetable garden. I was a red beet. During the whole parade the little boy walking behind me pulled my red pointed beet hat down. I felt completely humiliated.

Did you dress up for carnivals, Halloween, or make-believe? What was the best costume you ever wore? Did you pick it out or did someone else? Why did you like it the most?

Maybe there weren't life-shaping events at such an early age in your life, but I know those children's carnivals molded my values and beliefs. My self-concept, my brand, began to take shape. And I'll never eat beets again.

After the parade, we played every game imaginable, from three-legged races to wheelbarrow runs. And the best part of the carnival was that we were all winners. No child went home without a prize. Every year, everyone won! I suppose I won a prize for being the best vegetable. Do you remember when life was so simple and innocent? Back then I thought that those were the best days of my life. And they probably were.

Did you ever win a prize for something? What for? How did it make you feel to get that attention?

When the games were over, I remember watching the beautiful ladies up on the stage hand out awards and prizes to the children while we sat down on the clubhouse floor, eating ice cream out of plastic Dixie cups with those rough little wooden spoons. Eventually it was my turn to walk up onstage and receive my ribbon. It was a life-changing moment for me. I remember thinking then, at a very young age, "I'm on the wrong side of that stage."

I wanted to be the pretty woman in charge, dressed in the stylish jogging suit (clearly never actually used for jogging). She wore little sparkly earrings and a smile. From where I sat on the floor, she looked impressive, strong, and confident in her role as carnival leader. And I knew then that I was on the wrong side of the stage. I began my quest to develop myself into what and who would be up in front, getting all the attention: confident, strong, and wearing sparkly little earrings.

I've mentioned that I had lots of sisters. When girls grow up so close in age, as we did, it creates a very competitive environment. I'm not talking about sibling rivalry—I'm talking about fierce competition! We fought for and about everything. We competed for the last pork chop, the best bedroom, the latest bedtime, and eventually for each other's boyfriends.

Are you the youngest in your family? Are you the oldest? Did you compete with your siblings?

As the youngest, let me tell you how I fared. I was the smallest and did not get the last pork chop. I was the littlest and wore my sisters' hand-me-down clothes. I was the youngest and was always sent to bed 15 minutes earlier then my next oldest sister. And each year, as I was allowed to stay up another half hour for my new bedtime, it was still always 15 minutes earlier than my sister's bedtime.

I love being the youngest now, and I remind my sisters every chance I get, "You're older than me," but back then it was definitely a disadvantage. When my father remarried, I had a stepmother, three more sisters, and a brother to love—and compete with. My point is I learned the spirit and experience of competition at a very young age. These experiences shaped some of my values; I value winning.

What Do You Call Attention?

We all compete for something from the day we are born. Let me tell you what I've learned about competition. No matter what we are competing for, it's really always for the same thing. The goal, the trophy, the ultimate prize is *attention*. Isn't that true? Whether we win a carnival race or an Olympic gold medal, the real prize is the attention we receive. We might realize that we did a good job and be proud of ourselves, but deep down what we want (though some won't admit it) is attention. Call it self-esteem, respect, admiration, trust, good service at a restaurant, your phone call returned, a promotion, an endorsement contract . . . it is all *attention*.

Maybe the attention comes from ourselves and we call it self-respect. Maybe it comes from family or friends and we call it love. Perhaps it comes from your employer or associates in the form of a promotion or a nomination to be the leader. Maybe it is being chosen to join the team as you line up along the gymnasium wall. Whatever you call it, it starts with the recognition and the awareness of who you are. This is attention.

What are some different words you use for *attention*? What means more to you—the trophy, bonus, or employee-of-the-month parking space, or the respect, regard, and attention behind those physical symbols?

The next time you watch an awards ceremony, watch carefully what the winners do right before, during, and after they receive their awards. Watch them as they search the crowd for their mother or father or someone they love. Watch them as they say with their eyes, "Look at me. I did it!" And watch them as they see in the eyes of their precious loved ones a look that says, "I see you! I'm so proud of you."

We are all thirsty for it, but some quench their thirst with attention-seeking behavior based in destruction rather than improvement. But whether we are being criticized for bad behavior or applauded for achievement, our behavior is rooted in our need for—our addiction to—attention.

Attention has gotten a bad rap. There's nothing wrong with attention. We thrive under proper attention. We grow when we have our father's blessing. We become better when we hear the words "Well done!" For the longest time I denied it, but now it has become an affectionate joke between my friends and me: Like a plant that needs water and a dog that needs to be petted, we all need attending to. It not only keeps us alive, it makes us thrive. It makes us whole so we can give back to others.

Even though we all compete for attention, some of us are uncomfortable with that idea. For many of us, drawing attention is our greatest fear. In fact, public speaking is one of the top ten fears in life for most people. Something happens to us between our childhood, when we stand in the middle of a grocery store and loudly sing the words to songs from *The Lion King*, and our first job interview, where we stutter and shrink from a feeling of intimidation.

Attention and Humility Can Coexist

While some people love the bright lights and applause, others only want a nod of approval from their boss or associates. For some, humility and attention are mutually exclusive. It is easier to push the work or product to the foreground than to risk feeling too proud or conceited. But branding is at some level all about getting and sustaining appropriate attention. Attention comes from the recognition that you have something to offer. This is the kind of attention that translates into loyalty, influence, and satisfaction.

When we begin to see ourselves as something to share and worthy of being chosen by the world, we begin to be comfortable with the idea of attention. There's nothing wrong with attention. It's how you get it and what you do with it that matters. How much is too much? What kind is the wrong kind? Is the attention a reward or a punishment? When dealing with attention, those are important questions to answer.

When does humble appreciation and reflection become foolish pride? With any kind of brand, the most important thing to understand is that the attention we receive must immediately be returned to the one it comes from, in the form of honor and respect. That's what your customer, client, or audience deserves. Brands work best when they include everyone in an endless circle of respectful and supportive attention.

When we don't get attention (we aren't picked for the team, chosen for the job, or asked out on a date) we risk rejection that proves to be a self-fulfilling prophesy. "Well, I guess that proves I'm a nobody." Rejection quickly manifests as either defeat or conceit. Both are distortions of the truth.

Back in the 1960s, I grew up in an environment that set me on a course with one motto, one attention-getting agenda, one competition. It was the "I'll show them!" competition. I had entered the race to win.

My sisters had talents to marvel at. My sister Tess was such a remarkable softball pitcher and hitter that she would sub for the boys' baseball team throughout high school. She had her nose broken more than once when line drives came her way, and she was greatly admired for her bandaged nose—even at the prom. My oldest sister, Cindy, has the voice of an angel—just the voice, as no one would accuse her of being too angelic! She could also play any musical instrument she picked up. Talent oozed from these girls. Later, when I was in junior high school, my parents became guardian for a young woman I now call my sister, Mary. She, too, had talents I only dreamed of, and all the boys hung around our house to see her.

I, on the other hand, had decided that if I was going to get any attention, I would get ahead by studying. And so I studied. I didn't do what my sisters did. I didn't go out for the teams. I didn't learn to play the guitar. The fact is I didn't have much talent. So I read and studied and joined the debate team and science club.

What did you do in high school to get attention?

In high school, I was the student council president and class president. I quickly learned that when you were the president you got your picture taken a lot. I rarely joined anything that I couldn't become president of quickly. I would show them! And for better or worse, I'm sure I did.

My high school experiences served me well. I was the first in my family to get a college degree, but it wasn't easy. I got a lot of good grades, but I was the one studying in the library until three in the morning. I began my "I'll show them" agenda all over again. I decided to study the most difficult subjects—chemistry, biochemistry, and physics. I studied these subjects not because I liked them, but because I thought it sounded so smart to be a scientist. (Supermodel Cindy Crawford wanted to be a nuclear physicist because she thought that sounded cool!) Who knows what I would have become if I had followed my true calling instead of being who I thought I should be?

Did you go to school after high school? Did you study what you wanted or what you thought you should study? Did anyone tell you what you should be? How did you pick your career or college major?

Boy, was I poor. After my parents divorced early on, I grew up always worrying that our family would run out of money. As a result, I was especially determined to get ahead financially in life. Here is another example of how real experience shapes our values later in life. Throughout high school and college I had to scrape together money any way I could. I went downtown every Thursday to sell my plasma for the eight dollars they offered. I was probably the only 20-year-old raking leaves for extra money. And I had a job at the International House of Pancakes where I could eat all the pancakes I wanted. I worked 40 hours a week doing second and third shifts at a hospital. My experiences of putting myself through school and struggling for enough food and rent money instilled in me an appreciation for self-sufficiency, and I'm wrongly irritated with those I think have it too easy.

I eventually graduated with a major in chemistry and a minor in speech. And I thought, "I've really done it now."

Do you remember your first jobs? What did you do after high school? How did you pay your rent? Do you value money and security more or less as a result of these experiences?

I received and was promoted to job after job over the next 20 years, first as a research chemist, then in production, where I engineered manufacturing improvements for the Little Golden Book Company. But I was never completely comfortable as a scientist.

There was always somebody telling me, "You're too young, too extroverted, and especially too female." I longed to get into sales and marketing. "That's where the real money and glamour is," I thought. I'll never forget a vice president of sales and marketing who told me to come back when I had an MBA. "You can't run a business without an MBA," he said. Today, that company, Golden Books Family Entertainment, is bankrupt and out of business, while I ran one of America's most successful children's book companies—without an MBA.

In 1994 I was approached by a very successful company and asked to launch a children's book company for them. With a great team, including my husband, Rich, we created the company we named Dalmatian Press. We started on my living room floor in October of 1995. After nine short years, it has become one of the largest and most successful children's book companies in the U.S. mass market. I get to work with Warner Bros., Disney, and virtually every movie studio in America. I've worked in Chicago and New York, in Paris and Italy and China. I've worked on Wall Street and just down the street in Nashville. I figured I had really shown them now.

So I must have been happy. My gosh, I should have been one of the happiest people in the world. And I am happy now, but not for any of the reasons I would have predicted. At age 44 I discovered who I really am. And you should too. Here's what happened.

In 1993, I learned I had cancer. I remember the day. It was a late Thursday night in early November. I can remember hearing the radiologist saying, "Stop. Wait—that's not a cyst." When I found out that I had cancer, my Cinderella story became something like a Stephen King horror story. And I was the central character, written to be killed off.

I didn't know that I would be battling cancer for almost 10 years, six major operations, and four new hairstyles. Eventually, I stopped trying to look like my old self and bought a red wig, a blonde wig, and a long brunette wig. That was probably the beginning of my experimenting with who I really am. I traveled all around the country, from New York to Los Angeles looking for a cure. I even took a little trip down to Mexico. I continued in my competition to be the best at whatever I did, including fighting cancer. I fought with my sisters and called it holiday stress. I fought with my boss and called it ambition. I fought with everyone—the guy behind the McDonald's counter, the pizza deliveryman, the ATM cash machine, and especially with my husband at four o'clock in the morning when my mind played tricks on me and told me, "You're not going to make it." I ran all over looking for a cure. At the time I called it traveling, but I was really running.

During this time, while I was sick and weak, I was attacked in a New York City hotel and left bloody and bruised, to endure years of recovery. I fought a three-year criminal case to put my attacker in jail; against all odds, and with the help of great legal minds, we won the unanimous guilty verdict. It's easy to see how these experiences have created my values for safety and security in life. But, again, I was pretty stubborn about how I wanted to live life. On the outside I looked like I was holding up and winning the fight, but by this time my self-image was becoming a little twisted and tortured.

So on another night—ironically, a Thursday in November again—I was driving around the dark lakefront drive of Lake Michigan. An old, familiar song came on the radio, one I had sung a hundred times before. Amy Grant sang the poignant words, "In a little while we'll be with the Father, can't you see Him smile? In a little while we'll be home together, in a while." I had sung that song for years, but I had never thought of it like I did that night. At that moment I thought, "Father, I just want to be home."

I was tired of fighting. I was tired of running. And I heard God say, "I know. Stop running. You have all my attention. *Just be yourself* and everything will be better, easier, and improved beyond your biggest hopes and dreams."

In spite of everything, I had been privileged to have an amazing and wonderful life. I grew up trying to feel important, wanting to be chosen for the team, waiting to feel special. Because of my experiences I felt driven to make myself successful, as well as to make any company I associate with successful.

For most of my life, I created success because I had developed a special ability to make others feel important. I was always able to figure out what people wanted and then become it. When I became what the boss wanted, the company wanted, or the boy wanted, I got the best jobs, the impressive promotion, and I almost always got the guy. This made me feel pretty good about myself.

What was my brand? Whatever you wanted it to be.

A Higher Rung on the Ladder of Success

When I turned 40, I got tired of it. Even though I didn't exactly know what I was doing, I knew that it was exhausting. But anytime I stepped out of my comfortable role and tried to be *me*, I risked not being loved or popular or chosen or successful.

I slowly experimented with being "me," and in time I found out that there was a higher rung on the success ladder. This was a better kind of success. I connected to people and organizations, almost accidentally, as I began to share my life experiences and values with others. Although it was initially uncomfortable and awkward, each connection was real, deeper, and infinitely more memorable. It was a sustainable relationship, and it was all mine. I found out how to develop the best kind of personal brand. It is based on one incredibly simple yet deceivingly complex principle: Be yourself.

> *I don't know the key to success, but the key to failure*
> *is trying to please everybody.*[4]
> —Bill Cosby (b. 1937)

There is little about my life I would change, because I've learned that what happens to you in life really happens *for* you. All the experiences in my life have been carefully kept as treasures, sometimes hidden and buried, waiting for me to dig them up and share them. My experiences have created a story that I share to get others thinking and talking about their own true stories. When you find your personal or corporate story and learn how to share it, you'll build the most amazing brand identity that will catapult you into the spotlight of respect. And you'll gain more than the world's respect; you'll also have self-respect. Once you have self-respect, everyone else's respect for you is just icing on the cake. Wait until you see how successful you are.

What Does Sharing Your Story Mean?

Let's talk about sharing your story. The word *share* makes a lot of people nervous. It evokes thoughts of group therapy where they teach men and women how to get in touch with their feminine side. We wonder what we have to give up if we share something. It makes us laugh and cover our ears, screaming "TMI!" ("Too much information!"). I'm not talking about that kind of sharing. I'm talking about involving your audience and engaging them in two-way relationships.

When I show you how to share the values you've developed from all of your experiences, you'll learn how to build any kind of a brand with the power that comes from authenticity. This is the critical component for lasting success in today's world.

No one goes to college taking classes and seeking a major in branding and image making. There aren't any classes called Personal Branding 101. It is a subcategory of business studies, at most. So many people, like me, end up as accidental brand builders. We become builders, keepers, and protectors of brands. It is a science, artfully performed, and I love it.

I like the *Men in Black* movies. In the 2002 blockbuster movie *Men In Black II*, Special Agent K (played by Tommy Lee Jones) has his memory erased. As he reenters the life he had left behind, he does things and says things that make no sense to him at this point in his life. But something is compelling him to act out of habits long forgotten. His friend and partner, Agent J (Will Smith), gets it. He says, by way of explaining and comforting his friend, "Hey, K, you are who you are, even if you forget sometimes."

So who are *you*? Have you forgotten?

Your past is a powerful force in your life, for better or worse. With all its power, it must not control you but simply give you value, uniqueness, and clues to define your authentic self. Your past true stories only have meaning in relationship to the life happening here in the present. While your life goes on, you must confront the beliefs your past experiences have programmed into your mind. Are your memories a work of fiction that you've falsely created? You need to figure this out, because those memories will lead you down a pathway of experiences that only you have had. It is what only you can share with the world that creates the basis for your authentic, unique brand. How can you be your authentic self and your true brand identity if you don't know your truth?

> *You are who you are, even if you forget sometimes.*
> —Agent J (played by Will Smith), *Men In Black II*

Brand-Building Belief I

The only thing that can't be copied is the true experiences that only I have had. I will identify them and learn what they mean for my success.

Brand Builders

1. Do you enjoy remembering your past? Why or why not?

2. When was the last time you remember getting attention for something specific? How did it make you feel?

3. Have you ever written your autobiography? Can you do so now in 300 words?

4. What were some life-changing moments in your life? As a result of those events, what are the three things you value most, personally and professionally?

Chapter TWO

True Confession: Good for the Soul, Great for the Brand

"Men are born to succeed, not fail."
—Henry David Thoreau (1817–1862)[1]

Brands Matter. Brands Matter. Brands Matter.

As we define who we are, we'll understand how our past experiences shape our current beliefs. These beliefs can, in turn, shape the influence we have on the world by affecting our work and our business. Consider the following experiences and how they shaped values, beliefs and eventually success.

I began working for Western Publishing, later known as Golden Books and the Little Golden Book Company, in 1986. Who can forget characters like the Pokey Little Puppy, Saggy Baggy Elephant, and Tawny Scrawny Lion? The company had just gone public and was building its "golden" image. This company wove itself into the hearts of families with endearing, sentimental books. And books can have real power and influence over children and society itself.

By 1992 Western had revenues upward of $600 million. This came from more than market share and great product, although it had all that. The market share was gained in part from Western's reputation and promise. The little golden book spine with its adorable printed characters, like the Pokey Little Puppy and the Saggy Baggy Elephant, made wonderful memories. They even made heirlooms. From garages sales to eBay, Little Golden Books have a nice little price tag on them because of the memories that get stirred up when they are seen and remembered.

By 1999, divestments, poor management, and fierce competition resulted in declining revenues and annual profit losses of as much as $100 million. In 2000, the company had the option of either filing for bankruptcy (again) or selling. It did both. But the better story is that, while it was in a terrible state of affairs and losing money, it was able to leverage the value and promise of the Little Golden Book brand into an $84 million offer price. Random House, Inc., the world's largest English-language general trade book publisher and a division of Bertelsmann AG, bought into that brand promise and purchased the failing Little Golden Book Company—not for its current financial performance but for its brand promise.

The brand promised that a future generation of parents and grandparents would buy Little Golden Books because they had warm and fuzzy memories of them from their childhood. Random House believed that future financial value existed in the product franchise that most every mom and dad knows as Little Golden Books. They believed that the warm response people had when remembering their childhood with Little Golden Books at story time could be exploited into huge sales with a happy ending. I think they were right. In 2004 Wal-Mart rolled out a classic nostalgic line of the original Little Golden Book titles in the midst of America's love for all things nostalgic. The "LGB" brand promised a financial payout to Random House and that promise was, in part, fulfilled.

So now you've decided to work on your image. It's your brand. In case you need a little more assurance about the importance of this decision, this chapter will give you evidence of a brand's value and where that value comes from.

If you still think that branding is some obscure marketing department's project, then read on to be convinced otherwise. If you don't think that your image matters, just ask someone who doesn't have a good one.

A good brand is a huge part of anyone's success. A bad brand is the biggest part of one's failure. Good or bad, individual or corporate, everyone has one. Whether we realize it or not, everyone has a brand.

Almost everyone is familiar with the concept of brands as the way to talk about one's image, but most don't appreciate their full value. Most talk about their value in terms of the intangible goodwill associated with them. Those are the same people that still look at brands as graphic designs, logos, and clever taglines. Those are the people who define their image with the way they dress and the kind of car they drive. Brand identities are not what we look at. Brands are what we feel. But this isn't just some emotional psychology. Brands have *concrete, bankable value*. Here are three quick examples of taking a brand identity to the bank:

1. Consider a story in *Inc.* magazine about Joe. Joe was being considered for a major contract with a firm connected to the theme park industry. At the end of the bidding process the job went to one of his competitors. When Joe asked why he had lost the bid, he was told that they wanted to go with the bigger company. "That hurt," said Joe. "We are twice as big as the other guy, but they look bigger and we look smaller." Joe's lack of brand identity resulted in an important loss of revenues, as well as a damaged reputation.[2]

2. Coca-Cola reports revenues of almost $20 billion in 2002, and they estimate an additional $1 billion in licensed annual sales based on their brand—not their product. That's "the real thing," baby. They reportedly sell a half million Coca-Cola products every minute of every day.[3]

3. Americans give dozens of greeting cards to friends and loved ones every year, but they spend two to three times more when they "care to send the very best" and buy a Hallmark card. Paying $4.99 for a piece of folded 8×11 card stock? That's a powerful brand.

All of these examples illustrate that the brand is not some graphic design element flashed in Times Square or flown in the Macy's parade. The brand is the thing that makes people feel something. The brand is the influence over behavior. Brands matter. Brands have real value.

And who doesn't want to matter? We all want to be remembered. Our businesses depend on being remembered. As individuals we accomplish more and will become more successful when we are remembered. Unlike any other creature, humans are all about memories and being remembered. That is what managing your image and branding is all about. Individuals have personal brand identities that are every bit as valuable as corporate brands. The sooner you identify and characterize who you truly are, with all your belief systems and what has become important, the sooner you'll find the connection to your influence on your personal and professional success. Consider the following experiences and how they shaped these people's beliefs and work.

Actor Matt Damon, in the November 30, 2003, issue of *Parade* magazine, was quoted as saying that he was "obsessive about role-playing" when he was a child. His mother was a professor of child development and always told him what he would be doing six months in the future. Damon said, "You couldn't define yourself, because you already had been defined by her." This experience shaped his value to define himself as he wanted and was consistent with his decision to become an actor. Damon said he "felt such pain in wanting to belong somewhere and not belonging." Maybe becoming an actor "was a desire for love. . . . Isn't that what we all want? I think it was just a basic need for attention. It was an identity of my own."[4] Matt Damon has turned his need for attention into a personal brand that commands millions of dollars at the box office.

Politicians and presidential candidates from Eisenhower, Reagan, Nader, and Clinton to Bush and Kerry in the 2004 presidential campaign have been written about for the way they weave their personal lives into their campaigns.[5] At the 2004 Republican National Convention, vice presidential candidate Dick Cheney shared his grandfather's humble background as a cook working for the Union Pacific Railroad when he and his wife lived in a railroad car. He described how he went to public schools from kindergarten through high school. All politicians seek to make themselves likeable and someone that voters can relate to. Emotion-packed stories that reveal true lives become the foundation for political brands. And they'll be influential and effective if they're authentic. Conversely, if the stories are more fiction than fact, the truth will eventually come out and brand loyalty will be lost, as will the intended results.

Dennis Goldford, chairman of the political science department of Drake University, says this technique helps candidates form a bond with voters. Contenders are realizing that all the political platforms imaginable are only as effective as the person who stands on them. Anyone can say they want to lower taxes. It is their personal brand identity (perhaps even more than their professional party brand) that convinces people to believe in them and align themselves with them.

I disagreed with the political pundits reviewing the speeches given by the 2004 presidential candidates' wives, Laura Bush and Teresa Heinz

Kerry, when they said the speeches didn't add any value to the race. Of course they did—if not for content, then because they gave us a better idea of who the man running for office really is. We want to get to know more than his voting record. We want to know, "What's he really like?" If we can relate to him we are more likely to vote for him. Why else would Elizabeth Dole and Hillary Rodham Clinton publish their best cookie recipes in national women's magazines as a part of the election campaign in 2000? And why else would we read them and care?

To Matter You Must Be Original.
To Be Original You Must Find Yourself

In the first 10 minutes of the Oscar-winning movie *A Beautiful Mind*, John Nash gets to the heart of branding. He is talking about his fellow academic colleagues, all of whom are geniuses. He complains that they have already been published and that he doesn't want to read these "schoolboys'" work. He says, "I need to look through to the governing dynamics . . . find a truly original idea. That's the only way I'll ever distinguish myself. That's the only way I'll ever . . . matter." John Nash laid out the critical pathway to branding:

To matter, you must be original. To be original, you must find yourself.

Most people want to be remembered. We all like to leave our impressions behind us. And who wants to make a bad impression? From photographs to memorials, we leave our legacy in our personal and professional lives. Not only are we flattered and delighted to be remembered in life, but most of our businesses depend on it. Our memory lives on through our children, our contributions, and our work.

My father has started a professional memoir writing business in his so-called retirement. He can't keep up with the demand from people who want to leave behind their legacy for generations to come. "Dad," I say, "slow down." "I can't," he answers. "People want to be remembered forever before they die."

If you are reading this book, you are interested in how you are perceived as an individual and in what you can do to direct that perception. As my father interviews senior citizens and prepares their memoirs, one of the questions left for the final session is "How do you wish to be remembered?" Not one interviewee has replied, "I don't care how I'm remembered." They have spent a lifetime building an image that is their personal brand, and they intend to preserve that brand well into posterity.

Occasionally, an interviewee will throw in a curve that leaves the family momentarily speechless. A fervent Catholic centenarian told of her devotion to the church and then confessed, "I don't believe in God." A nonagenarian and a man in his 60s each confessed that his first child was conceived before marriage had been considered. A widow admitted that her husband of 60 years had not been her first choice and that she had always loved another man. A pillar of the community asked if he could safely confess to a capital crime after 50 years. When told that capital crime punishments were not bound by statutes of limitations, he decided to carry his past dealings to the grave with him.

All of these men and women were concerned with their brand even as they summed up their lives and prepared for eternity. They were concerned enough to examine every word of their memoir for the slightest suggestion that they had lived other than as "advertised." While a confession may have been good for their soul during an interview, the eventually published memoirs contained not a hint of earlier indiscretions.

Yes, we all want to matter.

We all want to be remembered at one time or another.
And we want to be remembered for the right reasons.

Why else build brands? Not just for their financial value to us. We also build them for the way they build our sense of self-respect and self-esteem.

Who Needs Your Brand More—You or Them?

My husband and I often stop at the grocery store on the way home from work. It was late one recent night, and I wanted to run in and quickly pick up some water while the car was still running and waiting close by the entrance.

Aisle 9 could have drowned an army with water. The entire aisle was filled with shelves offering jugs, bottles, and containers of every kind of water. There was distilled water, filtered water, purified water, sparkling water, flavored water, and more. And within each of those categories were brands that presented images designed to convince you that they contained the healthiest, purest, and best water for you. It was going to take some time for me to make the best water-buying decision. Never mind that a decade ago I never would have dreamt of buying water at all. Now I needed a brand to jump out from the confusion and solve my time crunch. There was too much water. What was I supposed to do? I left with a 12-pack of Diet Coke.

Curiously, the brand doesn't only matter to the one building it. It matters just as much to everyone else. In a world of infinite decisions and choices, brands are built for people trying to decide what to choose. Brands help us make choices more quickly.

Can you imagine going to a grocery store and making choices based on the true merits of a product? How long do you think it would take you to read and interpret the ingredients on every can of orange juice? The average American grocery store now stocks as many as 60,000 different products. There are more than 500 competing brands of soft drinks and cookies! Do you have time to learn about a company's philosophy and morals? Brands save us time. I may not be crazy about McDonald's hamburgers, but wherever I am in the world, I know exactly what I will get. That is comforting in a strange town or country. It allows me to make my choice quickly when I don't want to experiment with acid reflux and I am in a hurry. How do you know if you should support someone or some company? Brands and their images lead us to our choices quickly.

An exception might be for people over 70 years old who are wired to make their decisions based on long-ingrained habits or price. My father insists that on his senior citizen income it's all about price, and no brand is going to win his allegiance for symbolism over substance. Others say that they've been buying a particular brand for 30 years and they don't need any newfangled change. Senior citizens with limited incomes might be a kind of brand Teflon—resistant to any brands sticking to them. But here again, if the brand can make the senior citizen audience feel like the company respects their values and financial situation, then it's back to the power of the brand.

Secondly, brands can validate who we are and what we believe. When we associate with a company, we align ourselves with its bigger company profile. I feel better about myself when I choose to support a company with a history of sponsoring many worthy children's causes. I don't choose McDonald's just for its food (well, maybe the French fries). When I choose the McDonald's brand it's because it makes me feel part of the bigger company initiatives, like its association with the Ronald McDonald Houses. Good brands should make us feel like we are part of something bigger and more important than any one person.

The fact that our choice of brands validates our lives is important to think about when we begin to define people's personal brand
identities. We all know that some people are just more fun. We are
very conscious of the fact that some people make us look better just
for being in their circle of friends. Conversely, the wrong type of person can harm our reputation. How many times did your mom tell
you not to hang around with so-and-so? If we all had something as
obvious as a brand label hanging from our necks, then we would
know how much value each person had and what that person believed. It would make choosing friends and associates easy.

In many respects, we do look for these labels on people. We notice how they dress, their nationality, and what kind of house they
have. We make assumptions about their value, for better or worse. But,
just as with a brand label on a sweatshirt, where we don't really know
the quality of the garment until we live with it for a while, the same is
true of people. Whether a corporate brand or an individual's personal
brand, we need to get behind the label and hear the rest of the story.

Even as we support other brands, we brand ourselves.
By choosing brands, we are confirming what we stand for.

When we are chosen, we feel validated that we are worthy and
valuable. The branding cycle is unending. The key is to choose carefully. As far as our own self-worth is concerned, we should realize that
we are inherently worthy whether others outwardly choose us or not.
It just feels better when others pick us out of the crowd to be their
partner or friend or a member of their organization.

How Many First Impressions Can You Make?

Many of my best friends work at Disney. Disney is one of the most
well-known and powerful brands in the world. In March 2004 Disney
reported another strong quarter with a net income of $537 million,
up 71 percent from a year earlier. What great proof of a powerful
brand enduring economic downturns as well as controversy in its
management and film studios.

Some of my Disney-employed friends have told me candidly
that, surprisingly, the Walt Disney Company doesn't pay its employees as much as one would think. It requires them to sign a
strict, binding, no-compete, five-year contract. They work 14- to
16-hour days and often on weekends and holidays. Why do they

work there? The brand. All the Disney employees I know have exchanged the minimum five years of their lives for the prestige of being associated with this great company. They want the name Disney on their resume.

The experience of working for Disney creates many of their values, which in turn have shaped their individual brand identities. Disney employees, past or present, get something they value when they can say, "I've worked for Disney." It's part of their story—the wonderful world of Disney.

When Dalmatian Press started up, we slowly and hopefully pursued the giant Disney for the rights to publish their characters and stories. We were worried that they would be difficult and demanding to work with, but it didn't matter. We wanted to work with them. We believed that having Disney titles in our portfolio would enhance our image and make us more attractive to other potential studios. We believed that the Disney alliance would help us make a good impression on other Hollywood studios.

What the Disney brand stands for has changed over time. Some passionate artists assert that Disney is trying to fool people into thinking it cares when it hasn't since Walt Disney was alive. Still, what the brand does stand for is a legacy of creativity and professionalism that demands high standards from everyone who works with it. We believed that if Dalmatian Press could publish Disney books, it would help us make a stronger first impression with retailers who had never heard of Dalmatian Press.

It did. As we had believed, first impressions count, and they can save precious, expensive time in business. And, as it turned out, when we were fortunate enough to become a Disney publisher, it became and continues to be one of our most enjoyable partners.

A similar story with unique characteristics can be told about Warner Bros. This company does a superb job of building and protecting its brand. Therefore, our alliance with them makes Dalmatian Press look great.

We care about our image. We brand ourselves professionally and personally because we want to leave an impression on the audience. We want to impress. Good impressions lead to good memories and then to loyalty. And loyalty brings us our desired response: being the chosen one. Lest you think that wanting to be chosen is a conceited and totally self-absorbed endeavor, realize that until we are chosen we cannot give back to the world as fully as possible.

When your brand is brand-new, many things are uncertain. But there are defining moments. When you create a brand, it will leave an impression, just like an old-fashioned branding iron used by a cattle rancher to sear his brand on a new cow's skin. That mark was like a present-day tattoo, for all to see. But a brand is more than just what people see. It's what people feel when they see the mark. We must brand. We build brands and choose brands because, in a world with infinite choices, brands can lessen the stress that comes from having too many options and too little time and experience.

How Many Lasting Impressions Can You Make?

First impressions can last forever, but they are yours to constantly improve. First impressions can haunt you or help you repeatedly. Consider the following examples.

Case Example: MasterCard

MasterCard began using the 1970 Three Dog Night pop hit "Joy to the World" as the backdrop for their 2004 summer commercials. While they show us our common experiences of new homes, weddings, and the kids' unending expenses, the timeless, grooving song plays in the background: "Jeremiah was a bullfrog / Was a good friend of mine . . ." What kind of impression does this make on us? Does it make us baby boomers feel carefree, young, and hopeful again? Does it make us feel as if anything is possible, just like we believed when we were 13 years old? When the last stanza plays, "Joy to the world . . . / Joy to you and me," I'm ready to believe that MasterCard wants me to find my joy.

They make it easy for me to believe in their brand promise. I like associating with a credit card company that makes me feel delighted, not guilty, for spending money! The image they present is one that everyone can relate to, so it's a smart brand for the company. It's a brand that I will remember because it uses a favorite old song of mine. First I hear the music, then I *feel* the music. I feel part of a bigger movement that embraces the notion of acquiring "priceless" memories. The image helps me rationalize that it's not the material item I'm buying but the memories that will last a lifetime. MasterCard's branding efforts make a fun first impression and a lasting impression that works.

Case Study: Retirement, Anyone?

Consider the changing workforce in the United States. By the year 2015 the percentage of retired people could increase from 12 percent to 20 percent. Everyone is planning that next stage of their life. Are you? What's your exit plan? If you've built your personal brand identity carefully and with purpose, you can retire or change fields like Rudy Giuliani did. I've seen Rudy speak, and I know that he brilliantly teaches people about leadership—for $100,000 per speech. He built a great personal brand that influences people to hire him at huge fees. He has a personal brand that will precede him into any future professional endeavor for greater success. His image, developed from his leadership during 9/11, has crystallized into one that we can choose when we're looking for a hero brand. If you build your brand right, it will continue to make great first impressions forever.

Great organizations have great brands. Great people have great brands. Brands matter. Brands matter because they get results from the moment they make their first impression and for as long as they continue to impress. How's your brand working for you?

Most everyone uses caller ID now. When someone calls, we wait the second that it takes for our telephone screens to identify who is calling. Many of my friends have the additional feature that requires the caller to eliminate the caller ID block so that their identity can be revealed. That's how much we all want to screen our calls. When you see that telephone number or the caller's name, what do you think? Do you pick up? Do you let it go into voice mail? Whatever you think about the caller, that's their brand.

Your Brand Is *Everything*

Every company and each organization in which you are involved has a brand. Your brand is everything that people think of when your name or image comes to mind. Your brand is how people feel about you.

But here's what I believe is the essence of the best brands: truth.

The best brands are built on your authentic experiences and your true stories that no on else has ever had. You build your best brand identities when you know your true foundation and learn to tell it the right way.

Let's say you or your company is like a wood carving. This piece of wood has been carved, cut, and chipped away at. Like you, the wood carving starts as an unshaped form until a series of carvings results in the image we see. What has shaped the way you look? Remember your first job? Chip, chip. Remember losing that job? Chip, chip, slash, cut, and chip! This process of chipping and carving has resulted in your unique shape and identity. Others can try to duplicate it, copy it, or mass-produce it. But we want the original work of art, don't we? We want the one that is authentic. That's the one with the most value. In an art gallery or antique show, the original work always commands the highest price.

In London, 60 original works by impressionist and modern artists sold for more than $111 million at a 2004 Sotheby's auction event. I have a favorite Van Gogh print in my home which I paid $100 for, mostly for the frame. But here Van Gogh's original *Two Crabs* masterpiece commanded a price of $9.4 million.

It's always the original work that gets the greatest attention and is valued the most. It is our stories based on our real experiences that form our values and belief systems. They chip away at our development, giving us a shape that others see. They turn an unshaped beginning of life into a carefully formed and intricate creation that can never be duplicated.

> *You gain strength, courage and confidence by every experience*
> *in which you really stop to look fear in the face. You are able*
> *to say to yourself, "I have lived through this horror. I can*
> *take the next thing that comes along." You must*
> *do the thing you think you cannot do.*
> —Eleanor Roosevelt (1884–1962)[6]

If Your Brand Is Lost

Imagine you're walking through an enormous theme park, such as Disney World, and you completely lose your bearings. Or pretend you are shopping in a huge and crowded outlet mall, and you don't know which direction you need to go next. What do you normally do in these situations? If you're like most people, you look for the huge, freestanding map conveniently located for every type of traveler. On these maps, schematics with color-coded icons, arrows, and numbers jump out at you to lead you to your desired destination. As you stand there looking over the map, your eyes dart back and forth, trying to find the one anchor you can go no further without. What are you looking for? What do we all try to put our finger on?

We are looking for the words "You are here." Sometimes they get our attention with a big red star, sometimes there's a swirling arrow. But we all breathe a sigh of relief when we see those words, "You are here."

We're not relieved because we are "here." We're relieved because now we have the means to begin our journey, continue on course, and accomplish our mission. We no longer have to guess which direction to travel. We've got the most important piece of information to get exactly where we want to go.

Maybe you're in the theme park looking for your little boy's favorite Disney ride, Dumbo. Maybe you're at the mall and you have to quickly find the restroom, the Sharper Image store for the impossible perfect boss's gift, or the food court to get that free piece of chicken they hand out in front of the China Wok. Whatever your journey, go to the map. Only then can you plot the best route between your starting point and your destination.

Sometimes I'm in a hurry and I approach the search looking ahead in the direction of my destination. If I'm looking for the JCPenney store, my eyes jump to the big square blocks at the top and bottom of the mall map where big stores anchor the diagram. But after I find JCPenney, I am stopped in my search and compelled to go back and put my finger on the place that I am starting from. Our destination only has relevance in relation to where we start from. Where are you starting from?

Now imagine you are looking for your place in the world. What's your role in life? How many times have you asked, "Who am I and where am I going?" We constantly define ourselves and ask others to define us. Why? Because where we go in life depends on who we are.

Even if we define our goals, we can't actually begin to achieve them unless we understand the starting point. That's why every board game has a big game square with the word *Start* on it. Every race begins with a starting line that we touch with our toes before the starter pistol fires. In the business game, marketing plans begin with an analysis of the current situation. In our personal lives we have a million different measuring sticks to assess our progress, such as educational degrees, bank accounts, and even the bathroom scale. For example, when you go on a diet, you start by standing on the scale and determining how much you weigh to begin with. When you decide to save money, you count your pennies and get your current account balance.

Put simply, it is a waste of time to head toward any target without a good strategic plan. If your goal is success, then you need a plan. This plan must include the development of your brand identity.

By now you know what your brand identity is. It's what people think of you. It's the influence you have in the world. It's a kind of shorthand the world uses—in fact, must use—to comprehend and judge who you are. You wear your brand like a label whether you mean to or not. But when you do it with purpose and understanding, your brand can ensure your success on every level.

No matter what kind of brand you are building—corporate image, personal reputation, or professional status—the most important common denominator is always the same: the truth.

Truth is your "You are here" map marker. Your *true* experiences and your *true* stories are the key components for *any* kind of brand you create. Only when you truly know who you are will you know who you can become.

Let's go back to the big map on the wall in your shopping mall or theme park. Remember, no matter where you want to go, what's the first thing you look for? It's the "You are here" spot! Only when you realize where you're starting from can you navigate your best course of action. Then you'll get results! You must examine how your life has been carved and shaped to determine your foundation to build on. But this type of self-examination is the very thing that we typically avoid. It's hard to push yourself into this most vulnerable and uncomfortable position. I know. I've lived there.

In 1993 I discovered I had cancer. Imagine my life being chiseled away, shaping or misshaping my self-image. Chip, chip, chip. That doesn't make me special. Everybody lives with significant trials throughout their life. For 10 years, cancer has come and gone several times in my life, which has shaped many of my personal values. Cancer doesn't define me but it is part of my story. It's part of my brand. My unique experience with cancer creates a unique brand. The beliefs you form from your experiences in life can either hold you back or move you forward. Which way are you going?

Building brand identities on a foundation of authentic experiences rewrites some of today's common branding rules. Some other branding theories would have you build your brand by following formulas that have been successful for other companies having nothing to do with you. Some other branding strategies ask you to build your brand on being the first or the biggest, or some other feature that can be copied. And some branding experts ask you to copy someone else's success, even before you know if it is consistent with your true purpose and experience.

My process asks you to start with another practice that might break some traditional marketing and business school laws. It pushes you to define and tell your story effectively to build your brands.

Brands Are Better than Features or Price

When I started the children's book company Dalmatian Press, we began on our living room floor with the question, why start another children's book company? There are plenty of great books out there and over a hundred publishers. What will make our company different? Why should it succeed when so many don't? We began by rethinking the way the world competes. Remember, at the heart of competition is the quest for attention and being chosen. How could we get people's attention focused on our books? What would make people choose them?

In our modern world, we compete in three ways: price, features, and brands. We first compete with price. This is a tough way to compete. A good pricing strategy can always get you into business but can rarely sustain the business, much less grow it. It makes you just another commodity. Dalmatian Press was briefly in this competition when it first opened its doors. We caught the attention of retailers and customers with our low prices. As I said, it can get you in business quickly, but we knew we didn't want to live there. We love offering a good value, but we knew our worth was based on more.

Wal-Mart is a bit of an exception for having built a brand on a strategy of low prices. However, the fact that the business expresses itself with low prices to the consumer is the evidence of a deeper true story about Sam Walton. His story has been told again and again and we know it to be true. Therefore the Wal-Mart brand promises more than low prices. It promises more than an affordable lifestyle for consumers. It is about what Wal-Mart can do with its success, from charities to finding missing children. It is about an incredible business success story that entrepreneurs and Fortune 500 CEOs dream about and relate to. That's the emotional punch that propels the Wal-Mart brand beyond its low price image. Low prices are still just a feature that anyone can copy. It is the reason behind the pricing strategies and the promises you make with them that are your true brand. Many people don't know their own worth. We may not wear a price sticker, but we compromise and cut corners and cheapen ourselves all too often.

Second, we compete with features. Features are a good way to compete. At Dalmatian Press, we began incorporating special features in our children's books, like stickers and posters and inks that glow in the dark. Every corporation needs great features. Baskin-Robbins has 31 flavors! Glad ziplock bags introduced the resealable zip feature. But the problem with features is that if they're good, they will always be copied. Someone will come up with that 32nd flavor. Everyone has a ziplock bag now.

Dalmatian Press made product presentations every few months that I couldn't be prouder of. Shortly after, our competitors were in front of our retail buyers insisting, "We can do that, too!" Whatever we developed they were only too happy to copy. We were the first to create an activity on the back cover of a drawing tablet. Soon after, our competitors were manufacturing tablets the same way.

But our identity wasn't about features. Our experience was all about ingenuity and ideas. We built a brand on the ability and experience to come up with new ideas. I mentioned in the Preface a Rudyard Kipling quote given to me by my boss and mentor, Harold Anderson, which hangs over my desk. To paraphrase, Kipling said, "They can copy all they can copy, but they can't copy my mind."

The same thing happens with brands. You can build a brand (your image and reputation) on being the fastest, the smartest, or the best looking—but eventually someone will be faster, smarter, or better looking. It's true that we all have gifts and special features to share with the world. But their origination and *how* we share them is our true brand. So we need to move into the third and best way to compete: We compete with our brand.

At Dalmatian Press, we decided to build a publishing company unlike any other. We decided to build our company around a publishing brand to which customers, moms, and teachers would give their loyalty. It had never been done on a companywide scale. Sure, people know what titles they like. They might choose a book because they like the title, theme, or author. But rarely do they know the publisher of the book.

Everyone always asks me, "Why did you name your company

Dalmatian Press?" With our spotted spine and puppy dog logo, we connected to kids and customers everywhere, sending a message with the tagline, "Spot the difference." We connected to the world with qualities that people relate to. The Dalmatian puppy appeals to sensations of warmth, innocence, trust, happiness, and fun. "Spot the Difference" fosters a feeling of uniqueness. Anyway, can you imagine a children's publishing company named Hilicki Press?

We have stayed true to our original story of wanting to make a difference in children's lives. As we build on our authentic experiences we build an authentic and unique company. We share our true stories to build affection and loyalty to our company. And believe me, people will remember how they feel about your company before they'll ever remember any information you are trying to sell them.

One Good Brand Leads to Another

We built a strong brand, and we understand how to exploit the strong brands that we publish. Learn the facts and tell them with emotions that people will remember.

Take that big purple dinosaur, Barney, for instance. When our competitors had the contract to publish Barney books, they did a decent job. The books looked good. However, they had Barney on the cover in a space ship, or leading a circus parade, or playing basketball. That's not Barney! The essence of Barney comes from his "I Love You" song. That's his true story. And so we did something very simple. We asked, "What does his true story look like on paper?" Answer: We depicted him in poses hugging other characters.

Our Barney books, with the same page count and the same price as our competitors', placed next to them on the shelf, sold three times as well as our competitors'. Why? Because we told the true story of Barney. When his brand is built on his original story it is successful. Can you imagine Barney trying to change his image into an action hero just because action heroes were the new popular craze for children? That would be totally phony and, although attention-getting, unsuccessful. And yet that's what many of us try to do. We try to create a popular action figure image when that's not our true story.

We connected to our customers with emotions that they could trust and relate to. We took Barney's true brand story all the way to the bank. Dalmatian Press has had many similar experiences publishing other wonderful brands, such as Precious Moments, Disney, Scooby-Doo, and the American Greetings characters, Care Bears.

When Dalmatian Press acquires a new character license, many of us gather around the conference room table to analyze the true story of the brand. What is the essence of the character? For instance, when we began to publish books with the character Winnie-the-Pooh, we asked what were the most important characteristics of his existence and his popularity. He came with a multitude of costumed scenes and playmates that we could put on our book covers. As we went around the room hearing from our associates, I heard explanations about how cuddly he was, yet strong. I heard how vulnerable he was, yet heroic. Finally, one of our graphic designers, a big, strapping hunter who is usually quiet in our meetings, whispered, "He's all about hope and believing in yourself." He was right. We put Pooh on our covers in poses that could make kids relate to thinking bigger than you appear to be.

When we began publishing Batman, Superman, and other superhero books, we went through the same exercise. Out of our discussion came the theory that now more than ever, we are all looking for protection and safety. How does that look on paper? We chose Superman poses that depicted Superman standing tall with his hands on his waist, chin up, and legs ready to leap. We didn't have him flying in the air. We had him poised to guard us and keep us from harm. It looked as though he was saying, "I've got my eye on you and nothing will get between me and you that could threaten your well-being." The golden glow we painted behind him made us feel like the world would be a brighter place.

Does this sound like we're making a children's book into a psychology experiment? Does it seem silly to put so much effort into a $3.00 book that will eventually be thrown away? We know it isn't. We know from sales data that the book's cover sells the book. The cover presents the brand's image. We know it has to immediately connect with the customer and create an impulse that generates an emotional reaction and purchase. Whether it is a coloring book, fast-food packaging, or a drug company advertisement, the look creates the feel, and the feelings create the resultant action.

Bill Cosby is one of the biggest brand names in the world. His successes are almost too many to list. He is reportedly in discussions about the possibility of another big-screen feature film. Despite all of his unquestionable success in television, comedy, and publishing, he is not on the A list as a big-screen Hollywood actor. The essence of Bill Cosby has never come through in his movie characters like it has with his TV series character, Cliff Huxtable, and his cartoon characters, Fat Albert and Li'l Bill. Even his brilliant live comedy performance is more of a conversation than an act. I believe that until he incorporates his realism, the audience won't embrace his movies and he won't see the success that other movie stars achieve.

We love other movie actors in part because we only know them as actors. We can imagine any true story we want about Julia Roberts or George Clooney. But we have too much information about Bill Cosby, just like we do with Oprah Winfrey—and as much as we love Oprah, her talk show and magazine, her big-screen feature films have not been as successful for her. We don't connect with them as theatrical film actors because we think we know who they really are. (We probably don't but we think we do.) We associate their identities with authenticity based on their live performances we've seen for years. If they play another character, we respect them and recognize them, but we don't love the character as much as the person we really believe them to be.

At Dalmatian Press we know our story. We know who we are. We don't try to be what we're not . . . and we know how to compete with the other brands we associate with.

Dalmatian Press gets branding. We know how to build off of other brands to get results from branding. Today, Dalmatian Press is honored to be one of the largest coloring and activity book publishers in America's mass market. Since 1995 we have grown to a position where we dominate the market with prestigious partners such as Disney, Warner Bros., Sony, Universal Studios, American Greetings, Lisa Frank, and many other movie and art studios in America. There is only one Dalmatian Press. Other publishers can copy our product development, our titles, and our pricing, but they can never copy the way we express ourselves if it is based on the real experiences that only we have had. That's our story.

What's Your Story?

Let's talk about you—you the individual and you, part of the whole organization.

- You, like everyone, have a story of your own, whether you realize it or not. People are watching you and your story all the time.

- You have an amazing story to tell.

- The way you tell your story creates a brand identity that makes people think and feel the way they do about you. The way they feel about you will determine how they treat you.

- When you learn to put words to your story, you will recognize that you have unique value that defines you in a way that no one can copy.

- The only thing that cannot be duplicated in this world of personal ambition and professional success is you.

- You can build a better business, whether it's personal or professional, when you share your true story. This is the strongest foundation of your brand identity. And we've just underscored how valuable your brand is. So tell that story.

> *Words are, of course, the most powerful drug used by mankind.*
> —Rudyard Kipling[7]

When Brands Appeal to Our Senses They Become Sensational

The best brands are those with personalities.

It takes years to give an inanimate object a personality. M&M's candies were just chocolate candies. They got attention with a campaign featuring "melt in your mouth, not in your hands" qualities. But any candy can do that. Then they became animated green, yellow, red, and blue personalities. Once they started talking and walking, they worked their ways into our hearts and memories with a sexy green personality, a silly yellow character, and so on. But even with a multimillion-dollar ad campaign, it took hundreds of impressions on us before we enjoyed them as more than just candies. It takes the conditioning of our senses to build the emotional connection that brands have over generic products. How much more are you, a human being, able to build a brand when you already have a personality!

Building your brand image is at best a process of sending and receiving conscious sense impressions by stimulating hearing, vision, or touch. These sensations are the vehicles for emotions to ride. When we build a brand with sensory impressions and feelings, we can make a stronger impression than we can with facts and information. To be clear, facts and information are the foundation of any brand because that's what is real, authentic, and reliable. But the facts should be expressed with the kind of emotion that appeals to all the senses. M&M's doesn't build its brand with nutritional information. It connects to its fans via an emotional experience that is memorable and gets action.

This is a different approach to building an image. Rather than using facts and information, use emotion and sentiment. The way we incorporate human sensory outreach will determine how well our image is projected and received. The better we use human, sensory experiences, the better our image will be perceived. Sensory experiences are the most powerful tools we have when changing lives. And your brand can change lives.

A sensory experience is immediate. Intellectual learning is not. But we rarely use sensory experiences to their fullest extent in branding. What kind of brand can best integrate the human senses into it? A personal brand. Instead of building brands based on pricing or convenience or distribution tactics, we must use the human senses to compete. Instead of using personal features of beauty or wealth or intelligence, we must develop a personal brand based on our true experiences and told with all the senses the world craves. There will always be someone prettier, richer and smarter. But there will never be someone who has had the same true experiences you have had. Use all the senses to communicate your true story. That's the only way any brand will win the competition.

Keep reminding yourself that before using emotion to tell your story, you must know what the facts of your story really are. The story doesn't start with emotion—it is merely expressed emotionally. Emotion can make a wonderful servant but it is not the master. The starting point is the truth. Then you have the choice to make decisions based on your true experiences. Harness your emotions. Don't let them drag you along for a reckless ride.

The McDonald's brand does a good job of incorporating emotions into its endless brand development. It isn't selling its brand based on how good its hamburgers taste. In the past, it built its brand on its low prices. Occasionally it still competes with pricing. It has dollar menus and 49-cent hamburger days. So do all the other burger chains. McDonald's also competes with features; it has play lands and birthday parties and kids' meals with toys. The other burger chains have copied these. Pricing and features have sustained McDonald's business, but in order to grow it must exercise its brand

and build brand loyalty. How? With emotional promises woven into the brand.

McDonald's' jingle in 2003 was "We love to see you smile." It was selling smiles and the idea that it cared about our happiness. In the 1960s I sang along to the jingle, "Grab a bucket and mop . . . because McDonald's is clean." In the next decade we were told, "You deserve a break today." But "We love to see you smile"? I didn't buy it.

The *Wall Street Journal* reported in June 2003 that McDonald's realized its tagline was not connecting with its customers as hoped.[8] We didn't believe that McDonald's really cared if we smiled or not. In fact, this $300 million ad campaign coincided with the corporation's first quarterly loss in its history. How could we believe that it cared if we smiled, if we rarely saw a smile inside its stores on the faces of its employees? It sure felt like a broken promise to me. They were smart to reexamine themselves and what their true story was.

In 2004 McDonald's rolled out a new ad campaign with a hipper tagline and jingle, "I'm lovin' it!" What do you think? Does it move you to action? Does it make you feel like going to their restaurant? Although it tries to make an emotional connection, I wonder if we can all relate to "lovin'" McDonald's food.

I chatted with former McDonald's Corporation division president Kevin E. Dunn in August of 2004. He offered some insights into McDonald's and its future if the brand does not embrace some of the company's original story. "McDonald's has to offer more than just low prices. QSC&V [quality, service, cleanliness, and value] are the core elements that built the brand from its beginnings in 1955. But McDonald's became somewhat of a commodity, driven primarily by pricing strategies, offering customers games and discounts rather than focusing on QSC&V. Over time, that hurt the brand, in my opinion, and confused the customer."

> I think McDonald's lost some of the magic that differentiated the brand in earlier years.

Dunn believes that many people working at McDonald's today don't know the real McDonald's story and its rich history. "McDonald's needs to hold on to its traditional core values, continuing to revitalize the brand as the market and customers change," he said. "It must focus on the customer first and view the business through the eyes of the restaurant manager and crew."

Dunn went on, "McDonald's spent almost $1 billion last year in marketing and advertising, but if you asked 10 customers what the brand stands for, I'm not sure they could agree on what its message or its attributes are. McDonald's has a tendency to try to be all things to all people and in the process does not present a message that is clear, concise, and compelling to either its external or internal customer. Recent changes indicate that the company is working hard to refocus the system on QSC&V, and the past year's results show that this approach is resonating with the customer."

Dunn told me that he respects the current McDonald's leadership, who he believes values the "roots" of the brand and its core values. "The brand comes to life through the franchisees, suppliers, and restaurant crews," he said. "It's in the restaurant where the McDonald's brand really comes to life! That's where the real story is being written today, all across the globe, and that will determine McDonald's next chapter."[9]

The McDonald's brand will, of course, survive. It will thrive as it figures out who McDonald's really was and who it is now—and what's the relationship between the two.

The M&M's candy brand follows the same branding pathway. Thirty years ago, they promised that "M&M's melt in your mouth, not in your hand." It was a feature moms cared about. Today, they have developed a line of characters that we laugh at and enjoy. Before, their brand promised a clean candy. Today, it promises a cool candy that's fun.

These long-standing brands have changed their strategies from competing with functions and features, to competing with emotions that we relate to and become loyal to. A brand identity has to know who it truly is and tell its story with emotional strings that tug at our heart and soul. This is today's kind of brand.

Your brand identity will be noticed because of how you appeal to people's emotions. How do they *feel* about you—not what do they *know* about you. That's why the presentation of our written resume is as important as the words on the paper. Have you ever spent time trying to decide if your resume looks better on white paper or ivory paper? Elle Wood, the main character in the blockbuster movie, *Legally Blonde*, printed her resume for law school on pink scented paper. Memorable? Yes. In a good way? Only you can judge if that's how you want to be remembered. Still, that gives you an idea of how to incorporate all the senses into your brand.

There is only one thing in the world that will always be different all the time. It's not what you do. It's who you are. It's you.

Brands Are for Influence,
and Nothing Influences Like the Truth

When people remain unconvinced about the power and importance of brand development, it may be because they are not defining it correctly. I like to take those people back to the Ponderosa—not the restaurant, but the cattle ranch depicted on the old television show *Bonanza*, starring Lorne Green and Michael Landon. You may not be old enough to have seen that drama on prime-time television, but if you ever caught an episode on TV Land, then you know a little about image and branding. The family that owned and ran a certain cattle ranch was the Cartwright family. Wealthy? We assume so. Respected? Absolutely. The Cartwrights commanded personal and professional respect. They were regarded as good, moral, successful people and were praised for miles around. Their names and all that belonged to them were recognized, admired, and able to influence.

The Cartwrights put their brand on their belongings, specifically their cattle. Imagine the red-hot branding iron of Wild West days searing the skin of the cattle to identify them as belonging to the Cartwrights. Why did they do that? If someone came across one of their cattle—someone like a cattle poacher in the business of stealing cattle—he would pay attention to the brand. It didn't only matter what the brand looked like. What also mattered was that the brand was recognized and how it made people feel when they acknowledged it. How did that brand make them feel? What did those marks on the cattle's hide symbolize? That brand symbolized everything the Cartwrights stood for and all that their name promised.

The brand prompted feelings of power and influence, and made people feel like they could either be part of something bigger or against something bigger than they could handle by themselves. It was clear enough to speak for itself when there was no one else there to explain its meaning and intent. That brand would act as a kind of shorthand for the entire message of the Cartwright family. I imagine not too many people wanted to mess with the temper of Little Joe or the brute strength of big Hoss. Their brand got the results they wanted. It was based on the unique stories that made each character's personal brand special, and the Ponderosa brand impossible to duplicate.

That brand was powerful enough to jump from fictional television to a national restaurant chain. Hoping to evoke the same feelings of adventure, quality, family, and loyalty, Ponderosa restaurants sprang up everywhere in the 1970s and still conjure up the image of beef steaks grilled on an open flame and a feeling of honest fun and contentment.

Bonanza illustrates a humble beginning of branding. Even back then, a brand wasn't about the mark itself but the influence it had on behavior. Today's tattoos do the same thing. Eagles, Harley-Davidson logos, gang symbols, hearts, and butterflies—they're more about the feelings they're intended to evoke than how they look. A good logo is a visual representation of a brand so imbued with emotion that it acts as a visual trigger. That's what branding is and what it is for: influence. There is nothing more influential than the truth. True brands truly work.

Sales versus Marketing versus Branding

Where does true branding end and slick marketing and smooth sales begin? A lot of sales and marketing executives would stutter through an explanation of the difference between sales, marketing, and brand building. Sometimes the best definitions are the easiest. As we leap from corporate branding to personal branding, let's look at some business definitions that we can use in our personal branding strategies.

Sales is the function of convincing someone to buy something. It is being able to send a bill to someone and be paid (in whatever currency or exchange agreed upon) for what you sold him or her. You could be selling anything. You might be selling your idea or a product or a worthy cause, and you might be paid in money, time, or goods. You might be selling yourself as someone to trust or hire or love.

Marketing is generating more business, resulting in more sales. Marketing is done with the intent to sell something, and to sell *more* of something. Again, you might be marketing a philosophy or a commitment or a product. The way you dress might market you in a way that sells how powerful you are.

Branding is what influences behaviors, actions, or thoughts through the stimulation of thoughts and feelings. This is executed with marketing tools aimed at securing more sales.

We're talking about your image, but branding is not the actual visual image, the logo, or the emblem that is projected or worn. It is not anything that you can borrow from someone else. You can see an image in the mirror, but it isn't the thing itself.

Brand Backlash

Brands do have their backlash. More and more people (especially young people) are hesitant to give their complete trust to brands because they have been let down and lied to. Young people love to wear brands and align themselves with brands, but they will be the first to criticize them if they think they are phony. They don't want to be sold on anything. Maybe that's why young people don't like to dress up as much as older generations do. In their mind, black-tie events are just places where people come in costumes and act like the people they are not. They want to think that their choices are their own ideas and that they have not been manipulated. That's what creates fierce brand loyalty—free choice.

Brands have a backlash when they misjudge what the world wants. Through misguided marketing they build an image that might be shocking, promiscuous, angry, or even dangerous. They don't know who they intentionally or accidentally are, and they build a false image and reputation. They get attention, all right, but for all the wrong reasons.

Calvin Klein and Abercrombie & Fitch did it with nearly naked models advertising their apparel. That's a big disconnect: clothing brands building their brand with a lack of clothing. Tammy Baker got attention for all the wrong reasons with her huge false eyelashes, representing a false identity that was later revealed. When brands portray false images, eventually the world is offended, mistrusts them, and stops choosing them until they begin to tell the truth.

Everyone and every organization has a brand already. They just may not realize it. They may not know what it is or realize that they are expressing it with the way they live.

But our brand, our identity, is not how we look but how others feel and react to the way we look and the way we express ourselves.

It's how we express ourselves—through pricing, features, and emotional outreach that influences how others feel about us. It is those feelings that determine what kind of attention we get—good, bad, positive, negative, healthy, unhealthy, loyal, helpful, supportive, powerful.

Brands Inside and Out

There are so many books, web sites, seminars, and newsletters on branding that each must brand itself as the one that is special. Branding is trendy. But even when the trend slows down, you will always need to build your brand for a better business. You might call it something else in the future: image, identity, reputation, character, or the impression you make. But today it is called your brand.

Obviously, great organizations have great images and great brands. That goes without saying. Building brands takes an enormous amount of skill and talent. But I think it takes more than that.

Have you ever wondered, "Who comes up with all this?" Never mind who, ask yourself *how*? The answer to how is in the answer to *where*. Yes, where.

The difference between what brands are versus what they are not is where brands come from. Brands come from two places: (1) The outside, which is a place that imposes itself on the brand, or (2) the inside, which is where the true story and birthplace of the brand begin.

When something shapes and develops a brand externally, it's like pushing cookie dough through a cookie press. The press gives the dough shape. Building brands from the outside is like pushing your true story through a cookie press. When we build brands from the outside we use a mold that belongs to someone else. You can call it modeling or emulating, but it is duplication.

In the business world, we have management and clients who force their agendas on us. There are creative directors and account executives with political and executive objectives. There is peer pressure and self-pressure. All of this is a huge minefield compelling you down a pathway that will keep you from your true and best brand. This is *faux branding*.

An example of outside forces pushing a company through a one-size-fits-all mold is the low carb craze. In the 1990s it was the low fat fad. The potential financial uptick from a trendy marketing craze makes it tempting to follow. When low-carbohydrate food became the hottest food trend, virtually every food and diet company jumped on it. But is this the true story of bread companies or sugar-based food products? Is this what they want to be known for? When the essence of a company is delicious, obviously high-carbohydrate food, a quality that has defined it and differentiated it, should it be changing its story and confusing its customers? When the low carb or low fat trend is over, then what will these brands be known for?

Everyone was loyal to the Snackwell's cookie and cracker brand when it was the 1995 low-fat option of indulgence. We couldn't get enough of them. It built a brand on a low-fat foundation. Now that the trend has decreased, the loyalty is gone. Sales are down. In 2004 the company launched the Snackwell's CarbWell product line. Whether low sugar, low fat, or low carb, this company has a history of chasing features and following trends instead of creating a brand that makes us feel like we can trust its snacks as a solution rather than a short-term fix.

Krispy Kreme doughnuts reported their first decrease in earnings in mid 2004. The company explained that the low carb craze was significantly affecting its business since doughnuts are the epitome of a low carb no-no. Should it change its story from the tastiest doughnut in existence—the story supported by millions of personal experiences—to the doughnut that is healthier and has fewer net carbs? No. It should ride out this diet trend, which is only a feature that everyone can copy, and remain true to its true identity: hot, gooey, sweet doughnuts. If it allowed outside forces to mold it into something it's not, it may gain a different type of sale but to its valuable loyalists it would be selling out. Low-carb doughnuts—$5.00 a dozen. Long-term loyalty—priceless. I can see the bright orange "HOT" sign lighting up in my dreams.

Faux Branding

In today's marketplace, there is definitely a demand for faux products. Products such as faux painting, metals, stones, and building materials actually add modern-day strength of materials and cost efficiencies while maintaining the look and feel of traditional or historic value. Faux is in. Likewise, when economies are in recession, it's cool to find bargains and insensitive to be ostentatious. At these times, it can help your image if you buy faux brands *if* your true story is also about getting something for less. Why spend your money or your client's money on a higher-priced prestigious brand when you can get attention and be appreciated for finding a similar substitute and be applauded for saving money?

But faux *branding* is never a good idea when you are establishing a new brand, especially with personal branding. Faux branding means being fake, phony, and counterfeit. Branding is about authenticity. It should be your core identity seared onto your goods and services. It should be your fingerprint, traceable only back to you.

Because branding has become so trendy, faux branders are on

the rise. They take shortcuts in creating what they hope will have instant value by copying another, similar looking brand. Faux branders copy the look and feel of other brands to ride their coattails of apparent success. The key is, someone else's success will always be less than the success custom-created for you.

Even if copying someone else's brand wasn't wrought with legal issues, it is at the very least immoral. Laws and legal policies exist to protect us from copycats who would steal the hard-earned value of another's brand. Equally important, faux branders have taken the wrong path. They have focused first on who they want to become before they knew and laid claim to who they really are. Yes, we must have goals and dreams and role models, but too many brands start off by trying to be like the other guy instead of finding the greater value in who they truly are.

Without knowing the essence of who you are, you do not know what your raw materials are for growth. That is like a fish deciding that it wants to be a great bird. We can applaud the fish for wanting to fly, but let's not forget that it has gills and needs water to survive. The fish can be much more successful at swimming than as a fish that tries to fly. We've all seen flying fish, and it's a fleeting accomplishment at best. Know your true identity and *then* set your goals.

Here's the rule: The brand is not the image, but the influence the image exerts. The brand is how we feel about it, whether it is a corporation or an individual. Faux brands make you feel phony feelings. Being tricked into feeling something that isn't true is worse than the imitation product or artificial service. Frank Abagnale, Jayson Blair, Dick Strong, and Martha Stewart are examples of personal and professional brands that disappointed us. Some people said from the beginning that these brands seemed too perfect (phony) to be true. Their personal and resulting businesses weren't based on the truth, and when we found out, we felt empty and angry and needed to be convinced that our loyalty should remain with them. Some people feel that Rosie O'Donnell had a phony brand. Her audience of women felt she was a lot like themselves. They felt tricked or at least surprised when she came out as a lesbian and pursued an ugly lawsuit against her publisher over creative control. Ironically, at the heart of her complaint was her desire to protect her brand name.

Imagine building a brand image the same way you build an outfit to wear. First you pull on your Gap jeans. Next, you pull over your head your Tommy Hilfiger sweatshirt, and then you place your

New York Yankees baseball cap on your head. We wear brands in our society.

We decide we want to associate with the qualities of Gap, Tommy Hilfiger, or the Yankees. We put their clothes on to wear their brand of cool or hip or power or sophistication—whatever their brand says we are once we wear their product. It is much easier and faster to wear someone else's brand than to build our own. We begin by asking, "Who do I want to be?" then answer with, "I'll do what they did and I'll be like them." This is called *modeling*.

Management business schools have built an entire educational system with this concept of modeling. And modeling is great. But we should not begin with preformed conclusions. That's the wrong strategy. It's only building on a brand image that really belongs to someone else. This is a brand that is not your authentic self, and that will not produce the highest and most successful brand image you can have. Best-case scenario, it will be temporary. Worst-case scenario, it will be seen as phony and insincere, and may disconnect you from the very people to whom you wish to relate.

Now that we've looked at branding from the outside, we must ask, how does branding come out from the inside? You focus on your unique personal experiences and tell them with your branding strategies. I used to think that this process was unencumbered. I used to think this meant we had total creative freedom when ideas were produced originally. We could color outside the lines, run with scissors in our hand, and shout as loudly as we wanted because no one was there to tell us not to do these things. Weren't the best brands explosions of brilliance? Who could censor ideas that were truly original? Didn't we have the right to express them like the First Amendment allowed? Wouldn't these be the most brilliant and memorable brands?

Our Experiences Shape Our Values, Which Shape Our Brands

No. The best brands are built from the true stories that have been picked apart and analyzed and edited. Isn't that a contradiction? Not at all. Whether you are building a personal brand or your organization's brand, it should start with the true story of experiences that no one else has had. This, we established, will give you the foundation of a brand that cannot be duplicated and therefore satisfy one of the most important criteria for success: uniqueness . . . authenticity. But as we define our true stories and put words to them, it becomes clear that those experiences have gradually shaped our values, morals, and ethics.

For example, if you've had either significant money problems or success in your personal life or in your business, you may value financial success and security. If you've been the victim of crime, you may value safety and protection. If you've had a close family or no family, you may value nurturing and mentoring.

Cindy Hazen, CEO of the national recruiting firm Sales Executives LLC, had all these experiences in her business life and personal life. She was robbed several times. Her business was in debt. As a result she valued responsibility, dependability, and financial security. She had developed the belief system that she shouldn't take too many risks, a belief that obviously affected her business. But Cindy also was repeatedly named salesperson of the year, which instilled in her the desire to take risks. Initially she had been building a life and a brand with competing beliefs, security versus risk. One was limiting her and the other was moving her forward.

That's how belief systems work. Our beliefs and rules have a powerful impact on the quality of our lives. They don't change who we really are, but they do affect how we are perceived and how much influence we have in the world. Some of these rules hold us back. They keep us from expressing our unique, true brand identity. We protest and shout things like, "I'll never do that again." Some of our experiences are so difficult we make silent vows or public declarations like, "I'm never going to trust myself again!"

Sales Executives identified its true stories and the values and beliefs they led to. When Cindy focused on the values that were moving her ahead, she learned to use this book's process and translate them into a look, sound, and feel that her market could relate to and trust. Her brand didn't come across as phony. It used colors, images, copy, and sounds that personified responsibility, success, and dependability. She wove many other values into her brand development, such as constant self-improvement, nurturing, and humor, but all were based on her true experiences. Today Cindy Hazen has built very successful and profitable businesses that people trust and relate to and that cannot be copied because she cannot be copied.

When I was 25 I thought I was too young to be successful. I thought I didn't have the right postgraduate degree. So I emulated other people. I branded myself and my work from the outside, because my belief was, "I'm too young to be successful. I need a master's in business to be successful. I'm only a scientist. I can't be creative." Clearly, these rules were holding me back.

But rules are funny. They are often the basis for behavior, and they are considered sacred—but rules can be changed. Rules can be broken. And when I changed the rules from "I'm too young" to "I have more time to make all my dreams come true," I was able to express my true brand identity. I began to take pride in my youth and the energy that comes with it. That was my story. Ronald Reagan embraced his true age with humor and pride. During the presidential debates he told his opponent, Walter Mondale, that he wasn't going to make age, which he equated to inexperience, an issue. Everyone applauded and loved him for being himself. Are your rules holding you back or pushing you ahead?

Branding from the inside out isn't as simple as an explosion of your heart and soul. Even though it's the expression of the true you, it involves intense self-examination and editing.

People are almost always drawn to people or things that are natural. We believe that when something is called "natural" it doesn't have any hidden ingredients. Yes and no. Anyone who thinks that Oprah keeps popping up with award after award just because she is so naturally loveable, authentic, and honest is wrong. Yes, she is all of that. But Oprah is something else. She is like a private eye. She constantly examines herself and pays attention to what she finds. She does the work, sometimes painful and sometimes in public, and asks herself every day, "What do I know for certain? Who am I really?" Then, as she listens to her inner voice, she edits out all the rules that are holding her back and expresses the best self she is. She is brilliantly herself, branded as the only Oprah that cannot be duplicated. How valuable is that? There is only one Oprah. There is only one you.

So let's begin this intense self-examination that successful branding requires. It will take more than an off-site strategic meeting or a few minutes of journaling at Starbucks to determine who you are. To determine who you are (or where you are), let's look at the different ways to examine and edit your true experiences for the ultimate brand.

There is no agony like bearing an untold story inside of you.
—Author and poet Maya Angelou (b. 1928)[10]

Brand Building Belief II

I will build my brand from the inside out, with human qualities that express my values, for maximum influence.

Brand Builders

1. Who, besides you, is your brand important to?
2. What are the features that you are currently competing with to get attention? What's wrong with competing this way?
3. What is the first impression that you want your brand to make on others?
4. How can your brand communicate via human senses instead of information?

Chapter THREE

Brand-Stand: Your Platform for Success

Character is like a tree and reputation like its shadow.
The shadow is what we think of it; the tree is the real thing.
—Abraham Lincoln (1809–1865)[1]

Personal versus Professional

In the movie *The Godfather*, Tessio told Michael's men just minutes before they would kill him, "Tell Michael it wasn't personal." We all knew what Tessio meant. His betrayal was only business. Flash forward to the twenty-first century when Robert De Niro's hit men told Billy Crystal's character in the movie *Analyze This*, "It's nothing personal." Billy responded that he was wrong. Killing him was definitely personal. Tom Hanks told Meg Ryan in the movie *You've Got Mail*, "It's nothing personal." He had just run her small bookstore out of business. I love what Meg Ryan's character says next: "What is that? All that means is that it wasn't personal to you. It's always personal to someone. Whatever else it is, it ought to start by being personal!"

Business is always personal. Martha did it. Oprah did it. Bill Gates did it. Ted Turner did it. They made their personal brands their professional businesses. The best salespeople, dealers, agents, reps, and others who come into direct contact with clients and customers outperform the others when they make their professional business personal. Think about it. They all have basically the same things available for success. In our company everyone gets the same sales materials, incentives, and opportunities from the company. But it's the ones with the greatest personal brand identities who build a better business for themselves and the company. Conversely, a bad personal brand limits the individual's potential as well as the company's.

When I am at trade shows I am impressed, though not surprised, when clients or customers come up to me and sing the praises of their favorite Dalmatian Press salesperson. I hear comments like, "He's my favorite salesperson. I can always make time for him. I can trust him, and I trust him to make smart choices for me."

I know then that those salespeople are going to have the advantage over our competitors because they have made themselves memorable, relatable, and have built loyalty that takes action on their behalf. This only happens because they have turned an ordinary sales experience into a personal one. Just as much as the salesperson wants to be special, so does the customer want to feel special. The exchange of personal attention for the sake of professional gain is critical to the pyramid of brand building.

The best brands begin when you understand that your personal and professional brands need to be developed simultaneously and seamlessly.

Are People Choosing You?

If you're ready to do the work, then here is where it starts. Everyone today is familiar with the concept of branding products and services. But you have a personal brand first and last. Do you realize that your personal brand is another name for your reputation, which goes before you and follows you throughout your life, for better or worse? Your personal brand needs to be developed simultaneously with your professional brand for the greatest satisfaction in your life.

Why would we want to put ourselves under a kind of marketing microscope? Most of us are not developing and positioning ourselves as a product. We do not see ourselves as something displayed on a shelf or in a catalogue for others to choose. But that is exactly what happens to us every day.

> The reason people associate with us or do business with us is because they have decided that they want *us* just as much as they want any product or service we offer or company we represent.

Let's face it, most products and services can be obtained from many people and places. The world is also filled with many people who can be a model and mentor as well. How do we choose? Why do they want us? It isn't always about who we are as much as it is about what we can do for them. And what we *do* is give them a spoken or unspoken promise that their experience with us will meet their wants as well as their needs. Who wants a bad experience?

I have always told people who work for me, "Everyone has a lot of choices of who they want to work with. So be nice!" If you can choose to work with anyone you want, then you might as well work with people you like. Now perhaps you don't believe your brand is "nice" and you're not interested in being liked. But remember, your best brand is based on being true to yourself, and rarely are people or their business bad at the core. Maybe you've developed some belief systems that say you need to be mean or shocking or unpleasant because of the experiences you've had in life. But when you learn how to define your unique life experiences, either as an individual or within an organization's life, then you can learn how they may have misshaped your values that you express every day at work and play. In other words, I believe that you are inherently good, but perhaps you've been expressing yourself badly.

Whether the world is looking for a product, service, friend, or ally, you are the most important part of what they seek. How many times have you heard people explain someone else's success with the postscript, "Well, it's easy for him to get the sale or make the deal, everybody likes him." How many times do we teach others, "It's all about relationships"? Whatever the product, service, or business opportunity, people's choice almost always comes down to how they feel about the one offering it. And this is the brand.

What's in a Name?

Caryn Elaine Johnson changed her name to Whoopi Goldberg. Faith Hill's first name was Audrey. Michael Keaton was Michael Douglas, but that name was already taken in Hollywood.

Names matter. They are one of the simplest expressions of our brand. People and companies create and change their names because they connect their market with a certain image. And as people and corporations change, they may change their names to reflect that. Madonna announced in the summer of 2004 that she was going to change her name to Esther. Radio news stories reported her story: She said, "I was named after my mother. My mother died when she was very young. I wanted to attach myself to another name. So I read about all the women in the Old Testament and I love the story of

Queen Esther." Queen Esther was brave and beautiful, enduring much hardship as a role model. Madonna also said she wants to be part of order and not chaos. So changing her name reflected these changes, which began on the inside as a result of her experiences. Just on its own, a name can make people feel something when they hear it. The name Madonna has too much corporate entity value for Madonna to stop using it in business. But, to the extent she wants to feel differently because of her name, she will change to a different name. And what more does the Madonna brand stand for than change?

When something becomes branded it carries a mark, given to it because it is distinguished from everything else available. There has to be something special and unique about it or it couldn't carry the trademark. Can people be branded, too? Obviously people like Donna Karan, the Versace family, and Ralph Lauren have turned their very names into brand logos that others wear on dresses, suits, and shirts. Jennifer Lopez and Tommy Hilfiger do more than endorse products, they put their actual names on cologne and perfume and numerous products. The same can be said for Max Lucado, Billy Graham, and other spiritual leaders whose very names stand for the values and experiences that make us feel like we are part of something bigger and eternal.

These people have developed personal brands based on their personalities, and they manifest themselves in as many forms as the public will buy: books, CDs, clothing, and so on. From what we know about Jennifer Lopez, we buy into the promise that a perfume with her name on it will smell exciting and make us feel as electrifying as she is. These personal brands seal the promise for their corporate brands.

But when the personal brand tries to launch a professional business that is unrelated to and disconnected from its core identity, the public has a hard time trusting the business. For instance, when Madonna launched her line of children's books, the public didn't rush out and support it. There was a disconnect between her personal brand and her professional brand.

This doesn't mean that we should keep our personal brand a secret so that we can do whatever we want to professionally. It means that we will have greater success when the two merge and build on common denominators.

We are all familiar with designer brands and brand labels. We all know the difference between buying a brand-name product and buying a generic brand. We wear brands whenever we pull a Tommy designer brand shirt over our head such that people will recognize the designer brand label. We brand ourselves when we tattoo our body or pierce our nose, ear, or eyebrow. We define our look when we cut our hair a certain way. We brand ourselves when we choose a style of checks with a design printed on every check. If we carry around a Louis Vuitton bag or wear a Masonic lodge pin on our lapel, it labels us as a certain type of person. We represent ourselves with our stationery and return address labels.

In everything we do, we brand ourselves just like a major corporation does. Even our telephone numbers represent our identities. That's why we get upset if our number changes. Cellular phone companies are creating a whole new business value based on allowing customers to carry their old phone number to their new service.

How are you branding yourself? In 2003 new baby names were being used that were based on successful corporate brands: Lexus, Mercedes, Harvard, Rolex, Tiffany. Often a company has been named after a real person, but now people are reversing that, as if they could infuse the brand identity of the huge corporation into the tiny baby to ensure its success in life.

In Business, It's Always Personal

How are you running your company's brand? At Dalmatian Press we promise our retail customers that we run our business without excess or any extravagances that could be interpreted as mismanaging their profits. Our company car is a Taurus. We fly coach and our offices make people feel comfortable and special but they are modest with furniture from Office Depot. Our brand makes our retail customers feel like they can trust us to keep our overhead low and pass the savings on to them. This is also an extension of my personal value on saving money. It all starts with an individual's true-life experiences, which are then translated into the individual's own brand.

But are we wearing someone else's brand or are we really being our own brand? It is so easy to pull a brand on over your head in an effort to be everything that the brand says you will be—sexy, beautiful, cool, or sophisticated. It is so easy to start a business or take over a position and think, "How can I be just like them?" After all, case studies and models are what MBA courses focus on. This kind of imitation can become an attempt to wear someone else's brand. But the truth is that we are, in and of ourselves, our own unique brand identity. We are each a perfect brand that exists on the inside and just needs to be seen on the outside.

Go back to that original reason for your creation as an individual or as an organization. Remember the passion or at least the reason you felt you needed to start something new as opposed to copying something else. Go back to the moment when you felt that there wasn't another person or company that existed, able to do what the new one could do.

However we develop our personal brand, it should be in harmony with how we build our professional brands. Whatever we are, in terms of our essence and our defining characteristics, it should be carried through our organizations, corporations, and associations. These are the type of brands that endure through good times and bad times. Your truth is your greatest asset. Whatever your true stories are, they don't cease to be true when you walk out of your home and into your office.

It is easy for us to recognize brands on products, whether automobiles or cups of coffee. Everyone understands that BMW is a brand and Starbucks is a brand. When someone asks for detergent or a package of cigarettes, they are asked what brand they use or smoke.

Now make the leap from consumer products to people. Celebrities know well that they have a brand image because they've learned how much they need to protect it. Tom Hanks actively protects his brand by choosing the movies that he does and the merchandise that carries his name carefully. Oprah and Martha Stewart have extended their brand to everything from magazines to wallpaper. The moment they go "off-brand" is the moment they confuse the people they influence and the people who depend on them to make their lives easier.

It is easy for us to think of big movie stars and celebrities as a kind of a corporation in themselves and therefore having a brand. But brands are not based on the size of the entity. Brands have no minimum size requirement. And the worst thing to do is to wait until you become famous or you think you are important enough before you start taking care of your brand.

What will it take to convince yourself (because no one else can) that you are worthy of a defining brand that needs protection?

If We Knew Now What We Knew Then

For years I wanted to fit in. I wanted to be older than I was, so I always told business associates that I was 35 when I was 30, and 40 when I was 35. I thought they would take me more seriously. I should have known that part of my brand was what I had accomplished at a young age. I should have valued my youth while I had it and promised others the energy and passion that comes with youth. Instead I carried an erroneous belief that no one would respect me until I was older. It's funny how most of us imagine an ideal age instead of finding the value in our real age. I was 40 before I realized that 35 was a great age to be!

The average age that American women would choose to be is 34. The average age that American men would choose to be is 29.[2] I wanted to be older, smarter, faster. I was also 40 years old before I realized that a B+ was a good grade, a vice presidency was a great job, and 115 pounds was considered thin. I wanted all A's, the presidency, and to look like Audrey Hepburn instead of myself.

When I helped start Dalmatian Press, I couldn't wait for us to rub shoulders with the big publishers like Scholastic and Random House. Even as I knew we needed a unique brand to compete, I asked, "What are they doing and how can I be successful like them?" But knowing your enemy doesn't mean being like them.

In the 2004 hit movie *The Last Samurai*, Tom Cruise's character studies his enemy to such an extent that he eventually embraces his enemy and becomes a samurai. Do we lose ourselves in others' identities because we don't like who we really are? Do we forfeit giving the world our unique value when we focus on becoming like others instead of becoming more like ourselves? At the end of the movie these solemn, moving words are spoken by the young emperor, who is ruling his empire with the goal of becoming more like the Western world: "We have Western weapons and Western clothing, but we must never forget who we are and where we came from."

Who are you and where did you come from? You are a brand every bit as much as Bill Cosby or Katie Couric. Your personal brand identity can create meaning for your professional identity and your entire corporate organization. Maybe you don't have millions of dollars. Maybe you are not as well known. But what you do have in common with those big names is an identity that needs to be defended and represented carefully and with purpose. And when you do that, whatever you associate with or do in life can be an extension of that brand identity. Because when you build on your true identity you build on the only thing that is truly unique and different and emotional. And, as we shall see, that is the key to the future of branding.

People consistently cite the reason for their purchase, attention, or loyalty as the fact that the chosen product is different. Uniqueness is the reason that people notice and prefer something. But soon, everyone else starts duplicating the very thing that was once new and unique until the differences are all gone. We've seen it with fast-food companies that have all created kids' meals with little toys in them. Movie theaters are mostly huge complexes of 24 screens. Restaurants started copying each other's low-carb menus. When the first business starts to offer a unique feature, it gets our attention. But as everyone copies it, it loses its reason for standing out. It loses our attention. Part of business is simply keeping up with consumer demands with new features, but these are not ways to build brands. Don't be the same. Cherish your differences as your strengths.

Unlock Your Authenticity

My body isn't perfect. But I've had
success without trying to be someone else.
—Rock and roll star Melissa Ethridge[3]

Michael Jordan is a classic example of a person with a strong personal brand merged with an equally strong professional brand. He is undoubtedly one of the world's best basketball players in history. And he has built his brand with this extraordinary talent. But what's the real secret to his branding success? It isn't about his speed or how high he can jump. He hasn't gotten his image and name on hot dogs and T-shirts just because he is a great ballplayer. Even if he is the best basketball player, there were great basketball players before him and there will probably be many more after him. His brand has value and he is chosen because of more than *what* he does. His brand has power because of *who* he is, not *what* he is. He is the sum total of all his true-life experiences that have uniquely shaped his values and personality. He is a powerful brand because his true self sincerely shows itself throughout all his public moves.

It's not the fact that he is the best at his game. It's not that he has a winning smile. It's not that he is a savvy businessman. He has a valuable brand that will prosper because all these things are based on who he is on the inside. It is more about who he really is than what he really does. It is about what's behind the smile. Where does that smile come from? What is it that makes him happy inside that manifests itself as a smile?

There will eventually be another basketball player who plays as well as he does or looks better than he does. But there will never be another Michael Jordan who has the same personality—a personality that has been developed out of his experiences. His experiences are the one thing that cannot be copied. His strong personal brand makes a difference in every organization that he is a member of.

The principles of branding dictate that something be unique and authentic about what you're branding. Otherwise it is the same as others and not brandworthy. Your experiences may seem ordinary, but if they are yours then they are your brand.

It has been suggested by other marketers that personal branding take the same approach of building on a platform of special features. Fundamentals for personal branding could be that you have a special talent, intellect, or appearance, or that you have been the first to accomplish something or the best at something. Just like any product, this would make you noteworthy and special. But it wouldn't build a brand that couldn't be copied. And if your brand can be copied, it's not much of a brand.

Conforming

When we relish being ourselves we will find the organization that appreciates and enables that. When we are allowed to be ourselves rather than conform to a false standard, we can bring the organization value, and we find that the sum of the parts is actually greater than the single value of the whole.

At Dalmatian Press we go to great lengths to hire people who are different from others so that we fill in our voids and have a diverse set of values and experiences that better relate to our increasingly diverse customers.

Oh, people can try to act like someone else. Businesses can try to be like their competition. Most people do try to emulate or copy success. I bet if I asked a hundred little boys who they wanted to be when they grow up, at least a dozen would say, "I want to be Michael Jordan!" But we can tell when someone is a copycat. The truth is people's personalities are the result of the way they were created, how they were raised, how they grew up. Each personal experience will shape their values and result in their individual expression that we might call style or groove or personality. That's what cannot be copied. That's what makes people like Michael and Oprah and Cher memorable, for better or worse. They have personal and professional brands based on their true stories. They know who they are and they don't try to be someone else.

When you build your personal brand on your true experiences, you will become an authentic brand that cannot be duplicated. That's the true test of a brand: One that is truly unique cannot be copied and will survive the test of time. Authenticity is the true treasure of any brand, but how do you find this treasure?

Self-Examination

What are these treasures? Many times our treasures in life, home, and business are hidden. Hidden treasures are more than what you see in pirate adventure movies. Still, when we watch Disney movies like *Treasure Isle*, *Pirates of the Caribbean*, or *Atlantis*, we get drawn into the story of discovery. We want to find the treasure. We want to share the bounty or at least see that it goes to the heroes and not to the bad guys.

What about our search for our own treasures? Do we get hooked on other people's treasure hunts because it's easier to fanaticize? Do we believe that it could never really happen to us? Or is it just that we don't believe these treasures actually exist in our own lives? They do. The hunt for your brand is all about self-examination, which leads to the best brands. When it comes to self-examination there are four kinds of treasures that we typically keep hidden or hide from. What's your hidden treasure?

1. *Perfect treasures:* Some things seem so perfect, beautiful, and valuable that we keep them hidden for fear they will get used up, be ruined, or be stolen. Do you have something that you don't use because you are afraid you might break it or use it up? Something in your past may seem so flawless that you don't want to alter its seemingly perfect arrangement. We keep treasured old books on the shelf or special gifts in the cabinet because we're afraid that if we use them we might ruin them. We keep saving them for a special occasion.

What do you have that seems too perfect to use? A perfect record that you're afraid of ruining so you eliminate yourself from certain activities? A once perfect team that is in need of change but you're afraid to break up the group and what it used to stand for? Are you protecting some perfect record or achievement because you're afraid you can never do as well or better? Are you afraid that upon self-examination it may not have been so perfect after all? This kind of treasure is meant to be held up as a triumph and an encouragement to keep trying and never stop improving yourself. Beat that record. Improve that team. You can achieve more when you put these past treasures in perspective.

2. *Once-upon-a-time treasures:* Sometimes we bury something because it was so good that we hate to realize that it's gone and over. It's better not to think about it. If we think about it, we have to grieve that it has ended or died. Some people hang on to relationships at home and at work because they seemed perfect. They won't let go of them even when they become limiting and harmful because the belief is that "once right always right." While these kinds of treasures might have been perfect at one time, their real value lies in what they can prepare you for in the future. Their worth is their ability to serve you once you examine them and use them for what they taught you. You can be sad that your once perfect treasure is now not yours, but use it to serve you for a more perfect future.

3. *Painful treasures:* Some things are hidden because they were awful and it is just plain painful to keep them out in the open. How many painful experiences do we bury deep enough so no one else can see them, and so deep that we can barely find them, either? Even brilliant corporate executives and whole organizations tend to hide their bad experiences, calling them mistakes and keeping them out of sight to avoid the inevitable razzing, criticism, or anything that would communicate, "You're not good enough!" Let your pain serve you and you will have priceless treasures.

4. *Treasures right under your nose:* And some things are hidden in plain view because we don't realize the treasures they are. That's right. Your biggest treasure is probably in plain sight. It's you.

Deep inside our lives we have many treasures that are valuable, beautiful, and rare. They are hidden beneath layers of secret stories, past experiences, and deep, cavernous emotions. They lie waiting to be dug up, unburied, lifted to the light of day for all to see and share. But like many others, we let them lie, hidden from the light, the sun, and the fresh air we breathe. Why? If they are so valuable, why?

The president of Dalmatian Press seemingly grew up as an accountant. I mean, he seemed like he'd been an accountant his whole life. While he didn't actually wear a pocket protector, he always wore white shirts and kept a predictable schedule. Most of the 1,200 people at Western Publishing's Racine, Wisconsin, offices, his prior place of employment, knew that every day at 11:40 A.M. they could find him in line at the company cafeteria, ordering the same cheeseburger that he had yesterday. After knowing him for almost 20 years, I still don't know why he became an accountant. But more important, I don't think *he* knows why he became an accountant. He rose to the top of his field and had positions of prominence—but he was miserable.

Something about the way he grew up, his environment, his expectations (or lack of them) moved him into this career path that would provide him a predictable and stable life. He was a classic example of a man having treasures in his life that were unseen and locked up. He wasn't sure what to do—he didn't have the map. But he readily acknowledged that the accountant identity wasn't his true self. It was a successful life, but not nearly as successful as it could and should be.

At age 40 he began the work of self-examination, to begin to see what only he had to offer the world. There were so many people in his early life telling him that he shouldn't do this or that. There had been so many people who wanted to help him because they loved him and wanted to give him an easier life. Companies and bosses had boxed him into the stereotype of an accountant. The pliable clay that made up his young ambitions and character had become like concrete. His treasure was buried and out of sight.

A set of circumstances forced him out of his comfort zone and provided an opportunity for him to expand his business experience into the search for business solutions and repair of corporate business mishaps. His old belief system of who he was, based on what the world told him, was breaking down. Success after success created a new belief system within him. New experiences shaped his values for creative, alternative invention and production. He found his real treasure: the ability to creatively fix problems, counsel, and advise. Who knew an accountant could be creative? Maybe he was never an accountant after all. He found his treasures. He used his perfect scores from the past as records to better instead of impediments that unnerved him from trying something new. His treasured relationships were challenged, improved, and expanded. His painful experiences of life and loss were examined and used as beacons. He discovered and proved that he was more valuable than anyone imagined and that he possessed more reserves and assets untold.

> We sometimes end up being the person we think we should be and not the person we really are.

Today, the president of Dalmatian Press brings all of his experiences into the workplace.

We don't even know these treasures are here. We don't know what we hold in our own hearts, under our nose, beneath our skin, or behind our eyes that only reflect what we want others to see.

Stephen and Susan Polis Schutz are two very successful publishers. Their companies, Blue Mountain Arts and bluemountain.com, have sent out over 1.5 billion greeting cards. With their characteristic look these cards immediately make the recipient feel uplifted. Who would guess that Stephen's earlier education and work was in physics! He and I spoke at the launching of their book, *Blue Mountain: Turning Dreams into Reality*, and he explained that his experiences in physics were treasures that he still used in business every day: "Data and statistics need the same analysis in any endeavor I take on."[4] What if he forgot about his earlier life experiences? He found a way to make his past scientific experiences part of the treasure in his future liberal arts business.

I know that to a Fortune 500 company, the typical and easy definition of treasures is all about money and market share and equity value. Yes, they are part of the bounty but the low-hanging fruit is the treasure of your brand. The treasure is often buried or undiscovered. When we discover these treasures we'll learn that encoding the clues and following the map will take us on a very dangerous journey, albeit an adventure of mystery and excitement. These are the things that will make us richer than you can imagine.

The Treasure Hunt

Remember, the pure goal of a treasure hunt is to uncover that which is so valuable it has no right, and does no good, to be covered. And what is the purpose of uncovering something? Isn't it to hold it, know its value, and put it to use? When people find financial wealth they are quick to announce it and take ownership of it. Many can't wait to brag about their winnings. Can you imagine feeling the same way about your value that can't be measured financially?

What is happening to these treasures as they lie buried or hidden? What can the darkness do to them? Their value can decay.

Before you give it any more thought, which could only lead to trepidation, you must go and start digging. Dig with all your heart. Put your back into it. Put everything you have into it so that you feel every muscle straining. Your heart will be pumping and fueling the sharp, quick search of your life. Feel first. Then think.

This type of search can lead to either bitter disappointment or incredible power. It will be a treasure hunt steeped in either danger or exhilaration. This is where you need to push yourself past your comfort zone. Turn the discomfort into comfort. We can get used to anything if we practice it long enough. Practice constant self-examination and you will learn to become comfortable knowing yourself and your unique power and influence in the world.

What at first looks like labor will turn to pleasure. What feels like work and labored breathing from your hard effort will become a rhythm of sound and movement if you let it. Take something that belonged to the past and make it yours again. When done for the right reasons, that is an awesome accomplishment.

The key to opening up a treasure chest filled with your life is to treat it like an unexpected gift at an unexpected time. Enjoy the first vision of your treasure. That's absolutely the best moment. That vision, that moment is uncensored. It happens before anyone, including you, tries to analyze it and figure it out. It comes before fear or panic or sadness appears. It occurs before rejection of any kind sets in.

When we do this kind of self-examination, we will finally be able to build on a solid foundation. Only when we take out what is shifting beneath us can we plant our feet and set our hearts and minds on firm ground. No more surprise earthquakes. No more tremors. And what has been revealed can be examined and seen in the light of day, and recognized as the treasure it can be.

I worked with Thomas Nelson, one of America's most successful publishing companies, to help them define and build a new brand for a new publishing division. Before going through the brand-building steps outlined later in this book, they brainstormed over 50 possible names for the new division. The criteria for considering any name were that it sounded good, made sense, and wasn't already taken by another publisher. Many of the names sounded great.

We began the process of discussing the experiences of the division leaders and the company that had brought them to this point of launching a new division. Uncovering these experiences led to the discovery of their values of strength, history, leadership, excellence, and power that were common to everyone in the group and the company itself. How do those experiences and values translate to a new brand? Suddenly the initial list of new division names like Gathering Point and Creative Ink didn't seem to tell the true story. They didn't communicate the history, power, and strength of the people and the division.

The group ultimately chose the name Westbow. It is the name of their true story. In 1798 a young man named Thomas Nelson launched a world-class publishing company in Edinburgh, Scotland—on a street named West Bow. There's a story there that will be asked about and can be told with great passion, resulting in a memorable description of the new division. The logo contains the image of an archer that conveys the feelings of strength and excellence and the ability to hit a target. It has been well received and, even better, it is getting the response they wanted.

Your Experiences Have Profound Value

You are the ultimate treasure. Your experiences are valuable. Your memories, as well as your thoughts and feelings about those memories, are valuable to you and to everyone you come into contact with. There's a reason that job advertisements ask for "experience."

Remember skinning your knee? Can you remember feeling the sting and seeing the little red spots of blood popping up to the skin's surface? Today, you react immediately with sympathy and compassion to the small child you see falling on the concrete sidewalk, crying over his little skinned knee, because you can remember your own experience falling. When you see a child fall, you almost reach for your own knee and inaudibly suck in your breath as if you feel the sting, too.

Films and TV shows meet with the most success when the experiences of the characters tap into similar experiences we've had. If we couldn't relate to the actors, there wouldn't be the collective gasps when the hero gets smacked or the audible sighs when the heroine gets kissed. The extent to which you can recall and feel what you went through in the past is the extent to which you will be able to offer yourself and make a difference in the world.

The more you remember and feel your experiences, the better you will relate to others. A skinned knee is a relatively small thing. Just think about the value of your memories of success and failure, acceptance and isolation, life and near death. These valuable memories will shape your brand and the way it expresses itself.

Remember getting your first promotion? Remember how it felt to work all night to turn in a project on time and under budget? Remember being accused and embarrassed unfairly by a tyrannical boss? Remember how it felt to be fired? Remember how you felt when you were recognized as the best and were promoted? These are the true experiences that have true value. If you wince and push a memory away, stop. Remember it. These experiences and memories have value because they are the key to making your brand unique and relatable.

Men and women use their memories differently. Psychologist, expert, and respected scientist Pamela Peele reported on the *Larry King Live* talk show that a woman uses both hemispheres in her brain all the time.[5] She will see a child fall and think, "I remember falling when I was five *and it hurt and I felt stupid.*" A man, on the other hand, often uses just one side of his cranial hemisphere. He sees a child fall and more likely thinks, "I remember falling when I was five." Period.

For your experiences to add the most value to your brands you must try to use both sides of your brain.

Think about them and feel them. Some people are a little uncomfortable whenever they are asked to *feel*. That's okay. True development and growth toward greatness is bound to be uncomfortable at first.

Anyone who has been supported through an illness, job loss, business start-up, bankruptcy, death, or an assault of one kind or another knows that there is a special connection and a feeling of encouragement from talking with someone else who has gone through the same experience. That is the basis for the establishment and proliferation of support groups. And for all you who don't endorse the idea of support groups, even the group around the water cooler at the office is a support group. So is your church, the Rotary group, sports night, the gym, and anywhere else that people benefit from doing things together and sharing information.

Support Your Experiences

Support is good. Sometimes the most effective support comes from people who share their true experiences. When two people share similar experiences they can relate to each other. Loyalty is created. That's fundamental to building powerful brands.

After being brutally assaulted in New York City, I talked to a therapist, a shrink, friends, and dear family so that I might better cope with the aftermath. The truth was, I felt little support and wasn't coping well with that experience. Three years later, my best friend took me to a support rally for men and women victimized by violence. I didn't want to go. But then I heard respected politicians, doctors, scholars, and people just like me speak about their experience and their power to help. Ultimately I felt a deeper feeling of support unlike any I had before. Now when I see other such organizations I am inclined to listen to their commercials and take the action they request. I believe they have built an image and reputation based on truth and authentic experiences. Because of their experiences they have fulfilled a promise that they can meet my needs and anticipate my wants. They can fill in the gaps where support is most needed.

It is one thing to have someone offer you sympathy, but it is quite a different thing when you know that the one supporting you has actually felt what you feel, feared what you fear, hurt like you hurt. Then advice and understanding reaches you in a personal way. It makes a connection.

When you build the best brands you'll connect with your audience's wants and needs. You'll feel their hopes and anticipate exactly what they want because you have been there. Strong brands offer hope and relief at the same time. Strong brands offer a kind of support system.

It is support that we are looking for when we read biographies and great business books that tell us how they did it. We wonder and want to know, "Did they go through what I'm going through now? How did they succeed? Can I do it, too?"

It's the desire for support and understanding of what we are going through that makes us attend seminars and leadership conferences. "How did they do it?" we wonder. When reading self-help books we look for insight into our own lives.

We don't actually want to know how *they* did it as much as we want to know how their experience can help *us* do it. As we read someone else's success story we search for how it relates to our predicament. It's natural to read other's true stories and put ourselves in the other's situation to see if we relate and can get the same results. CEO groups and president's councils and virtually every other kind of networking group exist to help others by relating our stories to each other.

When we remember what we went through and tell others, "If I did it, you can do it, too," it's support that we're giving.

When you find the memories of your experiences buried deep beneath time, hold them up and look at them. Let the light shine through them like it shines through stained glass windows, throwing astonishing colors on those around you. That awful experience as well as every good one is yours to provide you with an amazing capacity to connect with someone in your life. And that is what makes you so very unique and special. That is what will eventually build your unique and authentic brand.

It is the entire sum of your past and present that makes you unique to everyone in your future. No one but you has experienced what you have. No one but you can bring these experiences and their valuable results to your organization. You won't be like the rest of the group. You'll stand out for all the right reasons in your organization once you know yourself and know how to make your authentic self known.

Strong personal brands are integral to a company's strength and success.

In New York City there is a well-known and respected prosecuting district attorney named Linda Fairstein, best known for running the Sex Crimes Unit of the District Attorney's office for two decades. She prosecuted the 1986 New York preppie murder case and the 1989 Central Park jogger assault. Ms. Fairstein took on my criminal case against a five-star New York City hotel, the Essex House, and the high-ranking security guard who attacked me. Cool and smooth, with her beautiful blonde hair and piercing eyes behind scrutinizing glasses, she was a walking brand of intelligent compassion. She didn't just use her brains for success. She was successful because of her compassion that brought out the best in people. She has influence for all the right reasons. Her experiences created a brand that promised justice and the power to get it. Her brand and its reputation eventually launched a successful author career of criminal suspense novels such as *Cold Hit* and *Final Jeopardy*.

Her assistant D.A., Martha Bashford, well respected for her cold hit investigations, saw me through four years of grueling trial law. Over the years I learned about her disabilities, her daughter, her husband, and heard about her win/loss record, which was mostly wins. I don't know her full story, but I know it resulted in her value of determination, expressed calmly as, "I'll show them." Today, Ms. Bashford enjoys uncommon success in New York City law. Her reputation enhances that of the public New York legal system.

Linda Fairstein and Marsha Bashford know the power of personal brands. Each time they begin jury selection they must look behind the image of potential jurors and determine what their stories are. With only a few questions and little information, they discern whether these citizens will be able to relate to their case. Will they be able to build loyalty and get them to take the action they want and vote in their favor? Your personal brand can help or hinder someone's professional goals, including your own.

Likewise, these attorneys hope that the true story of the one they represent will come across in the person's dress, voice, appearance, and everything that the jury sees and feels, to connect with the rest of the story inside. John Grisham had a number one hit novel turned theatrical success called *Runaway Jury*, based on this important principle. Our personal brands matter. We are putting our image and reputation out there for others to use or misuse, whether we mean to or not.

The decision for Bill Gates and Martha Stewart to testify or not testify in their respective lawsuits was the most important decision of their defense. Their personal brands extend to their professional brands and in fact define the conglomerates that they run and control. If the juries and decision makers like them and can relate to them, then the outcome of their trials is more likely to go their way. If the jury doesn't like them, then they will get all the wrong kind of attention and the wrong results.

You may not think you care if others like you or not, but what they think of you is your brand. If you want to get great results from your brand, then you need to know what others think of you. You need to know how your brand is perceived. Don't change your true self for others. Be who you really are—but examine what the results are.

New York City attorney Benjamin Fein supported my case with ingenious strategy and uncharacteristic legal compassion that could only come from his world of personal experiences. I've shared my theories of branding with Ben, and he has remarked, with humorous overtones of testosterone, "I don't bring my whole self to the office. I don't express love at the office." But I don't agree. His profound experiences of love and loss in his personal life have fostered his value of honesty, fairness, and compassion. His personal brand permeates his office and is seen, heard, and felt as the firm continues to grow. He is conscious of other people's needs and wants, and as a result his firm is better run, gets better results, and is extremely successful. Because of Ben Fein, people want to work there and give their best. That comes from his thinking more about others and giving in less to his ego.

His personal brand is a big part of the firm's brand. In the last five years, The New York City law firm Meister, Seelig and Fein has grown from a large successful law firm to one of the most successful law firms where New York competes the hardest.

These people's own personal experiences established each of their personal brands. Each of them developed a personal brand of success, determination, and intelligence. If you ask people what they feel when they see these individuals or hear their voices, they will say, "I'm in the presence of intelligence and persistence. There's a 'Never give up' attitude here clothed in compassion." That's their brand. And their professional brands, including the New York City court system and Ben Fein's law firm, are filled with the individual influence of these personal brands.

During my criminal case, when people entered the courtroom they felt a sense of victory, determination, and the spirit of a die-hard defender for the innocent. Linda Fairstein wasn't required to show up in the courtroom the day the jury was hearing summations. But when she made an unexpected appearance, the judge and the jury noticed. They felt the power of her brand. Her reputation preceded her. Her presence made the jury feel important, and that helped them take the action she wanted, a decision in my favor. We won the trial against all odds.

These people I've described connected with all their audiences—colleagues, defendants, plaintiffs, judges, jury members, or media. The emotional dialogue was constant, resulting in such a strong personal brand that they have all seen years of professional achievement and advancement. They don't leave their personal experiences at home. They carry them with them even though they don't know it. When they realize it, they will know the full power of their true experiences and make even better use of them as the treasures they are.

They bring their whole self to the office, and it creates a consistent image that gives everyone they know what they need, want, and expect. The world knows they're not phony and embraces them.

What do these stories have to do with you? Think about them in the context of your work. How is your personal brand infused into your professional work? How is it helping you build your business—or is it hindering it? When people see and hear you, they will attach how they feel about you to how they feel about your business.

Good brands don't just influence people. They change people's lives.

You Have a Story to Tell

You have a story. You are a story. And although we don't all come with architectural plans or blueprints, we certainly all leave behind a life that can be seen, written about, or illustrated. We leave behind us a myriad of stories that have been told and retold to those in our lives. We tell them with words and with photographs. We tell them with resumes, medical records, and our old school transcripts. We tell our stories whether we mean to or not.

People are watching you, even when you don't see them watching. People are reading the story of you. Our story is told by glowing recommendations and references. It is also told by rumors and gossip, whether wrongly or accurately. It is told by the way our children live their lives. And it is told by how our company succeeds or fails, and especially by how it responds to success and failure. We all have a story.

People have different comfort levels when it comes to telling their story. How many times have you sat on an airplane or waited in a doctor's office and been surprised, embarrassed, or bored to hear a stranger tell you his complete life story soon after you sat down? Some people *love* to tell their stories, don't they? Most people love to hear stories. We wait through the commercial to hear Paul Harvey's "The Rest of the Story." Virtually every business meeting I have begins with someone asking me, "What's your story? How did Dalmatian Press get started, and why did you name it Dalmatian Press?"

You may see the opposite in men or women who have been married for 20 years and have yet to open up to their spouse about a childhood trauma. They may not even tell their story to themselves, much less to another. That's a buried treasure.

We may consciously tell our story on job interviews or on first dates. We can write it out in business plans and journals. We can leave our stories at the office and try to dissolve the day in a drink or in front of the TV at night. However we choose to tell it or avoid talking about it, we *always* tell the truth by the way we live and by everything we say and do or don't do.

Control Your Story

Once you realize and understand that your story *is* being told, whether you want it to be or not, you will want to take some control of *how* it is related. In this case, control is more of a responsibility and an opportunity than anything else. I've learned to tell the Dalmatian Press story so that it effectively lays out the American dream in a way that relates to whatever audience is before me that day. The truth of it creates a brand and a memorable experience resulting in interest and loyalty. This is what helps lead to the purchase order in a world where dozens of publishers are competing with similar products and services.

So examine the following:

- What is your true story?
- Why should you tell your story?
- How should you tell your story?
- How are you telling your true story now?

Memories

If our experiences are so valuable in building our brands, then our ability and willingness to remember them is equally crucial. Why on earth do humans have the capacity to remember? Memories only exist because we have this uniquely human ability to make them, and then to remember them.

Never before has the phrase "Why on earth?" meant so much to me. Why on earth do we have so much to remember in this lifetime? Surely we could wait until the next life to file and retrieve so much that has clogged our mind's limited space. Surely we could postpone remembering those painful memories that hurt and twist inside our minds and somersault through our body. The moment a painful memory comes to mind, we turn our heads away as if we could actually see it in front of us. And what about all those things that we want to remember, like a name, directions, where our keys were laid? Why can't we remember those things?

What we do remember is impressive. But what about those experiences we push out of our minds because the pain and hurt and confusion of them isn't worth going through? These are the memories that we have placed a price on that is unrealistic and unfair in any value system. We think the price is too high to pay for those memories. But what will it cost us if we don't recall them? If we understood what these memories were really worth we would dig them up immediately. If we understood that the ugly memories are the precious ones that are intended for great things, we would hold them up, dust them off, and discover what they looked like in the light of day.

Our deepest fear may not be that they are too awful to recall, but that they are powerful beyond measure. The courage and stamina it takes to remember difficult memories is daunting, even knowing the benefits they could bring us. Whatever has happened in the past isn't meant to lie in darkness. We must uncover what our mind tries to forget. We must shake it out and let it be seen in the right perspective and through the sight of forgiveness and wisdom that gives meaning beyond our small, present-tense living, so we can make use of it in the future. Too often our ego puts up obstacles to remembering what might have been foolish or unsuccessful events. Lose the ego and your foolish pride. Stop worrying about what people will think of you.

Reach for the next rung of success, the one based on truth and not on what the world says you should be.

Difficult memories include betrayal, hate, greed, pride, loss . . . Our memories run long and deep under the ground we think is solid. Memories of loved ones dying, trusted ones betraying us, illness tricking us, team members abandoning us, bosses criticizing us, have all been pushed so far back that we can say we don't remember them. We testify, "I don't recall." But we should. The purpose of memories isn't to let us cling to a life of victimization. They shouldn't excuse us from the work of building a better future. Memories help us know that something bad happened and something good is going to come from it, maybe not today, but soon.

Somehow, thanks to the intrinsic design and wiring of our body, soul, and mind, whatever happened in our past will affect our future. Our thought processes will manifest the very best that is within us. And that is why some memories are golden.

A Return on Your Investment in Branding—We Want More

The branding cycle, personal or corporate, is about either wanting more or wanting to be part of something more. Building a brand is asking for attention. Some ask passively and some ask aggressively, but the relationship between brands and attention cannot be denied. Does everyone have a desire, perhaps unspoken and even unacknowledged, to be part of something more? I know that doesn't sound independent or self-sufficient enough for this tough business world. But I suspect that I am not alone in wanting more.

Being *more* comes about in so many ways. We can create it. We can be it. We can look at it and feel a part of it. When I see something exuding excellence, something pure, something exquisite, I just want to associate myself with it any way I can. Isn't that why many of us are constantly drawn to new opportunities? We want to be part of what we think is more.

Professionally, I want more. I want to exude the kind of excellence that I see in those who are at the top of the game. They are quick witted, calm in chaos, smarter than imaginable, and able to see through any problem instantly to save the day. People hang on their every word. Small crowds gather around them, and when they move on, a new group forms around them. They make us feel like we can be better. That's their brand. It's not about how they look or their nickname or the clothes they wear. It's about how they make us feel.

Build the kind of professional life that makes others feel like they can do anything. Build a brand that will go before you so that when people come into your presence they already believe in the promise your brand has made.

As much as I love the exhilaration I get when I see something extraordinary and beautiful, I feel a little sad too, because it also stirs my feeling of lack in the beauty category. I suppose it is a yearning to be more.

It is also a longing to *give* more. Giving more would result in being appreciated more, if not by others than by myself for doing the right thing. So there it is: a circle that you and I spend our waking lives trying to close. It is the circle of giving and receiving, spinning around a core of appreciation. And that brings us back to being chosen for being special and authentic. Once again, we are back to building brands.

This is so important that I'm going to say it again: There's an endless feedback loop in branding, composed of giving and receiving attention, with the goal of choosing and being chosen for all the right reasons.

When you're trying to create and become more, what does it look like in your life? What is keeping you from developing more or expressing more? What is your ratio of giving attention and getting attention? How are giving attention and getting attention related?

The first step in building your brand is to do the work of self-examination. There were a lot of memories that I would have liked to wipe clean like a blackboard. But whatever kind of brand you're building, be it personal or professional, individual or for the whole company, dig up those memories until they are so thick in front of your face that you have to brush them aside to see past them.

Remember why you were created. What was your purpose? What were the experiences that collected in the form you call life? Take some time to remember the small victories that shaped your dreams and goals. Take more time to look back at the mistakes that you called failures but that created your values of determination or pride, or perhaps your fears. Examine them, inspect them, study and scrutinize them to learn from them and know their worth. They are your treasures to invest in and to anchor you in your unique and powerful beginnings.

There's a reason we use expressions like "Remember where you came from," "Don't forget your roots," "Don't get too big for your britches." Lines like these became clichés because they're truisms. When you are looking for the "You Are Here" signs in your life, sometimes you have to go back to the "You Were There" sign.

Where are you?

> *Try not to become a man of success*
> *but rather to become a man of value.*
> —Albert Einstein (1879–1955)[6]

Brand Building Belief III

I will define and control, to the extent that I can, my personal and professional story because it provides for my success and the success of others.

Brand Builders

1. What are the different ways your personal story gets told? What are some of the ways your professional story gets told?
2. Which parts of your story are told by you and which are told by someone else and out of your control?
3. How do you formally or informally support others with your expertise from your experiences?
4. How do you define *more* in life and how much more do you want? How can your brand help you get more?
5. What are a few of your treasures that you keep buried and why?
6. Do you believe you're successful enough and therefore don't need the help that self-examination could give you?

Chapter FOUR

Bring On the Brand

*Somehow I can't believe that there are any heights that can't be
scaled by a man who knows the secrets of making dreams come
true. This special secret, it seems to me, can be summarized in
four C's. They are Curiosity, Confidence, Courage, and
Constancy, and the greatest is Confidence. When you believe a
thing, believe it all the way, implicitly and unquestionably.*
—Walt Disney (1901–1966)[1]

The Race Is On

The 16-year-old boy's age had been found out. He was prevented
from enlisting in the military, but at least he could join the Red
Cross and drive ambulances overseas. No ordinary ambulances
though—instead of a routine camouflage paint job, his would be
covered with cartoons.

His military experiences no doubt shaped who he was and how
he lived. During World War II, 94 percent of his already successful Disney studio facilities were engaged in special government work, including the production of training and propaganda films for the armed
services, as well as health films that are still shown throughout the
world by the U.S. State Department. The other 6 percent made films to
raise the civilian morale. Walt had begun drawing at an early age, selling his first sketches to neighbors when he was only seven years old.

Walt Disney believed in believing. When his name or image
comes to mind it conjures up feelings of hope and optimism. He is
one of America's greatest examples of a self-made success. Walt Dis-

ney isn't only a twentieth-century legend but his name is shorthand for rich imagination.

It has been said that Walt Disney did more to touch the hearts, minds, and emotions of millions of Americans than has any other man in the past century. Since his time, many others have created animated characters, theme parks, studios, and film productions. Some have even done it better than Disney. But it is the sum of all his experiences that created the unique Walt Disney and Disney Company brands. Certainly our world will know but one Walt Disney.

We've all heard the expression, "Live and learn." In other words, we all learn what we live. And so we must improve the way we live, and improve and improve again.

Practice doesn't make perfect. Practice makes improvement.

It's never too late. In order to improve our brand and its impact on the world, let's use Walt Disney's secrets for making dreams come true as we allow our brand to tell the truth:

- *Curiosity.* Be curious and discover and define our specific abilities, qualities, and gifts that uniquely define us.
- *Confidence.* Have confidence and believe that these discoveries are rare and valuable. Don't just know about them; know that they are yours, and uniquely yours. *Own* them.
- *Courage and Constancy.* Have courage and teach yourself to live with yourself, constantly and persistently. The most important relationship you will ever have isn't with your family or friends or even your customers—it is with yourself. If you treat yourself well, I promise you, so will everyone else.

If your business relationships aren't bringing you the results you want, it's probably more about you than anything else. Restore the relationship with yourself. Stop playing roles like "struggling businessman" or "poor entrepreneur who never got a chance." Believe that your personal and professional story will have an ending that allows you to live happily ever after. What are some of the roles you are playing? If someone were describing you, what character would they say you play?

The price for improvement is paid in time and effort and, yes, some pain from your discoveries. But not asking these questions will cost you dearly in terms of focus, authenticity, and results.

Janis Ian voiced our fears when she sang the popular soulful song from the 1970s, "At Seventeen." She sang that she "learned the truth at seventeen/that love was meant for beauty queens/and high school girls with clear skinned smiles."[2] A million young girls, and no doubt women of all ages, cringed when they listened because they believed that we must pretend to be what we are not or try to look like some beauty queen in order to be loved.

Those false beliefs, constantly reinforced by the media, keep us perpetually trapped in the beauty brand. Even great corporations fall into the trap and create beautiful but false images, thinking that their customers will love them more for their opulent lobby or impressive uniforms or gorgeous offices, stationery, or whatever.

All our lives we try to be what we think the world sees as perfect, in order to stop the pain of being less than others. We try to stop the pain of being left alone and unchosen by being not who we are but who we think we must be.

Listening

She sat in his waiting room, waiting. Forty-five minutes past her given appointment time, she still sat and waited patiently. She was a busy executive herself, with little free time and always juggling an overloaded schedule. An hour now after the two o'clock appointment, she fidgeted but knew that waiting for Dr. Doug Brown was worth it. His brand, his image, his reputation was that of a doctor who listened. His brand made his patients feel understood, respected, and recognized as deserving attention. These were in fact the qualities that he valued and that were translated into doctor-patient appointments that exceeded the normal 15-minute office visit.

This wasn't just a satisfying experience for his patients; it was smart business, too. When he listened to his patients they responded by listening carefully to him. By listening carefully and thoroughly to them, he could anticipate what they needed, but more important, he knew what they wanted. He gained loyalty, which resulted in patients taking the actions he wanted. And this actually made his medical practice more efficient in the long term. I asked him once why he was such a patient listener and he said, "It's one of the things I value most in life—being listened to."

If branding is all about your stories, then think about the flip side of telling them. For every story told there should be a listener.

Listening is as important as the actual telling of any story. Remember, we have two ears and only one mouth. We know that we all have stories to tell. If we are to build loyalty, a crucial component of any great brand, then we must not only tell our stories but we must listen to each others' stories, too. When we listen carefully to someone's story, whether personal or professional, it should make an impact on our ideas, opinions, and feelings. We will then be able to anticipate their needs and wants and be a better brand.

Listening is as important an act as telling. Both acts are essential and revealing. The way we listen tells as much about us as the way we tell our stories. And only when we stop and listen will others be able to tell their stories to us. True stories mean so much less if they go unheard.

Not only should we listen to each other's stories but we should find a way to hear our own voice. Listen to yourself. What are you saying? How are you saying it? What do you think you sound like to others? Listening completes the branding cycle. It reminds us that the life of the brand grows on two-way communication.

When Dalmatian Press was competing for the Warner Bros. master publishing activity book license, we made a different kind of case. We highlighted our financials, product line, and distribution attributes of our company, but then we talked about their company brand and ours. We told our story and why it made us different. We discussed our experiences in which retailers, moms, investors, and many partners listened to us and how that called attention to the belief that listening was as important as talking. Everybody knows that, but we were living it.

We pitched the idea to Warner Bros. that in a business environment where most of our competitors were offering the same features that we offered (although we believed we did it better), we were also offering a resource that was in short supply. We were a listening company and one that created knowledge from listening. This was our brand. This was our experience and one that shaped our belief that listening is power. I don't think the people present then remember that speech, but I believe that at that moment we affected the emotional tone of the conference room. We were involving our potential partner in our very human experiences that went beyond inventory control and selling terms. Our brand, shared via our experiences, broke us out from the features and price structures that our competitors competed with.

How Your Brand Is Born

Whatever you are and all that you will become is summed up for you and the world to see in what we call a brand. Just like Kodak or Nike, you have an identity. Your brand is whatever people think or, more important, feel whenever your name or image comes to mind.

You have an image that serves as an instant message for all who look to you for help, for knowledge, for inspiration. Those around you use your image the same way we use shorthand. It quickly encodes what lies beneath and what takes more time to understand.

What is your brand identity? And, just as important, what is your brand awareness? Make no mistake that as you uncover your stories your brand will change forever. The very means by which you take on and go about this search will differentiate you from the rest, including the old you.

As you define your true stories, put words to them, and *feel* them, you will be changed. You will become more relevant to your everyday friends and business acquaintances as you apply your own experiences to theirs. You will be infinitely more appropriate, approachable, and meaningful. Hopefully you will also become more compassionate.

How you live with your newly discovered stories will recreate your identity. So ask yourself what feelings you want your presence, even the thought of your presence, to evoke in others. What are the senses that you appeal to? What will you stand for? What's your brand?

The more your brand affects someone's well-being, the more critically it is evaluated.

People are willing to pay an enormous amount of money for an aspirin brand that affects their health. They may not care as much about dish soap. Therefore, we are much more likely to pay for a brand-name pain reliever like Tylenol or Advil, whereas we shop prices and make do with a generic brand of dish soap.

How much more are we willing to pay for a doctor or lawyer with a big brand name, because they can make such a huge difference in the quality of our life. Never mind a doctor—think about how much we are willing to pay a hair stylist because of what we think they can do for us!

It was a natural product line extension for Dalmatian Press to publish educational workbooks. They are more ink on paper, are sold to the same retail buyer, and use the same manufacturing and art production process. In fact a lot of coloring book companies produced educational workbooks. Many of our competitors used their everyday cartoon art and put simple educational text under the picture, such as "How many ducks can you count in this picture?" This they called an educational line! This was a way to make additional revenues for their company. But what about the brands that these workbooks were published under?

Dalmatian Press had established a brand that made people feel positive and happy. We hadn't built a brand that made people trust us for our ability to teach their children. Putting our little puppy dog on an educational line wouldn't offer much educational credibility. So we birthed a new brand called Home Learning Tools. The key to its success is more than great content. It has a logo than proclaims an alliance with Harvard and the chief of child development on a child-friendly gold ribbon. Our covers are fun but, unlike our competitor's, they are not funny.

Our competitors have printed kangaroos and clowns on the cover, which have no bearing on learning. They are merely meant to entertain. If the brand stands for trust, then what does that look like as an educational workbook? Not clowns or kangaroos. It looks like the best content possible that parents and teachers can relate to and kids will enjoy. It looks like the actual interior pages delightfully depicting learning with characters and colors that will never look outdated. What's more credible than the DP brand? A brand extension of DP called Home Learning Tools, coproduced with Harvard's chief of child development. This is what it means to know who you are and what you value, and translate it into the right look and sound that your audience can relate to and be loyal to.

This new line is a big success, but only because we examined what Dalmatian Press stood for. We know who we are, and our customers count on that. We didn't try to make the brand be something that it's not. However, it was the strength of the Dalmatian Press brand that opened the doors with retail buyers to make a sales pitch about our new Home Learning Tools brand. To that audience, our Dalmatian Press brand stood for good service, good quality, good prices, and an overall good experience that made them feel valued and important.

The point is that educational material is on a different playing field than coloring and activity books. It can have a greater impact on children's lives, for better or worse. So parents and teachers are going to place more importance on the brand.

In 1994 Western Publishing (Golden Books) was so desperate to cash in on the popular Power Rangers license that they made a deal with Saban Entertainment's licensing agent to publish educational workbooks. Another publisher named Modern already had the rights to publish coloring books, so the only way Golden could partner with the Power Rangers was by inventing another children's book category. Do you trust the Red Ranger to teach arithmetic and reading to your child? They make the best action figures and coloring books, but their brand doesn't stand for education. I might trust Sesame Street to teach my kids, but not Shrek or the Flintstones. They can create great new opportunities for companies to make money, but it's a bad use of a brand.

How much more would people pay for the valuable brand of a friend or a trusted mentor at work, if there was such a thing? Well, there is. It is the image that you emit. It is the image that you create and protect. It is your reputation. It will surely change now that you have found and reclaimed your stories, once hidden and untold. You can now consistently protect the essence of all that you want to be.

Now you will get attention because you will be known as the one who understands, the one who gets it. Whether you are building your personal brand or your professional brand, you will be chosen for your ability to relate to other's wants and needs. With such a reputation, you will be trusted with amazing stories, not just to listen to but also to react to. People will choose you or your organization, expecting something in return. They will expect results from their encounter with you.

Your brand will go beyond managing people's needs and wants. It will manage people's expectations. Depending on who they are, the results desired will range from success and solutions to love and compassion. But what they know is that by associating with you, they will get better and faster results. The outcome of an encounter with you will be more satisfying than once hoped for. And the domino effect of such encounters will be unending.

Brand Reconciliation

In creating a brand we too often speak of the external things. We are mostly conscious of our accomplishments. Whether it is our human appearance or our company's balance sheet, we only see the physical manifestation. We focus on our behavior and on visual signs. The science and practice of branding seems to emphasize modifying outward behavior and signs. So the notion that brands can succeed or fail depending on how we think about them may seem like a stretch. This may be because it is far easier to focus on external behavior than internal feelings. It's a lot more complicated to figure out the essence of the behavior or the reason for the accomplishment.

But when we figure out that the internal affects the external, we'll see that any shift in our beliefs creates an external shift in our brand. When we figure this out, then we are approaching the root of the brand—our own brand. The reasons usually go back to the true stories we examined in the last chapter.

And this is exactly what we must do. We should not just build a brand that makes us feel better or look better. We should not create a brand just to get the attention we want. I'm all in favor of feeling better, looking better, and getting what we want, but we must reconcile our inner self with our outer brand. When there is disparity between what we say we are and who we really are, then our brand will fail miserably and we will be miserable. We will be unsuccessful.

BMW operates admirably in the zone of brand integrity. Few industries depend on brands as much as the automobile industry does, and BMW does it well. Helmut Panke, CEO since 2002, was quoted in the *Wall Street Journal*: "As provocative as it sounds, the biggest task [in building your brand image] is to be able to say no. Because in the end, authentic brand management boils down to understanding that a brand is a promise that has to be fulfilled everywhere, at any time. So when something doesn't fit, you must make sure that it is not done."[3] When BMW had to decide whether to get into the hugely successful growth category of minivans, it said no. The brand didn't fulfill the BMW brand values. Minivans would have broken the brand promise. This is an important example of a company knowing who it is and knowing what its customers need and want from its brand.

Perhaps two of the most important questions we can ask are these:

1. How were you designed to live, and what does that look like?
2. How was your company designed to be, and what does that look like?

If you were a ship meant to cross oceans, you would know what that would look like. You could imagine an ocean liner or an exciting cruise ship. If you were a boat meant for middle-aged men to relax in and eat peanuts and chips on a lazy Saturday afternoon, you would look like a pontoon boat. What are you created for? What does that look like?

When I was sick I thought about hanging up my hat and resting on my success. It would have been the safe thing to do. I wanted to be like a ship safe in harbor. But one of America's most successful business managers pointed out to me, "You weren't made to rest in a harbor. You were made to cross stormy, wild waters and reach new destinations."

The Competition

She is known, somewhat to her frustration, as the blind girl who sings contemporary Christian music. That's her brand, and she wanted to change it and take control of how she is perceived. The fact is she is an amazing Dove Award winner and entertainer. True, she's blind, but that's not *who* she is. That's just something she does. She is also everything that being blind has shaped her into.

Her name is Ginny Owens, and we began working together under difficult circumstances. What made it difficult is that in the music business there are a lot of different handlers that don't really understand branding or care about the artist's brand. They care about the immediate sales opportunities, charts, and bullets. That's why so many music labels use a formulaic method for producing new artists: When something works, make more. If a thin, blonde, belly-revealing girl sells a lot of music, then the label will put out more of the same. Before you know it there are a dozen artists on the radio who all look and sound the same. There have been a lot of one-hit wonders who followed the formula—and we loved them for a moment—but it is the unique performers who sound and look different who survive and succeed. Country music did it. Christian music did it. Rap does it.

It's hard to get people to understand the value of the brand until they see proof that it affects the revenues and profits. Ginny understands branding, but label producers and graphic designers are in the business of creating an image that may or may not be based on authenticity but is definitely based on potential sales.

Ginny and I started the work of examining her experiences to see what her authentic brand should sound like and look like. A dominant theme of mischief and freedom surfaced from her life's experiences. What does that look like? What does that sound like? For example, it doesn't look like a still photograph on the cover of her new CD. At the very least it looks like hair blowing and a little movement. The colors and shapes should be less traditional.

When we began discussing how her brand might make people feel, Ginny said something pretty profound and brave that most mature corporations wouldn't dare to say. She said, "I don't want to *make* people feel something. I want them to be able to feel whatever they want."

What she didn't understand was that she had just defined her brand brilliantly as the brand that made people feel free. She can compete in her business best when she competes with her brand. As she defines herself with her true experiences, the world will see her clearly. She will see herself more clearly, too.

Few of us venture in and out of business without the goal of making a living. Some of us are in nonprofit businesses, but we still pay salaries along with all the other expenses—rent, office equipment, the water cooler. Some people have enough money to be in a business purely for the joy of it, bringing an important service or product to people's lives. Some feel a calling to perform a mission. Some do it because the world desperately needs this service, and being selfless in a selfish world is reward enough. (What's their personal brand?)

But most people provide services and products for money. And so we compete against others who are providing similar services or products.

Besides the obvious competitors, we also compete against ourselves, our past selves, and our ghosts.

Brands live with or without competition, but they often come to our attention because of how competition exists. The fact that humans are social animals sets us up to live with competition. We are not meant to live in solitude. Other animals may survive that way, like water buffalo and leopards. But humans form families, societies, and organizations—and this makes us vulnerable to each other.

A word of criticism may be remembered forever. Why should it matter what others say? Why do we care so much about what the competition is saying about us or what the reviews, press, and editorials say? It just does and we just do. How much more do the words of a trusted friend or associate mean? As much as criticism can damage, praise of our brand can positively affect us for the rest of our lives.

Intimacy makes brands more susceptible to competition. In our modern world, we don't just live with a lot of change; we thrive on it and desire it. This creates a heightened state of desperation to be appreciated. Everywhere we go, everyone and everything is competing for attention—however you define it.

I can live for two months on a compliment.
—Mark Twain (1835–1910)[4]

How Brands Live

One of the best branding campaigns in our consumer product history was Coca-Cola's "I'd Like to Teach the World to Sing" campaign. The nation loved how those commercials made them feel. Coca-Cola became more than a beverage.

Branding has a ripple effect. We all know that one bad apple can spoil the whole bunch. Can a brand have a similar effect on whomever it touches? Can a bad brand infect its audience with meanness, apathy, or rudeness? Can a brand that tells a story of purity, fun, and goodness create the same in its audience?

Absolutely. When we tell our story or seek out stories of beauty, broadly defined as those in which we see humanity's better side, we will create a current of positive emotions. Everyone responds to their environment, for better or for worse.

Jonathan Haidt, an associate professor of psychology at the University of Virginia, researched the physiological response to what he calls moral beauty. His research showed that recalling or witnessing such acts as an 11-year-old boy helping the homeless made the subjects feel "a warm glow in the chest." But what is more remarkable is that he actually documented a responding change in their physical heart rhythms.[5]

The most powerful branding element we have as humans is to incorporate our human emotions that generate human responses. Positive responses will trigger a current or swell of action that you may not realize. Whenever you make a determination to bring whatever is good and most worthy about yourself, you will be benefiting yourself, your brand, and undoubtedly the audience who connects with and gets involved with your brand.

Branding Up

My term *branding up* describes the effect that uplifting brands have on the audience.

Consider the Hallmark brand. When you "care enough to send the very best," you send a Hallmark card. Their commercials begin by validating the act of recognizing someone as special. We say, "You're special" with a Hallmark card. This might be acknowledging anything from a birthday to an anniversary to the death of a pet. Whatever the occasion, the card gives the recipient positive attention. And when we watch those Hallmark commercials we feel better. We become motivated to give a card. We see images of love and laughter, hugs and joy, and our hearts beat a little faster. We are inclined to take action, the action they are suggesting. We buy a card, a Hallmark card. We spend $4.99 on those little cards. Now that's great brand power.

Lately television commercials have begun to show advertisements that do not talk about the product but about the quality of life people have when they use the product. Publix food stores have produced commercials that show a rich, traditional Thanksgiving gathering filled with golden moments of the family's preparation. They show the precious son coming home unexpectedly from college. Grandparents hold babies on their laps, and small animals scurry around the yard filled with fall leaves, eating nuts and berries shared by family and friends. It makes you feel good. They don't talk about the store. They don't even talk about the food in the store. They just show what the food from their store leads to: a happy Thanksgiving. Brilliant.

Their 2004 spring ad campaign made it even more personal. A woman shopper says, "When I shop at Publix I get more than groceries. I get attention. I bet I'm not the only one who feels this way."

Publix combines the two most important elements of branding in the shopper's two comments: We, as customers, want the brands we choose to give us attention (respect), and we want to *feel* like they do. Give your audience attention and they will give it right back to you.

The Cattlemen's Beef Board uses the same strategy with their campaign of "Beef. It's what's for dinner." The American Cotton Association does it with the ads that say, "Cotton, the fabric of your life." GE does it with an ad campaign, "GE: We bring good things to life."

In every case, the positive images generate positive emotions and brand us up to take positive action.

Branding-up is all about your personal true story that needs to be shared—not just told, but *shared*. The difference between telling and sharing your brand is that sharing signifies the act of *involvement* with each other. And when we incorporate the very best of ourselves into our brand, as only a brand filled with human emotions can do, we create a ripple effect of positive and uplifting responses.

Does your brand just tell a story, or does it *share* your story and get the audience to pay attention and get involved?

Our beliefs, when truly expressed, have a domino effect on everyone they come in contact with. So our beliefs may manifest in the people around us. The reality is that in some way this makes us all connected, right down to a molecular level.

Let's talk about the human qualities of your brand. Besides the fact that they should be born directly out of your humanness, the best brands will indeed make hearts beat faster and incorporate as many sensory experiences as possible. The best brands understand and connect to people's deepest emotional desires. Humans bring to the product what no inert piece of marketing copy or clever packaging design can do. They bring emotion. And when you bring true emotion from true stories, it will define your personal and professional brand as successful while other brands create only a reaction of indifference—that is, no reaction. Successful brands are able to establish a unique kind of trust with their audience.

Successful and unforgettable brands are always associated with character, and character is something that a pretender can't give. Character comes from the true stories and authentic experiences in one's life, whether it's the life of an individual or within the life of a corporation. How easy it is for us to forget that the product must ultimately be inspired by people's wants and desires! Anyone can give them what they need.

The best brands know what people want and promise to fulfill those desires. We may think about shelf space, billboard size, cost, shipping procedures, or delivery policies. And of course we have to think about profit margins, investment strategies, and resources. But until we immerse our brands in our own humanness, we will have a disconnect with our audience. Only when we begin a kind of emotional dialogue with our audience can we call ourselves a brand.

When we brand ourselves and our organizations on actual experiences that no one else has ever had, we are uniquely able to connect with people, not based on price and need but based on desire. It's the true stories of founders and why they started companies that we listen to and remember.

A charitable organization called Boot Straps sought to build its brand because it needed the kind of attention that could turn into charitable donations. We reviewed its true stories and uncovered the story of the founders, who had started off in life under the worst of circumstances. They pulled themselves up by their bootstraps and became notable, recognizable successes in their community. Their experiences shaped their values and made it important for them to support hardworking kids who didn't just deserve a break but who worked harder than most to earn a break. When they related this story to me, I asked them how often they told the story to their contributors. How often did they connect their audience to the emotions and human heartstrings of the original people behind the brand? "Rarely" was their response. They showed pictures of the kids who were helped, but the world is full of kids in need. What made their brand unique was the initial life experiences of the organization's founders followed by the important stories of worthy kids and the events that occurred as they grew.

They went on to create an elevator pitch, logo, and tagline that reflected the true stories of the founders as well as the mission. The logo was proposed to show arms lifting upwards with a spinning world placed in view to symbolize how one life will affect the whole world and keep it turning as progress is made. And the story of how and why the organization was formed will be told to make it real and memorable.

Because they had identified some of their actual stories and experiences, they had identified their uniqueness. No one else had those initial experiences. Putting a name and a face to their organization made it seem more real and definitely more human. This, then, their audience can relate to and remember. We love true stories. Boot Straps wasn't just a philosophical organization. It really happened. It was brought to life with the founders' unique human experiences.

Our society has been moving away from dealing solely in terms of objective and rational goods, into a world of desire and the subjective. You are uniquely able to transcend material satisfaction and experience and provide emotional fulfillment. Why? Because you bring the human experience to the brand. A brand is brought to life by the personality of the product or service the brand stands for. And these things don't have personalities in and of themselves. People do.

People's personalities are most powerful when they are a composite of all their experiences. It is the people behind the brand that bring it to life with their true stories. How people feel about the people behind the brand is becoming increasingly important in our society when most products offer the same thing. We have to pay attention to the people behind the brand because these days, bad people and bad companies can break the trust of the brand. Even good people can break the brand promise, and that's bad, too.

The People Inside the Brand

Consumers today expect the companies they support, their chosen brands, to know them and understand their needs. How is this possible? It is only possible when you, the person behind the brand, become real to the customer and begin an emotional dialogue on whatever is most meaningful to them.

Remember, it's not about you—your brand is about *them*.

However, being able to make the connection is still dependent upon you meeting them.

It all comes back to you sharing yourself. In order to serve the whole person, I believe you must bring your whole self to the brand. Those who do not will be less successful.

Home Depot founder Bernie Marcus, now a retired CEO and billionaire, was a young boy when his mom taught him to donate his nickels to help plant trees in Israel. He says, "My mother taught me to give back. You have to help people who are less fortunate."[6] He went on to build one of the most successful brands ever.

The Home Depot brand is rooted in community service. If someone comes in to buy supplies to build a wheel chair ramp, chances are that Home Depot will help them build it. Marcus says, "We all felt so good about it, it became part of the culture of Home Depot." Today there are over 1,500 stores and $58.2 billion in sales. What his mom taught him he uses every day. Bernie Marcus and Home Depot have invested more than $25 million in neighboring communities. That certainly gets my attention. What a great brand.

The world is so full of brands that it is brand-saturated. It is like a dripping wet paper towel, soaked and drenched, but still sitting on top of a giant puddle. How much more can we absorb? We're brand crazy. The brands that stay on the top are not always the pretty ones. Sometimes they are the oily, gritty ones. If you stay in the brand competition business long enough, you begin to feel like you are living in the wake of boasting, bragging, bad brands. As we are assaulted with brand images of the ugly and violent and controversial, we feel overwhelmed with stereotypes and false claims.

New brands have appeared so routinely that we can't help asking if there really is anything new to see and discover, anything that is unique anymore. All the new brands must fight harder and harder to get our attention. They compete with new advertising media, new sensory perceptions, and new shock waves of information. This is our competition. Individuals aren't much different. People compete with the same power clothes, teeth-whitening kits, and hairstyles. People compete by following each other to the same self-improvement seminars, picking up the same pop lingo and living styles. It's fast, it's easy, and it makes us fit in, but does this one way of living fit all?

We don't know what to do with all these brands. We don't know how to process them. As a brand expert, I don't even know how to write about them all. Branding colleagues look for new angles to glamorize the need for branding or sensationalize the stories of brands that have been damaged.

We are fascinated, not by all the success stories but by the failures. We all hang on to the news stories about what took that company down. We talk about the scandals of corporations and what they did to us to lose our trust. We boycott and protest and wait for the mighty to fall. This isn't just about who we compete with but about *how* we compete.

The growth in branding is relentless. Brands have become as common and impersonal as some generic commodity businesses. Imagine that branding strategies are so common they are generic! Could it be that the only way to compete is to limit the playing field? Is that why we tear down other people's brands? Is that why they get the press coverage?

Why don't the good and respectable brands make more headlines? Sometimes there is what's called a good news/goodwill story that captures the heart of America. Some small underdog company has done a good thing and we rally around it. But even in these cases, what they have often done is brought to light some wrong that they are trying to correct. And then the focus returns to the ugly side of the story.

There is a wonderful international organization called Cops 'n' Kids, founded by Julia Burney of Racine, Wisconsin. Cops 'n' Kids operates out of police cars by handing out books to bookless children in the inner city. Ms. Burney has built a connection between patrolling police squad cars and inner-city children. Where kids once ran *from* the squad cars they now run *to* them, calling out, "Police officer, do you have a book in there for me?"

This wonderful story was brought to light by Oprah in a three-part series about how Julia saw a problem and did something with her own life to improve the world around her. Her personal brand and professional brand are the result of her true life experiences of living in poverty and living without books and the opportunities books bring. Besides all the good work she is doing, I asked, "Is the Cops 'n' Kids brand successful?" Well, how many brands are lucky enough to be discovered and endorsed by Oprah? Only a powerful brand can rise to that level of attention. Only true brands that are authentic and one of a kind can become noteworthy and remain noteworthy.

The brand grew and grew and grew. There are now more than 26 Cops 'n' Kids programs around the nation and the number is still growing. When you see their logo, attributes like achievement and accomplishment against all odds come to mind. This brand makes you feel hopeful. It connects to everyone's hopes and dreams for a child's better life.

When I interviewed Julia in October 2002, she was speaking to a Delaware group of politicians, police chiefs, volunteers, and cops on patrol. "I was a bookless child," she said. "People wrote me off as a future failure but here I am today as your keynote speaker. Give books to kids and you give them a chance to get out and up in the world."[7]

Julia Burney tells her true story every day with her organization. Its brand delivers a promise based on the experiences she has had in life. And because it is authentic in every way, it delivers success in every way.

Don't let her emotional story fool you. She is one savvy business woman who captured the hearts of Ethan Allen, Barnes & Noble, and computer stores by using her brand to influence their actions. She branded them up into donating thousands of dollars of materials for kids everywhere.

Today as the brand and organization grow, reporters cover the growth of new local chapters. But what are they focusing on now? They tend to focus on the problems of the inner city. Yes, there are reasons that these kids are bookless, as Julia presents when establishing the need for the centers. But now, instead of focusing on the changes and improvements the book program is bringing to neighborhoods (which Julia also proves and discusses), the media focus on the pain and trouble and violence in the homes of these kids. That's the story the media report on. Again I ask, do we limit the field of brands by focusing on that which is negative?

It is the rest of us who have tolerated, encouraged, and even embraced this culture of negative news reporting. Why don't we want to see more of the healthy, award-winning brands? Why don't we promote and talk more about the brands that build and improve lives? Today, watch your news and count the number of "brands" that are reported on for their poor performance and negative influence in our world. There will be more than you can count. And there is no sign that this is about to change.

Brand Pressure

I spoke to a large group of teenagers about branding. Kids get brands. Kids love their brands. They wear them, listen to them, eat them, and model themselves after them. I was talking to them about their own personal brands and asked them to consider that they are just as valuable as Tiger Woods and Madonna. I explained that they have a unique story to tell about who they really are. *I urged them to realize that their authentic personal brand was far better than pretending to be anyone else.*

This particular group was a special group of kids at a teen center, hired to be role models, teachers, and mentors to other kids. I said, "Be yourself. Don't give in to peer pressure. Don't try to be like the other guy. Your value comes from all the unique personal experiences that you have had. Your brand is what people see and feel whenever you walk into their presence. *Don't just fit in. Stand out with your own unique story that no one else can tell."*

One girl raised her hand and said, "My sister is 15 years old, pregnant, and trying to stay in school. Why should she tell her story? Shouldn't we wait until we have a really good story before we tell it?"

Wow, I thought. What a great question. She made it crystal clear that we don't think we have anything worth sharing unless it's a success story. It's not just individuals who feel that way. Many organizations and companies hide their stories, waiting until they feel they have a story that will impress their customers or investors. Many new sales people, real estate executives, marketing entrepreneurs of every kind think that they have to wait for measurable success before sharing and building their brand, when just the opposite is true: Share your story correctly and the success will come.

First of all, we are telling our story with every word and action, spoken or not spoken, taken or not taken. Whether we realize it or not, people are watching us. They are reading our story and discovering who we really are.

Most of our customers or clients don't know or need to know all of the events in our story, such as the young girl's pregnancy or perhaps a corporate scandal. What they do need to know is how you behave and what you believe as a result of your experiences.

Second, it is all of our stories, good and bad, that make us memorable and relatable to the audience we wish to influence. It is "the rest of story" that people are dying to hear—how we overcome obstacles and go after success—that keeps them rooting for us and loyal to us. We all fall down. It's the getting up that gets the best attention. We'll discuss how and how much of your story to share in Chapter 7.

Oprah didn't wait until she became successful to start sharing her struggles in life. Nor did tennis stars Serena and Venus Williams. Not even Sam Walton. They shared their struggles and true-life experiences first and *then* became successful, famous, and loved because we felt like we knew them and could trust them. We loved them even more because of their honest portrayal of their difficulties.

When you build your brand on truth, you will have more influence than the most successful fabricated story on earth. If troubled organizations would share their true stories before their demise, would we root for them and stand behind them to help them make it back to the top?

A corporal in the U.S. Army was honest about his shortcomings and, as such, perhaps affected the outcome of our military's position and strength during the Korean War. This particular soldier was trained by the Army to be an interpreter of the German language. During his tour of duty in West Germany, he was called upon to interpret for an Army general at a meeting during the early stage of negotiations with the population of a small village where the Army wished to build a strategic site. The villagers were concerned about anything that involved the military. It's quite possible that they reacted to the United States' brand with suspicion, fear, or even hatred.

The young soldier had not used German for many months and knew that he was not fluent and probably was not the individual to serve as a critical go-between. However, the regular interpreter was ill, and he found himself in the staff car with the general and his colonel aide.

At the meeting, all went well as he read the opening comments to the sullen-faced villagers. Not a smile was on anyone's face. A villager raised his hand and asked a question that contained technical wording. The soldier had not been trained in such vocabulary and he halted when he came to translating that word. There was an embarrassing silence on both sides until a villager spoke up and offered the word in English. The American soldier smiled and thanked the German villager, receiving a smile in return, and completed the question. The general replied, bringing in more technical language. Again, the American soldier stalled until another villager helped out with the German counterpart.

After a few such exchanges, the villagers began to chuckle over the corporal's amateur status. By now he was also chuckling and smiling more and more as he stumbled from one language to the other. The general, a highly competent officer, recognized an opening and gently chided him. Some villagers jumped in on his side, explaining that technical terminology in German was not easily learned. The corporal sighed and rolled his eyes, causing further laughter on each side of the room.

Eventually, a villager who was fluent in both languages offered to step in and finish the translation. Both sides were now relaxed and laughing, occasionally asking the American if he would like to come back into the conversation. He declined amidst much more laughter.

Now that they were more relaxed, the villagers and Army personnel came to know each other outside of their advertised reputations. Because they were being themselves and not trying to be the arrogant, tough, and intimidating military that they might have pretended to be, negotiations proceeded smoothly. Each side saw the other with a new, previously unrecognized brand of reasonable adults discussing reasonable situations to find reasonable solutions.

On the drive back to the Army base, the general shook his head and said he would not bother the corporal again to interpret. But, he added, his bumbling translations probably did more to improve the image of the German-American relations than anything else that day.[8]

Remember the four C's. You must be curious or you wouldn't be reading this book. Now with confidence and courage you can build your brands through the constancy of self-examination and branding up.

Brand Building Belief IV

I will use my brand to move people to positive action.

Brand Builders

1. How does your brand demonstrate that it listens? Is it capable of receiving feedback? Does it respond to feedback?
2. Does your brand inspire people positively or move people with fear?
3. Does your brand involve others or does it *tell* its story without *sharing* it?
4. How does your brand incorporate human elements and character? What are the human elements and character it incorporates?

Part TWO

Build the Brand

Chapter FIVE

Making a Brand Impression

There is confession in the glances of our eyes;
in our smiles; in salutations; and the grasp of hands.
—Ralph Waldo Emerson (1803–1882)[1]

Emotional Experimentation

I love to carefully dabble with people's emotions. I love to do this because for me it is a kind of chemistry experiment. It is throwing in a little of this and a little of that and seeing what reaction occurs. It is about conversation, gestures, and facial expressions. It's a little like putting your name in a hat and putting your best foot forward to see what happens.

Branding is the art of emotional experimentation. When we play with people's emotions we leave them with all kinds of impressions, both good and bad. We always make a first impression and perhaps a lasting impression. Making impressions puts us in the business of advertising ourselves. How do you introduce yourself? When we do, we use lines, slogans, and catch phrases. What's your favorite line you use to advertise yourself?

On the highest-rated hit TV sitcom series, *Friends*, my favorite character, Joey, always introduces himself with the question, "How you doin'?" He says it in such a way that there is no mistaking his sexual innuendo. It is his signature line. Before he even utters the words to someone new in his sight, the audience smiles in anticipation. His brand promises amusement and pleasure and doesn't disappoint. We are forever loyal because he makes us feel a full range of sensations from his brand identity. The underlying emotional dialogue is as important as any verbal dialogue.

Many business professionals have developed a reputation such that their audience just knows what they will say when they enter a room. The anticipation can stir up any mixture of emotions, from dread to exhilaration. The feeling that others have as they anticipate your arrival, as they think about you and prepare for you—that's part of your brand. The feeling we experience as we are about to walk inside a place of business is more the brand than any corporate logo hanging on the wall.

Here's a favorite line that I almost always use with a new client, customer, or anyone I want to sell something to. I say, "I really want to impress you," and as many times as I might say it I always mean it.

This remark is usually met with a look of total surprise and appreciative laughter. My audience never expects it. People are surprised that I am so forthright in telling them that I want to impress them, maybe because too many of us try to play it cool in business matters. The fact is we need to make the encounter more about them and less about us. The fact that I want to impress them tries to make them feel special and important, respected and valuable. It leaves them with the impression that my approach to business is unique.

A good brand makes an individual feel like he is the most important person in a given moment. A great brand actually *believes* that this individual *is* the most important person at that moment.

Making people feel important is what making good impressions is all about. The root word of *impression* is *impress*. I am not embarrassed to tell people that the purpose for my presentation, pitch, or conversation is about making a good, strong, and favorable impression. My words have meaning and are spoken to influence, persuade, convince, or affect people in a strong way. Think about it this way: If a brand is like a rock being thrown into the water, we should concentrate on the way the water ripples in response. Leaving an impression should be less about us and more about what or whom we're trying to impress.

The Secret Service of Brands

Behind the brand lies a secret. Behind every brand, whether your personal brand or your organization's brand, there are undoubtedly a few secrets. Every individual and every organization has them. The problem with secrets is that they are easy to make up and hard to keep down. They live lives bigger than our own. We think that they are just little things that won't amount to anything, but we're wrong. We don't just make secrets—they end up making us, and they want to be heard. They want out. The problem is that when they accidentally escape they can wreak disaster. If they are revealed with the intention of shocking the listener or getting revenge, they can instantly devalue a brand.

Sharing secrets can get you the right or the wrong kind of attention. You know that phrase, "a well-kept secret"? Secrets are rarely, if ever, well kept. So whom do you tell your secrets to? Successful branding finds a balance between secrets and truth.

The truth is something that constantly tries to make itself known. It wants to be seen and heard. Trying to bury it will eventually (and sometimes immediately) create isolation, compulsions, and harm. A brand that exists in isolation is hardly a brand at all.

Why does your brand ultimately need to reveal your secrets? If you read about the psychology of confession you will learn about man's deep need to declare himself. This makes sense when you realize that we all have a deep need to be accepted for who we really are. The best brands are authentic brands, accepted for what they really are. Even if you pretend to be something or someone you're not, you wish you could relax and just be yourself, but that's a hard thing to be. It's hard to base your future or the future of your company on yourself. Behavior expert and motivational guru Tony Robbins says that all of our fears can be summed up in these two questions: "What if I'm not good enough?" and "What if they won't like me?"[2]

Who you really are is the composite of all of your true stories, some of which have been pushed into hiding because they're ugly. But remember, you can never be truly accepted as long as you keep yourself hidden.

Sanction Yourself

What do you hide? You hide those things that you think others will consider inferior or horrible. But the more you hide your secrets, the more you hide yourself, and, in the end, it is that very effort of keeping secrets that makes our secrets surface. The tension of what's inside wanting out and what's outside pushing it back in creates such a stressful situation that we can't help but blurt out the truth. It could come out in dreams, in Freudian slips, in joke telling, or in rambling confessions to strangers on airplanes. In business, secrets can be revealed when efforts to hide them create suspicion, investigations, and sometimes even hostile witch hunts.

Recently I was interviewed by the *Wall Street Journal*. I had anticipated a few dicey questions, so I asked my husband for his advice because he is the most ethical and honest person I know. His words always bring me back from that gray area. "Remember," he said, "the truth will always out itself." In other words, just be you.

Our hesitation to do this often comes down to one prevalent thought: No one would want me (or my business, service, or company) if they knew who I really am. Psychologists (and many corporate management consultants) agree that the single most effective healing process in easing the pain of isolation is to tell your secret. Only then can you make the necessary connection. An isolated brand is painful. It lives a life unnoticed or unchosen. The single most effective solution in fixing a bad brand that seems to be hopelessly disconnected from its audience is to define its true identity. Uncover the mystery of the brand. Don't let your audience wonder, be confused, or come to the wrong conclusions about what your brand is really about.

But what secrets am I really encouraging you to confess? What secrets am I talking about? As far as your personal brand is concerned, no one needs to know what you look like in the morning or the real color of your hair. This kind of information is private, not secret. Regarding your professional brand, not everyone needs to know your cash flow or bank covenants. That's confidential, not secret. What we do need to share, though, is the essence of our being; that which makes us authentic.

Actions Speak Louder than Logos and Taglines

The best revelation, as seen in branding, is what we show people about ourselves based on our values. In other words, reveal your secrets through the behavior that your experience has taught you. Here's how it works. The fact that I had cancer is not a routine part of my conversations, but my values shaped by my experience with cancer permeate everything I do and say. Living with cancer and its long-term aftermath is part of my story and, consequently, my brand. As a result of being very sick I value strength: physical, emotional, and spiritual strength. What people see and hear about isn't the illness. They see that I lift weights, I pray, I eat right, I surround myself with emotionally healthy people. The way I take care of my body and soul from the inside shows on the outside. That's how I reveal my true story about my illness.

When people see me they feel confident because I appear strong on many levels. The world responds differently to people who appear weak and frail—not necessarily disrespectfully, but differently. I don't have to share all the details of being sick. But people connect with me based on vitality and strength. It comes through in my personal brand and connects with my diverse audience's needs and desires. It lives on in the way I run a business, which in turn creates part of the Dalmatian Press brand.

Another secret I've kept is the secret that I was a poor reader in elementary school. I, a publisher of children's books, was a poor reader! Now that's a story I didn't share much! But this experience created for me a world in which literacy became extremely important. I didn't even realize the path I was on until 40 years later. Through my business I began helping the world to read and to value reading. My true experiences created beliefs on which I have based my personal and corporate brands throughout my life.

My personal branding extends into my professional brand with the same valuing of dynamic power and strength. I can relate to a huge portion of our society's demographics because I don't hide from my personal experiences. I use them to reach people by anticipating what they want in life. I've been there and I use those experiences and values to connect with people in ways other people cannot.

When people ask me where my strength comes from, I can then share the details of my experiences with life-threatening disease if I so choose. It doesn't make me special—in fact I'm reminded every day that everyone has something equally significant that enables them to connect with their clients, customers, and everyone they deal with.

Rudy Giuliani, Bill Cosby, and Jack Welch have all had life-changing moments that we've read about and talked about. Oprah is another huge brand who has had amazing experiences from her young life, including struggles with money, struggles with her weight, and sexual assault. Have these people's experiences shaped their values? Absolutely. They all value control, success, and strength of character. And all of their values are beautifully and brilliantly incorporated into their personal and professional brands. No one has had the same experiences that they have had. Their experiences have made them unique and no one will ever be able to copy them, as long as they continue to be authentic and not someone else. And why would they want to? They are successful beyond compare.

Oprah was struggling to make a living and connect with her audience just like the rest of us. How did she do it? By building her identity on her true experiences and being herself. She didn't wait until she was successful to start sharing her personal stories. She became successful *because* she first shared her true self with the world. And we listened because we related to her and made the emotional connection with her.

The Emotional Connection

We need to reveal our truths in order to make an emotional connection. The environment of truth provides the opportunity to make this connection. Get it straight: *You can never really get connected with people as long as you are concealing your authentic self from them.*

Telling your true story is risky. When you tell your true story some people will reject you. But these are the relationships, clients, customers, or others that have been requiring extraordinary energy from you to keep up to this point. You will replace them with 10 times the number of relationships that are naturally drawn to you and all that you offer. The sense of connection will be so satisfying and bring results you didn't think were possible. By sharing your authentic self, everyone will benefit.

And here is the miracle of truth. Truth can change the world, unlike any well-hidden secret, because it becomes the lighthouse of hope to others. When people know that you are telling your true story they will come to you, and come back to you, because they trust that you have gone where they want to go and have made it back again. When others hear your personal stories it will change the way they think of themselves—and vice versa.

Whether we hide our true stories or create stories that are not true, the result is the same: Both keep us from reaching our highest potential. Denying our true stories in our personal life and within our professional company will keep us from moving forward with the greatest speed and will rob us of every kind of wealth.

In January 2003, *Inc.* magazine featured Barbara Corcoran as one of New York's most successful real estate professionals. She started her business with $1,000 that she borrowed from her boyfriend. Ten years later she sold her business for $76 million. She started it for $1,000; she sold it for $76 million. Not a bad return on her investment. She attributes her success to several key principles, but the one that caught my eye was this one: Share your secrets. She said, "When you share your secrets with people, the most amazing thing happens. They share their secrets right back."[3] I believe this is yet another crucial competitive advantage in business that comes from building brands on true stories: You know their secrets.

Telling your true story is an act of trust. It is the utmost you can do to be all that you are.

In 2003, award-winning country music superstar Tim McGraw had a new number one hit called "She's My Kind of Rain." The particular lyric that caught my attention is this line: "I confess like a child."[4] I was reminded how children share themselves so easily and honestly with anyone and everyone. They can't keep secrets, can they? Whether it is the Mother's Day present that Dad is trying to keep hidden or the fact that they took the cookie that they shouldn't have, their secrets come falling out of them. The kind of honesty that children have is typically met with a smile of appreciation for their simplicity and purity.

As you define your personal and professional selves, you'll become more committed to your newly defined brand identity. The proof of your commitment is seen in the results. As George Washington said, "Anything will give up its secrets if you love it enough."[5] If you really love yourself and what you're doing, you will give up your secret identities and become a successful, loved brand identity.

This chapter opened with a quote from Ralph Waldo Emerson: "There is confession in the glances of our eyes; in our smiles; in salutations; and the grasp of hands." Ralph knew branding.

Wherever You Go, There You Are

If you are building a brand or choosing a brand, you are an evangelist. Everything you do makes an impression on somebody that tells others about who you are, what you like, what you stand for. You tell others what to wear, where to vacation, what books to read. Sometimes you do this with words, sometimes by example. Often we insist on what people should do, shouldn't do, where they must go, and what they can't live without. If we are sincere we do it with passion, and the way we live our own life is the basis for persuasion.

Some of us don't see ourselves as a type of evangelist. Others recognize that they are either experts or some kind of authority and like to be asked for their opinions. But whoever we are, no matter what our age and level of experience, we are all being watched, even when we don't know it, by others who want to know the answer to the question, "What should I do?!"

Every time your company or organization tells its employees to fly a particular airline or stay at a certain hotel when they travel, they are spreading the word (actually they are spreading the brand) of that chosen and endorsed company. You are being more than loyal. You are being an evangelist.

A client or customer who is loyal to your brand is more than someone who just frequents your store, buys your product, or uses your services. Some frequent shoppers are repeat customers just because you are convenient or have the best price in town. You don't want frequent shoppers, you want loyal shoppers. You don't want convenient friends, you want loyal friends.

You are an evangelist from the day you become aware that there is a world around you, and that you are not the center of the universe. For most of us that is around age two. (Some people never become aware of this and continue to operate as if the world revolves around them.) From early on, we repeat our behaviors that we become known for and impose our own beliefs on others as a function of everyday life. We promote our own beliefs by the way we live.

As people see and recognize the repeated behavior, they make the connection between that behavior and us. They say things like, "That is vintage Cindy," or, "Theresa always does that." Our repetitive behaviors are largely habit, a little bit choice, and a lot of innate expression of who we really are. And as we repeat ourselves over and over, it often converts people to our way of thinking. We are self-created evangelists for others and for ourselves. We tell our story over and over again.

Brand Conversion

A business traveler noticed as he boarded his Southwest Airlines flight that he had his parking garage ticket in his coat pocket. This presented a problem, because his wife would be picking the car up when she returned home on a different flight. If she didn't have the parking ticket, she would have to pay a very high fee to exit the garage or be charged with car theft. As soon as her husband landed at his destination, he began working with the airline to contact the city, terminal, and gate at which his wife might be waiting. Gate changes, late departures, and the long distance made it a complicated series of calls. Any one of the Southwest employees could have just said no to the request to track down the woman who didn't know she had a problem on her hands. Eventually contact was made, the information was exchanged from one city to another, and from husband to gate attendant to courtesy phone to several other gate attendants, to the wife.

This businessman, Rich Lindner, is a sales and marketing training coach, and he tells this story of excellent customer service at the beginning of many instructional speeches. His loyalty to Southwest Airlines has created more business for the airline than can be measured. To him and others, the brand is shorthand for making travel easier when you have had a really hard day and nothing seems to be going right.

I have a similar story about Northwest Airlines. I never felt any loyalty to the company because my experience with them was late arrivals and the most expensive flights from my hubs. But one of their employees found a notebook of mine filled with important handwritten information and telephone numbers that I would miss dearly. I didn't even know it was missing until I received a phone call saying that she had found it and would be mailing it to me. I don't know how she found my name or phone number because it wasn't in the notebook. I don't know how she tracked me down, because I had recently moved. But I know she carried the book home with her, packaged it, and put it in the mail on her own. Even though this was simply the act of an individual, I will be more loyal to Northwest because of it. I guess I believe that in addition to this woman's character of caring, there is something in the company that encourages her to perform with excellence and rewards her for her superior customer service skills. I will tell this story often when speaking about brands. I will fly Northwest and encourage others to do so, too.

Two different airlines with the same foundation for success. It's not their prices, frequent flier system, or food. Those are just features that any other airline can copy. Their success and the success of any airline competing today will come from brand loyalty. When airlines can all compete with prices and schedules, the only thing that is going to set them apart is personality. And personality comes from people.

Most branding is a kind of conversion process.

Based on how the audience thinks and feels when they see our brand, we inform, persuade, share, comfort, and teach. And the more we believe in the message of our brand, the better our chance is of converting others. What about your brand? What could we believe in more than ourselves?

Unfortunately, too many people don't believe in themselves or in their company. Therefore their chances of getting the right kind of attention and creating loyalty are limited. Build your brand on yourself and your authenticity. You should have such a strong emotional connection to yourself that you believe in yourself passionately. The stronger the belief, the more we are compelled to tell others. And that is why we are, or should be, evangelists, spreading the good news about our brand. Truth creates beliefs, which inspire evangelism, gaining converts, and this translates to success.

This reinforces our own brand image to ourselves as well as to others. And this creates a certain kind of buzz about who we are. It is called having charisma; it is called making an impression. It lets you make an entrance before you even enter a room. It perpetuates your self brand and builds a reputation that will support your company or organization through good times and bad times. Contrary to popular belief, charisma isn't something you are born with. Charisma is definitely something that is developed.

As this continues, others become evangelists for you. And wherever you go, you are already there! What does that mean? It means that the people who have asked for you already believe in you and hence believe in your product or service. Their turnout for your appearance affirms that they have made the right choice in joining you. They recommend you to their friends. They purchase your products not just for their use but as gifts for others. They enjoy not only the substance of you and your company but the symbolism as well. They provide you with unsolicited praise. And, most important, they feel that being in your presence makes them a part of something bigger than themselves.

Most people miss branding success by about 18 inches. That's the distance between your head and your heart. When you put your heart into your brand you'll be a successful evangelist.

Tommy Lasorda is an ambassador for baseball. You can see it in his eyes, the way he lights up when he talks about it. He loves baseball. His personal charismatic brand is the result of each baseball game of his life. No one has experienced the same wins, losses, injuries, training, and exercises that have resulted in who he is today. He didn't toss those out and try to be like Joe Dimaggio. He built his identity on his own true stories. His brand is uncompromised because no one can ever copy what they didn't experience. Supposedly his wife said to him, "Honey, I think you love baseball more than me." He hesitated, then answered, "Well dear, I love you more than basketball." He loves baseball. He is devoted to it. How devoted are you to what you are doing?

Many books and films have been made about Babe Ruth's home run record. Roger Maris, Sammy Sosa, and Mark McGwire have all broken the record. These great athletes have great personal brands, but their brand isn't defined by their home run record. Records can eventually be broken. The brand is how they broke the record. Their brand is about how they lived and how they converted followers. If you build a following on one of your features your followers won't stay with you for long. They will follow the feature.

Loyal customers are made, produced, created. Accidental loyalty happens, but why wait for an accident to happen? You can make loyal customers. Let me show you how to start.

The Elevator Pitch

Know, write, and practice your elevator pitch. *Elevator speech* is an expression for the speech you could make to a stranger in an elevator as you ride from the top floor to the lobby floor. The speech is your proposition, or your unique selling proposition (USP). And the amount of time spent in an elevator ride is about as long as the average attention span of your customer. An average adult's attention span is just two seconds longer than a child's, or about eight seconds. As you are telling your story, are people nodding along in understanding? Or are their eyes glazed over with confusion or boredom?

As you write this short presentation, remember to tell it with the emotions that are based on the facts of your true story. Remember that your listeners will carry with them your emotional pitch more than a lot of facts about your company. Remember to connect with them by sharing yourself and helping them believe that, for that moment, they are the most important people in your sight.

Then test your elevator pitch. You are successful if your client or customer can communicate what you have told them to another person as well, or better than you did. Is it easy to understand and repeat? Don't just hope that they got the message. Ask them to tell it back to you. The message isn't the only thing that counts; what matters is the passion that they have been infected with and that they pass on to their listeners. Believe me, they'll catch your emotion and will be able to deliver that better then the facts you tell them. Then they are your evangelists. These are the people who are your personal and professional brand's first and last line of defense. They protect you. They guard you. A strong defense surrounds you so that you can win brand loyalty.

Brand's Don't Want Just Satisfaction

Is customer loyalty more important than customer satisfaction? Yes and no. Customers won't be loyal for very long if they are not satisfied. Any brand must deliver on its promise. But they can be satisfied and never be loyal. A customer can be very satisfied with your service or product and still change providers for no other reason than that they want to try something new. But loyal customers are much less likely to leave you.

Brand image expert Marc Gobé wrote that the biggest misconception in branding strategies is the belief that branding is about market share when it is about "mind and emotion share."[6]

Purchase decisions are made largely for emotional reasons. Emotion moves the brand promise to the brand reality. Emotion gets attention more than any facts. Emotion should live inside of your employees and show in their behavior. People form emotional relationships with people. People put the service into customer service. People put the quality into the brand. People create the experience of the brand. And as we have seen, brands are about experiences. Loyalty is a wonderful experience to foster and give to your brand.

> *Never underestimate the power of a satisfied customer.*
> *It's why Ford has more repeat buyers than any other make.*
> —2004 Ford Motor Company commercial

Great Brands Create Loyalty

A 1996 article in *Marketing Review* by Jeff Resnick stated that companies can command prices that are four to seven percent higher than weaker competitors, resulting in three times the profit if they excel in creating and maintaining loyal customers.[7] Now that's a powerful result from building a great brand.

A brand is in many ways a living, breathing thing. It is more than just visual, or rational—it is emotional and behavioral in practice.

Evangelists of your brand, both within your organization and outside, truly live the brand. The first part of this book has discussed the questions below. Now, test and confirm the brand loyalty to you and your organization. Ask your employees or associates the following five questions:

1. Do you understand our brand's promise and how it delivers the promise?

2. Do you know what makes our brand different? (Hint: it's you.)

3. Can you clearly explain our brand? And most important, do you know your role in relationship to the brand and your role in protecting it?

4. Do you add to the brand experience or detract from it? Do you brand up?

5. Do you buy into the fact that everyone's actions impact the success of the entire organization by way of the brand?

Loyalty Starts Inside

Ask yourself the same questions! If the answers are yes, then your employees become associates, or members, or family. Wal-Mart doesn't have employees. It has associates. Disney has "family" working with them. Companies that succeed don't have mere employees. And as that kind of an organization, they all work hard at becoming the brand together. Loyalty starts inside. The way employees treat each other is the way they treat customers and customers treat them back.

In spring 2003 a *USA Today* article reported, "After several high-profile corporate scandals, U.S. teens are taking a hard line on business ethics. Nearly nine out of ten students surveyed online by Junior Achievement say they would refuse to work for a company accused of wrongdoing, while three out of four say they would not even buy a product from a company accused of unethical behavior."[8] Increasingly, young people are looking at job opportunities as more than a paycheck or simply a good job. They see companies as brands and ask themselves if they want to be part of a particular brand experience. They consider whether the company's brand is an extension of their own beliefs and personal brand.

In fact, I'm disappointed by how many companies profess to be devoted to their brand identity and go to great lengths to express it with media campaigns only to have it fall miserably short in the lives of its employees. Employees of all ages should reflect the company's brand, and this happens best when individuals align themselves with companies they share experiences and values with.

If you are asking your client or customer to have a relationship with your brand, is there any reason why you shouldn't expect the same, or more, from your employees? How does this happen? How do employees learn to be brand builders?

They learn the story of the brand from you. And you don't just tell it, you share it in every way. You share it in a way that involves everyone in the organization.

Brand building is everyone's job. If you're not building it up, then you are breaking it down.

In the mid 1990s, when Firestone found itself in the middle of a mess of defective tires that were allegedly causing accidents and bodily harm, its brand became shorthand for "unsafe." Its brand made people temporarily feel nervous. They felt they couldn't completely trust the brand. Who forgot to take care of the brand? When accountants started seeing claims come in, did they think about the brand? When repairmen started replacing tires, were they thinking about the brand? Since 2002 they have done a remarkable job of rebuilding their brand and defining their future on the values they learned from their true stories.

Oren Aviv, Disney's studio marketing chief, told the *Wall Street Journal* in February 2003, "I don't think people make their decisions to see a movie based on whether there's a Disney logo there or not."[9] Is he kidding? And how much did he just discount the Disney brand? Brand erosion is faster than that of oceanfront property.

Ask yourself if you have everyone around you in your organization and in your life building your brand. And don't be afraid to ask them directly if they know and accept the job of doing so. Ask yourself, and say yes.

Brand Building Belief V

I will choose to engage an emotional connection with my brand for faster, lasting, and more meaningful results.

Brand Builders

1. What do you think people are thinking and feeling as they anticipate your call or entrance? What comes to mind when they see your name on their caller ID or in their e-mail in-box? Are they excited, nervous, scared, or energized?

2. How do you know if you've made a good or bad impression?

3. Can you think of a time when you were a satisfied customer but not loyal? Can you think of a time when you were loyal even though you weren't satisfied, either personally or professionally?

4. Who, besides you, is taking care of your brand? Whose ultimate responsibility is the brand?

Chapter SIX

Brand Relativity

When the character of a man is
not clear to you, look at his friends.
—Japanese proverb

Does Your Brand Relate to Others?

Philosopher and writer Anaïs Nin wrote, "We don't see things as *they* are. We see them as *we* are."[1] That doesn't say much for the communication process. When we build a brand we have a goal of getting across our message as we see it, not how someone else might see it differently. When we communicate we hope to send *our* message clearly. We don't set out to reinforce what the receiver may erroneously think. Often we want to change people's perceptions or their thinking to our way of thinking. We want them to join us in our conclusions. And yet we can all agree that perception is anyone's reality.

What is the pathway that branding takes? To what end does it work? Are brands only meaningful and effective within small communities where we all think the same way based on common experiences? If personal experiences are the best foundation for brands, what if we can't relate to each other's experiences?

Remember these three steps in the branding pathway:

1. Defining your story is the first step in branding.
2. Making your story relatable is the second.
3. Translating it into something people connect with and feel an emotion for is the third step in the branding pathway.

120

Tom Hanks is certainly relatable. He is everyman's casual pal. He is every woman's hero. He grew up loving the astronauts and did the Oscar-winning movie *Apollo 13*. We get the feeling that what we see is who he really is. He shocked America and the Hollywood crowd when he gushed over his wife, Rita, and ended one of his Oscar acceptance speeches with "God bless America." He's not too good looking. He's not arrogant. According to a 2002 *Vanity Fair* article, he is today's Jimmy Stewart.[2]

What about Tom Cruise? Devilishly handsome, he drives a Porsche and flies his own Gulfstream airplane. He defines the United States as "terrifying" and doubts whether he would ever raise his children here. His pet cause is to save Scientology in Germany.

Who can you better relate to? I see both of their movies but I can definitely relate to Tom Hanks and his world better than I can relate to Tom Cruise's. Being able to relate to Tom Hanks makes me feel closer to him and therefore more loyal to him. I sing his praises easily and gladly. When I choose him, I feel better about myself because I am proud to associate with something seemingly good, moral, and fun. I want to be with someone who seems to be such a good husband and makes me feel a little giddy, too. Being his fan makes me look good. Going to his movies makes me look good. And that ends up making his personal and professional brand more successful.

How many companies can you think of that you don't do business with because they don't seem like your type of people? You can't relate to them. They are too big or small or stuffy or religious or sexy or too something. On the other hand, some brands feel just right. You search for brands the way Goldilocks sought the perfect dish of porridge, chair, and comfortable bed. You want what is just right. Isn't that why we choose the restaurant or the bank we do? It's not just about the food or the money. It's because some feel too stuffy and some too casual. We need to be able to relate to the places where we do business.

On the runaway reality-based television hit *American Idol*, the judges keep telling the young performers who are struggling to win, "Just be yourself. Find your own groove. Make that hit song your own." Simon Cowell continually criticized several contestants for hiding behind a façade as they try to sound like Whitney Houston or Barry White. He said to one of the top ten female contestants with a fantastic voice, "I feel like I don't really know who you are. I can't connect with you." She was voted off the show on the next episode.

The country music industry saw a huge increase in popularity in 1998 and it continues to grow. According to a recent study, each week 41,893,000 adults listen to country radio stations nationwide, and more radio stations continue to program country music than any other format. There are 2,139 country radio stations, followed by 1,167 news/talk and 1,136 adult contemporary stations.[3] Offered the choice of rap and metal, many fans report that they just can't relate to those stars as well as they can to country music stars.

One woman explains, "I need to be able to make out the lyrics and relate the stories in the songs to my own life. . . . You can really tell how authentic and nice the country stars are just by listening to their acceptance speeches at award shows." In fact country artists are used in national ads and corporate promotions by Bud Light, Coors Light, Dr. Pepper, Chevrolet, Ford, Slim Fast, and more. These corporations use country stars to build their brands because the greater public can relate to them. Metal and rap, for all their success, relate to a niche market, not a mass market.

Is there a relationship between how the country music business *relates* to Americans and its popularity and increasing loyalty? Absolutely. The artists tell stories about themselves and with their songs. They are relatable. They translate their stories into something that provokes an emotional response. They become memorable and loyalty is born, with success following.

Garth Brooks was finally experiencing fame in the mid 1990s and, along with it, all the fast and seductive temptations of the road. He and his band members have described the nightmare that was happening to them as husbands. I watched his televised biography, in which he opened up about the concert that forever changed his life and his career.[4] He was in Missouri in 1989 and opening with his hit song, "If Tomorrow Never Comes." As he began to sing the first words, "Sometimes late at night I lay awake and watch her sleeping . . . ," he stopped unexpectedly. He waited until the crowd was silent. Then he said, "I can't sing this song because of what's going on in my life right now." And then he told the mesmerized audience about his life of cheating and adulterous affairs.

He cried. The whole band cried. The producers waited, unable to imagine the reaction. "And so you see," said Garth, "why I'm having trouble singing this love song." Then he publicly recommitted himself to his wife, Sandy, and sang the song in earnest. The crowd went wild. They gave Garth Brooks his first standing ovation. Not only did he share his secret, but he made it relatable and appealed to every human emotion so that there was nothing but a heartbeat between him and tens of thousands of people. They loved him for making himself human and connecting to them on a very real level. He defined his true story. He made it relatable. And he translated it in a way that created a powerful, emotional tidal wave of loyalty.

When you tell your true stories through your brand, you must appeal to human sensations and feelings that people can relate to. Be yourself, but be real. In other words, just because you are in front of a group of comedians doesn't mean you should try to come across as funny when your true brand identity is more serious and earnest.

Don't try to relate by asking the question, "What do they want me to be?" Relate by being human. Relate by being yourself. Your loyal audience will be drawn to you because they recognize the real thing.

You might get a temporary customer base by pretending to be what they want, but no one, no organization, can keep that up for too long.

Rock and roll star Melissa Etheridge was probably smiling when she said, "Luckily, I was signed for my music instead of my looks."[5] She was talking about her personal brand identity as related to her successful business in rock and roll. Back in the 1980s she gained steam with her raspy, hard-hitting, heartfelt sound. She played in T-shirts and jeans. "Every time I've strayed from that, thinking I had to be somebody else, I haven't gotten very far." Still, various managers and image stylists tried to make her look like what they thought she should look like. Looking back on some ridiculous hairstyles and outfits, she now knows not to trust strangers with her self-image or her self-esteem.

She says, "My body isn't perfect but it suits me, and I've had a certain success without trying to be someone else. I'm about the music." She has stayed true to who she really is, and to her vision of a future based on that. She has taken her true experience of music and all she values and created a business phenomenon. She attracts a loyal audience that relates to her and responds to her with all the emotion that successful momentum requires.

Most of us have dressed the part to look like a successful businessperson. In the 1990s women wore spunky little banker's ties with their suits and men wore the latest power-color tie (1992, teal; 1993, yellow; 1994, Ferragamo). We tried to look like what we thought "successful" looked like. Most of did so without giving it too much thought. Different clothes, like different marketing tricks, can make us popular for a while, but unless your brand stays relevant you don't really get it.

I think that's why we enjoy hearing about small entrepreneurial companies. When we read about a huge corporation it is hard to relate to it. When Martha Stewart first began her climb to success, women got wrapped up in the seemingly ordinary, everyday way she was making a living: cooking, decorating, and cleaning. These were things that everyday women did and could relate to. She attracted loyalty and so did her company, with all its products.

There's a moving company called Two Men and a Truck. Many people see the company name and feel like these guys could be just like them. What if we found out that this was a multimillion-dollar company owned by people who never did a day of hard labor in their life? What if Ben and Jerry turned out to be skinny, lactose-intolerant dieters? Brands must be relevant to the audience and we must be able to relate to them.

As Martha Stewart's business grew and stories of her harsh leadership were revealed, true or false, we stopped relating to her. We still loved her products and ideas but the loyalty diminished. We remained satisfied customers but were ready to switch our loyalty should a better product come along, or a new domestic heroine.

We relate to people and companies when we realize that they have gone through the same type of things that we have gone through.

When a corporation builds its business through franchising, it is critical that the lead corporate office or store tap into the common experiences, frustrations, and success stories that each franchisee is bound to have. What a shame it would be if we never learned that someone who had experiences similar to ours turned them into enormous successes.

When direct marketing companies such as Avon, QuickStar, (Amway), or Southwestern Books train new representatives for success, they are actually starting a new business with every new individual. These brand-new companies depend on being able to relate to the lead company. They thrive on hearing their true success stories because they try to put themselves into the story and imagine arriving at the same success.

Corporate business people, managers, mentors, and any other leaders shouldn't tell people to be like them. They should tell them to relate to them and see the common experiences that can lead them on a pathway to success.

We relate to brands because they strike a chord of familiarity from our past and of hope for a better future. When people can relate to your brand, their attention will last and you will be able to turn their attention into the kind of action you desire.

How are you telling the story of your brand? How is your brand telling your story?

Alignment

A global qualitative brand study was conducted in 2003 by Research International Observer (RIO).[6] The biannual study questioned 1,500 consumers in 41 countries and 52 cities about the existence of global brands. What they found was the affirmation that people do like brands and they consume them to be affiliated with them. Kristine Kirby Webster of the Canterbury Group recapped their findings in her web article "Branding: The Third Wave Is Here." As one survey respondent from New Zealand said, "Global brands make you feel part of something bigger and give you a sense of belonging." A Japanese participant felt that brands "increase the value of the one who uses them," and a Hong Kong resident noted, "You feel you are above others if you own a Louis Vuitton product." When we relate to brands we are apt to align ourselves with them.

> We align ourselves with brands based on our personal values that we project onto the brand.

Furthermore, we actually believe that the brand will then project these same values onto us in the perception of others. For example, someone who values wealth may project that onto the brand Rolex. And they in turn believe that Rolex will project that value and wealth onto us in the view of the rest of the world. This is further proof that the development of a brand is based on perception. Part of the brand's meaning comes from the company or the individual, but ultimately it's about what the world wants to project onto it. Brand *accuracy* increases when the brand story is relatable and able to connect with real people's own experiences.

Let's look at people who value being taken seriously in life. This value has been shaped by both the positive and negative experiences in their lives. Dick Strong of Strong Funds was one of the big five in its category. Dick Strong was fired from previous companies, and he vowed to create a company that was more successful and that would make the financial world take him seriously. Not only did he succeed, but he gained a reputation for rewarding his employees with the kind of attention many workers dream of: award banquets, free lunch, and beautiful grounds and offices. He had a reputation as a hard-as-nails businessman, but he made his workforce feel special. The reciprocal attention he received made Dick Strong feel more special. Ironically, he was the focus of the wrong kind of attention when he was accused of wrongdoing by the SEC. His company was bought by Wells Fargo, and his brand will be indefinitely diluted.

Over years, the desire to be taken seriously becomes lodged in the very being of many people, to the extent that their behavior follows and reinforces activities that make them feel like they are being taken seriously. They are no longer someone to be brushed aside or thought of as insignificant. The clothes they wear, the cars they drive, and the coffee they drink reinforces their values, as if to say, "I am not a flighty bimbo or inexperienced airhead. Don't laugh at me. I am significant. Give me your attention!"

Some of us drink Starbucks Coffee because we are serious and sophisticated coffee drinkers. Only experienced coffee drinkers can handle the strong, rich flavor. They know rich Columbian beans from freeze-dried generic brands of coffee that taste like dishwater. We project our values of drive and sophistication onto the Starbucks brand. When we tease my dad about the diluted, weak coffee he prefers, it is as if we are saying, "What's the matter? Can't you handle the real stuff?" Or, "Can't you afford it?"

Starbucks, in turn, has built a company that makes us feel indulgent, affluent, European, and appreciative of the finer things in life. When we open the door to Starbucks, we are saying that we are worthy of walking into the upscale coffee shop and lingering to see and be seen as Starbucks consumers. No gas station coffee for us, with three sugars and cream. If it's cream we want, it is whipped on top of a latte. When others see us going into the Starbucks store or holding a Starbucks branded cup, we subconsciously hope that everything we believe and feel about Starbucks, they will believe and feel about us. (Burger King actually made a drinking cup in August 2004 printed with the slogan, "This cup makes a statement about you. It says, hey, look at me.")

Now we can get a pretty good cup of coffee anywhere these days. But when my friends travel 650 miles from Madison, Wisconsin, to Nashville, Tennessee, they smile with relief when they see the neighborhood Starbucks. We always pull over for a cup of sophistication and indulgence. Is there a secret Starbucks handshake? Even if there is not, people feel that they are part of something bigger when they associate with this worldwide brand. And it somehow reinforces the values that have been shaped by their life experiences. They are worth the higher price the Starbucks coffee commands. They deserve the break the Starbucks brand promises from the hassles of their day. Starbucks has brilliantly built a brand based on the company's story of being superior, which relates to everyone who values a feeling of excellence. And who doesn't want to feel worthy of excellence?

As a side note, the Starbucks brand makes different people feel different things. It alienates some who feel it is a symbol for the disappointing homogenization of coffeehouses.

> The very reason some love the brand is the reason others don't want it on their block—the brand has become too generic for them.

As revealing as how individuals align themselves with brands is how corporations align themselves with other corporate brands. In 2003, Loews Cineplex, freshly emerged from bankruptcy protection and with renewed optimism, established partnerships with General Mills popcorn, the Susan G. Komen Foundation, and others. These alliances didn't just draw attention to its partners but drove foot traffic into its 250 plus locations.

A similarly named company, the super home improvement chain Lowe's, ran a 2004 campaign that built its brand on the basis of providing its customers with other brands. Their ad slogan was, "Lowe's makes it easy to get organized because we have more brand solutions than anyone." Their TV commercials are as much about promoting the fact that they offer their customers more great brand selections as they are about promoting their own brand name, Lowe's. Great brands can build other great brands if they share common stories and promises. More important, they can turn attention into successful business by converting it into sales.

In addition to aligning yourself or your business with another entity, it is effective to align yourself with traditions and memories. Macy's will forever be associated with Thanksgiving. We've grown up watching the Macy's parade on television every Thanksgiving morning, and we see it again in *Miracle on 34th Street* while eating turkey leftovers. If Macy's could not convert the relationship into sales and a base of loyal, repeat customers, all the strategy and alignment would be wasted. This is what branding is for: to be in the mind of your audience such that you give people a reason and motive to take the action you desire.

The Misfit

McDonald's aligned itself with Disney, which made a lot of sense. A large portion of McDonald's' business comes from its Happy Meals and preschool loyalty. What a perfect fit between the two huge corporate brands. McDonald's has been putting exclusive Disney toys in Happy Meals for several years. However, Disney is beginning to put its brand on more and more of its movies. Disney is expanding the definition of a Disney-label movie and releasing a flood of new movies bearing the Disney brand. The result will be a test of what the Disney brand means. Studio Chief Dick Coke says, "This is an idea for the company to regain control of what the Disney name means, rather than allowing it to be pigeonholed by increasingly narrow audience expectations."[7] This is smart for Disney but may make its alignment with McDonald's a questionable fit. If the Disney brand becomes better known for either movies that adults know, such as *Hidalgo*, or for movies that are flops at the box office, such as *Treasure Planet* ($38 million in ticket sales) or *The Country Bears* ($17 million in ticket sales), then the alliance becomes a misfit.

Comedian Carrot Top is a spokesperson for 1 800 CALL ATT. This alliance I don't understand. He is a talented comic and does funny sight gags, but what does that have to do with saving money and communications companies? His brand is slapstick. When he comes on TV to plug the use of 1-800 CALL ATT, it just doesn't make sense. There's nothing funny about AT&T. I don't relate to the partnership, and it distracts me from feeling anything but confused. A great brand knows exactly who it is and doesn't confuse its audience about that identity.

Visibility and Credibility—See and Be Seen

Businesses are always anxious for new ways to make money, especially in a poor economy. Some companies try to reinvent themselves when they look for new revenues, which may be good for their financial business but bad for their brand. Smarter is to increase the brand's visibility by expanding with on-brand new categories. Gap, the United States' biggest specialty apparel chain, started with a great line of basics under the Gap brand. They stayed true to their brand identity and expanded into Gap Kids and Baby Gap apparel. Their new product line benefited from their brand strength, and their brand benefited from increased visibility of their brand label. Pressed for time, more consumers are focused when they shop.

According to the International Council of Shopping Centers, some 60 percent of consumers are purpose-driven shoppers as of 2002, compared to 43 percent in 2000.[8] When time matters and focus counts, brands are a key factor to the purchase. Therefore, the one we see is the one that stands the greatest chance of getting our attention and being chosen.

We've discussed constancy and clarity in your brand development, but they aren't enough if it's not visible. You have to strive to be visible to your audience, constantly. There are few reasons to decrease your visibility. You may be shy and not good at it but you can overcome that and find the right type of visibility for you. There are times when you or your company may want to fly under radar to surprise your competition, and for that reason I'll agree that visibility to the world can wait. But make yourself seen and heard to those who matter from day one: yourself, your employees, and those who can help you. Soon after, when the competitive situation is right, be seen and heard everywhere.

Don't hide your brand. Humility and visibility can coexist.

Dalmatian Press snuck up on its competition by quietly building and improving its product line until we appeared in the market as a force too big to be brushed aside. When we hit the radar screen we were firmly entrenched in the retail and home environments, preventing our competition from preying on what was a smaller and more vulnerable presence. We didn't join the clubs of "who's who." We didn't go to all the industry events and parties. We didn't give interviews. However, we did immediately begin with a branding strategy internally. Our first converts were the company associates and our board of directors. Without loyalty at home the brand story would have quickly faded into an unhappy ending.

Controversial CEO Richard Kovacevich, banker and turnaround expert of the profitable Wells Fargo & Co., is known for bucking trends. He said, "I'm not on the radar screen. I don't do high-profile anything. No one knew about Wal-Mart, no one knew about Home Depot—until they dominated."[9]

Who is your target audience? If you're Microsoft, it's the world. That is why we can't make it through a day without being exposed to its commercials, logos, or advertisements. Television, sporting bill-boards, charity sponsorships, retail signage, and people carrying their laptops in airports all scream, "Microsoft Windows!" Considering it's a relatively new brand, Microsoft is one of the world's strongest brands. But let's not confuse advertising with publicity. Publicity gets you attention. Advertising will then build the brand you are getting attention for. Both are useless without visibility.

Chances are your brand's target market is a lot smaller. At Dal-matian Press we put Dalmatian spots everywhere—not just on the product but on presentations, shipping materials, labels, business cards. Associates at Dalmatian Press understand that every piece of paper that goes out of our offices is another opportunity to link the substance of the message with the symbolism of the brand.

We meet with important New York licensors at the International Toy Fair every year. In the rush to prepare the accounting statements of royalties in time for one meeting, the reports had been printed out on plain white paper. Rather than hand those out, I chose to leave them in the briefcase. Plain white paper lacked the brand imprint and our trademark spots up and down the left margin of the paper. With-out this branded stationery, the accounting numbers only told half of the story. They lacked the ability to share the history of the company and make the reader feel emotions like trust and loyalty that we had worked so hard to build over eight years. Never ignore the power and potential of tying your work to your brand.

Consider visibility at every opportunity. When you prepare a 20-page report, consider the probability that there will be one page that the reader focuses on. Perhaps they tear it out, photocopy it, and send copies to others in their offices. Did you have your brand on that page? If you routinely have it on *every* page, you won't worry that you missed the chance to stand behind your work and send your brand out ahead of you to spread the story behind the presentation. We send stuffed animals ahead of and after our meetings. These Dalmat-ian toys bark and make people smile or at least shake their heads. We elicit an emotional response. People remember us. We don't want to have to wait for someone to read the words "Dalmatian Press." They feel it when they spot us. Many companies send thank-you gifts to customers. The question is, do they tell your story and represent your brand or are they generic?

Newspapers put their brand on every page via their name. We take it for granted when we look at a torn-out page we've saved that we can find the name of the newspaper it came from. This is what all of our personal and professional marketing materials should do. If you want your brand to get attention, put your brand everywhere it can be seen. This isn't vanity—this is branding. Science has shown that there are over 750,000 separate thoughts bombarding us every day,[10] and many of these thoughts run well-worn patterns. It's hard to make new thoughts seen and remembered without a lot of repetition. A brand that is repeated over and over will not only influence someone's reality, it will *become* their reality.

How does your brand do?

It's sad but true that visibility is credibility. The temporary absence of talented movie star John Travolta between movies *Saturday Night Live*, *Grease*, and *Pulp Fiction* made us wonder, "Is he any good? Was he ever?" We think that if a brand was any good, it would be everywhere. If McDonald's stores started to disappear we might think it was because they weren't wanted any more. If they weren't wanted, it must be because they weren't any good. If a movie star isn't seen in a major picture for a while it must be because he's no longer any good, rather than because he just wants to take time off. Perception is definitely people's reality. And if we don't see a brand than we certainly don't perceive it.

In 2003 Dalmatian Press decided to close its New York City office because the person working out of that location left the company. We didn't need the office anymore. Some people in our business world wondered if we might be having financial problems and might be closing our whole business. I heard rumors. I got phone calls from good friends in the business asking, "Is everything okay?" I felt it was important to increase our visibility in other ways to offset the lost visibility in New York. I traveled coast to coast to make our presence felt with important associates and partners. We simultaneously launched major book product lines, including Veggie Tales and Strawberry Shortcake, two of the hottest children's character lines of that year, to make our presence seen through product rather than with an office space. Visibility comes in many forms.

Conversely, when something hits the radar screen we believe it's hot. Business analysts wait and watch to see if a market introduction becomes a trend. But which comes first? Do products and services become fads because they are advertised and promoted? Or do they have a grassroots, growing popularity until they hit our brain waves and finally get public relations via a feature news story? It is visibility, forced or natural, that stirs up our thought process and gets us wondering, "What's up with that?" Being in the public eye gets people's attention, and brands thrive on attention.

What does this have to do with you and your brand? How do you take your experiences and make them visible in a way that is authentic and thus successful?

The Truth Stands behind the Brand

Whatever you do for your brand, if you're not true to yourself then it just isn't worth it. We all know that no matter how successful and rich we are, it is unsatisfying if we are miserable in life. As my personal and professional brands grow and evolve, I don't want anybody to be able to take my happiness away from me. Chances of success are just that—filled with chance. So if an organization is built and it is unsuccessful, at least it should have had fun trying and knowing that it was authentic and not a phony attempt. If we labor for something that is criticized and fails but is a labor of love, then there is some satisfaction in being able to defend the time and effort we spent on it.

It is far easier to live with the brand results if we have been in control of its true substance. There's no second-guessing our strategy if we based it on the truth. When Dan Quail was George H. Bush's vice presidential candidate, he had a lot of handlers. Everyone around him created an image for him to try to become. The image was based on what they thought the public would respond to rather than who he really was. When his image failed (as did the reelection bid) and years later he regained control of his brand, he said, more than once, that if he had just been allowed to be himself he would have been far more successful. At least he would have been less frustrated with the failure. If he had still failed he wouldn't be left wondering whether the world might have embraced the real him.

It's hard enough to fail, but it's harder to live with your failure when you've been something or someone that's not you. You'll always think, "I know I could have been better." You'll always have the what-ifs that can haunt you forever.

What Will You Do for Your Brand?

Brainstorm about how you can make your brand more visible and affect people's perception of it. If I could do whatever I wanted to make my brand visible and audible, I would do whatever expressed my values and my character. When you perform the following exercises you will stretch the way you think about how you present your brand to the world. Keep asking yourself, "How does my audience see my brand and hear my brand? How can my brand get attention for all the right reasons?"

Here is the first of three examples to trigger ideas for building brand visibility. Two more will be described in later sections of this chapter.

Create Billboards That Translate Your Values for Others to See

Billboards are anything that puts your brand out there visually. Thinking about my brand in billboard terms is a natural extension of who I am, as you will see shortly. I am a billboard watcher. I love to look out the car window and react to the various signs. I critique them in every way. Is the type too small to read while driving by at 60 miles per hour? Is the color wrong for the various changes in sunlight? Can the image be immediately recognized and remembered? Do I understand the message?

I would love to create billboards that drill the image of my brand into people's memory. I want to provoke a strong feeling for my brand. Remember, the reason we named our company Dalmatian Press was because it is a whole lot easier to remember a Dalmatian than it is a Hilicki. A Dalmatian Press puppy can trigger a lot more smiles and emotion than a Hilicki can. A brand billboard is most effective when it makes an emotional memory.

Creating billboards is a natural extension of me. Not only does it feel right because I love billboards, but it is a natural outgrowth of my creative abilities in the publishing industry. When I was a little girl, my favorite sitcom was *Bewitched*. I still look for it on TV Land. I imagined the advertising job that Darren Stevens had as the ultimate job. He was an advertising guy who always came up with the perfect slogan and concept to connect his clients to their audience. All those days of watching *Bewitched* have made me appreciate that kind of advertising creativity. I appreciate the ability to come up with the perfect sales pitch to sell a product. Creating brand bill-boards expresses part of my true story as the little girl dreaming of having an advertising job, who grew up to create a line of books that have to advertise fun.

Do you like to watch commercials? Do you read book jackets and magazine covers? Do you read billboards while driving and ana-lyze them for effectiveness? Once you see cereal boxes and Christmas cards as a kind of brand billboard, you understand that all packaging is a way to present your brand to the world.

My personal and professional brand makes the promise to im-prove people's lives, personally or professionally. So how can I create billboards (a visual presence) that can communicate this with a glance? Would it be with color or humor or an image that evokes an inspiring feeling? And how can I unmistakably tie the billboard's im-age to my brand?

One of the reasons I put a graphic design of books into my per-sonal marketing logo was because books are always associated with value, and I love the idea that my name is likewise associated with value. The world buys books and gives them as gifts because people believe books can make lives better. We look for books in the offices of successful doctors and lawyers. We love to see beautiful libraries in Hollywood mansions with rich mahogany bookshelves and beautiful original editions. It is a sign of status and prestige when a former pres-ident of the United States establishes a library in his name. And since people connect me with books because I am a publisher and an au-thor, it makes sense to visually represent myself with books.

But even if people don't know that about me, I believe they will feel a sense of empowerment and betterment when they see a stack of books. I deliberately had the top book drawn as if it were opened to a new chapter in one's life. A billboard filled with images of books could inspire people to feelings of achievement, improve-ment, and progress.

As an experiment, you might decide to design a small billboard. Small billboard opportunities are everywhere—benches at bus stops, bathroom graffiti, signs, fliers, and even your entry doors. Billboard opportunities are available via the Internet. You might have a web site or be linked to someone else's web site. This experiment isn't so much about reaching the most people but about experimenting with the graphics and the feel of a billboard.

The experiment should help you answer these three questions:

1. Did they notice your billboard? Did it get their attention?
2. How did they feel when they saw it? Were they confused?
3. Could they repeat the message to someone else? Did they remember it 10 minutes later and a day later?

If you have a product that requires packaging, realize that it is one of the most significant vehicles of your brand. The package is shorthand for everything your brand stands for. The package must portray much more than the product information. There are some brilliant examples of this in the perfume industry. UPS has even personified its signature brown color in their packaging and uniforms, with their ad campaign that simply says, "Brown can do it."

I worked with a remarkable CEO who was one of McDonald's' first female supplier/vendors. She has a powerful self-image and a string of successes to her credit. As her company, The Tennessee Bun Company continued to grow, she began receiving inquiries outside of McDonald's for her buns and English muffins. Costco representatives said to her during one meeting, "We like your brand." She called me soon after and asked me, "What's my brand?!" She had all that success in spite of brand uncertainty. Imagine her success with the added power of the brand—not to mention the fact that any additional, intangible value would boost her company's value far beyond what she billed her customer.

We began to work with the entire company to define the experiences that made it what it is today. Again and again I heard stories about honesty and family: honesty in problem solving, work ethic, accounting; family values around hiring practices, benefits, and the nurturing attitude of the owners were an important part of the company's story. How did these company values of honesty and family translate to the brand? What should it look like and sound like? Well for one thing, it doesn't look like a the trendy brown wrappers that a lot of bread companies use to symbolize the Old World bakery. Honesty doesn't hide the product. And it doesn't use illustrations if possible. A "billboard" or package that depicts honesty should actually show the product. So their packaging did just that. Instead of an illustration of the English muffins, a large open window was left clear in the package so the customer could see the real product. The package design said, "We have nothing to hide here." The family values were communicated with a simple phrase on the back of the package under the ingredients: "From our family to yours." In fact, e-mail signatures within the company now conclude with that tagline. Every chance you get to further the look and feel of your brand will further your influence. Cordia Harrington's Tennessee Bun Company brand was always there but now she has birthed it. How she raises it will determine how her company respects it and how the world values it.

How do you feel about having your name out there with no way of knowing who's looking at it? Do you wonder what questions they might have when you are not there to respond? Does this make you nervous? Or do you feel confident that your billboards effectively communicate who you are and create the feelings you want in the observers? I am comforted knowing that if there is a question about what I mean, I can answer it during a meeting. That's not the case with your brand billboards.

Size Matters

Think of yourself as a presence much greater than your person. That is the very reason why companies have T-shirts printed and magnets and calendars—to be in more places than they can be as individuals. Your brand goes before you and should open doors to relate with and influence everyone it touches.

When you begin to think of everything as a type of a billboard, you will get into the habit of reversing the sizing in your mind. In other words, if a business card is one form of a billboard, then imagine it enlarged and blown up to the size of a billboard looming over the freeway. Imagine how your logo on your card, stationery, or imprinted coffee mug would look 30 feet wide by 20 feet tall. Every nuance and choice of type, color, and spacing would big enough for everyone to see. Nothing would go unnoticed, especially your mistakes and especially the things that you aren't sure about. All the things that you kept putting off, like corrections to the address or updates to the language, would all be huge! If your little billboards can't stand the test of enlargement and expansion, then they shouldn't be seen in their small size either. If your brand can't stand the test of sizing up to a billboard, your brand needs work. Conversely, if your billboard can't stand the test of downsizing to the size of a black-and-white business card, then your brand isn't clear enough.

This brings us to a second idea for building brand visibility.

Represent Your Brand with the Way You Dress and the Way You Look

When I was letting people know about the children's book company Dalmatian Press and my involvement with it, I actually bought black and white clothes. From Armani to Target, I found suits with Dalmatian-spotted collars and cuffs, blouses, and jewelry. I even found a Dalmatian-spotted soft briefcase in Lord and Taylor one year. Lucky for me, Dalmatians have been very popular in the consumer product world since the 1996 Disney release of *101 Dalmatians*. (Oh, wait a minute. Was that luck or was that according to my branding plan?)

Although it may be a little too cute for you, my choice of clothing was appropriate for me. Remember my confession in Chapter 1? When I wore spots, my appearance was definitely noticed. Clothes have always been a big part of my reputation, probably because of the way I grew up in the wake of hand-me-downs and secondhand-store clothes throughout college. So I pulled the Dalmatian clothing appearance off with style. Since many of my true experiences throughout life have revolved around clothes—getting them, and getting reactions from them—it's a natural expression of my true identity to express my brand with them.

Steven Spielberg has a look. He is known for his signature look: baseball cap, leather jacket, and jeans. He looks fabulous in his Oscar attire, but he's expressed that the jeans and ball cap are the more natural extension of who he really is. His brand, both personal and professional, makes us believe in his promise to take us on a journey of strength and honesty. His movies, from *Jaws* to *Schindler's List* to *Catch Me If You Can* to *Shrek*, all illustrate fabulous and meaningful moral messages. Just like his appearance, they are more about reality and less about glamour.

His brand permeates his Dreamworks campus in Pasadena, California. When I visited there I was struck by the feeling of Mr. Spielberg's values seen through the casual dress code of his employees. Amusing live topiaries whisper of his deeper values on the campus grounds of his studios. There is a green shrub cut to look like a child sitting on the moon with a fishing pole, just like his movie logo. This reminds us of the dreams we all fish for in life. He and Dreamworks have done a great job of presenting the brand in every way possible. And therefore there are many more ways for his audience to come in contact with the brand and all it stands for. Spielberg and Dreamworks get our attention and we feel branded up to take the action they are looking for.

If the Shoe Fits

When meeting me for the first time in airports or in convention centers, my contacts were amused and relieved when they spotted me. It is still a great icebreaker and conversation opener when I show up in my black suit with Dalmation spots on the collar and cuffs. It has become my signature look. When I am seen, the company name, Dalmatian Press, immediately floats into their mind. Many people have logo lapel pins made up to billboard their company name. Some companies make up signature ties. A lot of people, especially men, groan if asked to wear a tie that has a picture of their brand on it. I remember the sales team at Lyrick who were asked to wear ties with a big purple Barney on them. That illustrates my earlier point that for me to wear funky clothing is consistent with the real me, but for a hunky, male senior vice president to wear a Barney tie—well, there's an obvious disconnect with who he really is and who he is dressed up as.

Building brands is about loving your image and getting it in front of people again and again. Luckily for me, I could do so with some amount of fun and class in my clothing. Don't ask me what I would have done if I worked for Bozo the clown.

When I had cancer I studied the benefits of positive imagery. I learned that different colors could affect my mood and my energy. I began to surround myself with pink because of how it made me feel— positive and healthy. I had pink walls, pink clothes, pink everything. One year my husband gave me a pink Christmas. He surrounded me with everything from pink garbage bags to pink light bulbs and pink cotton balls. My friends turned out in pink to surround me. Today, the color is associated with me to the extent that my friends will ask me why I'm not wearing pink. This is a simple example of a true life experience that shaped my values for health, which were then translated to a visible look and feel.

Nancy Zimpher is a powerful and immensely effective businesswoman in Milwaukee, Wisconsin. She was the Chancellor at University of Wisconsin, Milwaukee, and was heralded for the improvements she made to the image of this urban university. When she left that position in 2003 for a life in Cincinnati, the funniest question journalists had was, "What will she do with all her black and gold clothes?" Nancy Zimpher had always worn the school colors, from her early morning walks to evening society functions. She purposely used her clothing as a walking billboard for the school. Wherever she went she raised awareness and thus sparked conversations about the university and its plans. She opened the door for provocative and influential conversations just by showing up in clothing that said, "Here I am, go ahead, ask me about my school." It was a great way to get attention for her business. When she left, she donated her black and gold wardrobe to charity, which reflects yet another level of her values—turning symbolism into substance.

Norman Rockwell painted a portrait of Harland Sanders, the founder of Kentucky Fried Chicken, in 1978. His attire, white hair, and beard are so legendary that only Santa competes with it. What is really significant is that this is the clothing he wore before he became famous. He turned his real-life look into a marketing icon. While other boys were playing baseball he was cooking at age five. At age 40 he was serving chicken off his own dining room table in a gas station. Today there are more than 7,000 KFC restaurants around the world. Do you remember when they were called Kentucky Fried Chicken restaurants? He kept his true story but simply changed the way he communicated it to the new health-conscious world. During the 2004 preelection days, the company ran a hip ad campaign calling KFC "Chicken Capital, U.S.A." Whatever it is called, we will always and immediately know what to expect when we see the white suit.

Music Magic

I was one of the women who planned her Monday night schedule around the *Ally McBeal* television show in the late 1990s. And it wasn't a show just for women—I was joined by the men in the family, absorbed by the show's comedy and sexuality. This comedy/drama allowed us into the intimate circle of a law firm with its own interesting brand. Their brand was associated with greedy, selfish, quirky, and ambitious people, all desperately seeking attention and a meaningful relationship. Well, of course that requires a lot of therapy. And the hilarious therapist, played by Tracey Ullman, had an unconventional practice that used music therapy. She required her clients to find a theme song that depicted their true story. It wasn't a suggestion or a piece of advice; it was a prerequisite for therapy with her. The choice of the song was as much to tell them about themselves as it was to remind them to get on with it, get going, and make some headway in your life.

Ally made several attempts at picking her song, which were rejected by the therapist. I was appalled. Who was she to tell the client what her true theme song should be? But here again is the lesson that how we see ourselves is often very different then how we are seen by others. So there is some benefit in having others look at your logo, your 8×10 photos, and your theme song. The therapist told Ally that what she had picked was too whiny, sad, and slow. She told her that she was focusing on her sad stories and on what had happened *to* her, not *for* her. At last they picked a song, which Ally loved and I loved. It became the perfect theme song for Ally and for the series. People listened to it on the radio, in clothing stores, and over PA systems everywhere. With just three opening words and three beats of music, we thought, "Ally." And we felt the promise that if she could make it, so could we. How many other theme songs are out there that you recognize after just three beats? The theme from *Cheers*? *Mash*? *ER*? When you hear the beginning of the song, do you realize what emotions the song is triggering?

The Brand Plays On

Just for a moment, experiment with choosing a theme song for yourself and your company. You don't have to tell anyone or use it, but go through the exercise of choosing the music or song with lyrics that capture the spirit and character of your brand. This isn't just to have fun. This is smart branding. Music is one of the most memorable aspects of branding. Music can create an emotional mood instantly. And as a song gets stuck in the listeners' minds, so will your brand be stuck in their minds. Without even seeing your logo or your product, your name will come to mind with the emotion of music over and over again.

Think of some of the theme songs most memorable to you.

Movies, sitcoms, dramas, and commercials all use them. Even the shortest pieces of music can have the most impact. The opening lick to Jerry Seinfeld's TV show is incredibly recognizable. With its crazy montage of pops and buzzes it stays in your mind. Plus it is so unusual that anyone trying to copy it will be accused of doing so, which in a way just brings the listener right back to remembering the *Seinfeld* show. Intel has a catchy few notes at the end of its commercials. So does McDonald's.

Music is so important that the rules of copyrighting continue to create a billion-dollar protection and regulation business. When creating a new song, there are only so many notes that can be used from another similar song before it is called infringement. That is how valuable music is.

Music is so important in branding that companies spend huge amounts of money researching the effect it has on shoppers. As you walk from one department into another in a large retail store, the music will change to reflect the demographics of the typical shopper in that particular department. The brand of music has to change to tell the different products' stories as well as relate differently to different shoppers. Music motivates the purchase.

Companies hope that particular songs will be associated with the store to such an extent that when you hear the songs elsewhere, you will be reminded of the store's name and shopping experience where you first heard it. Many stores now even sell CDs of the music selections that you hear during shopping. They categorize them as "women's daydream" music, "girls having fun" music, or "men at the sports event" music. It is a little weird if you analyze the whole mind-control process they are trying to create. But the results are clear: music subtly gets attention, whether it's conscious or subconscious. Music stimulates your memories, your memories flood you with feelings, and you take action based on those feelings.

If I could use music to bring attention to my brand, I would create a theme song that captures my spirit, energy, movement, and passion. The music itself would have the whole range of notes, played both slowly and quickly, to tell the story of ups and downs and eventual success. It would be about being born to fly. It would inspire others that they can do it too, no matter what it is. It would get the heart rate up even before I appear to speak or conduct business. It would be remembered after I leave and would keep my brand in their mind for as long as possible. And it would seem vaguely familiar without in-fringing on any other writer's work, so that I would come to mind in all possible situations.

Seinfeld, Intel, the Super Bowl, even weather alerts on TV all have sounds that put you in a particular state of mind. When the brand sets your state of mind, it can set the course of your action.

Now that you remember the true stories of your life, what would they sound like in music? Can you think of a song that com-municates who you are?

> Music can actually be your chance to express yourself with more honesty than you'll ever allow yourself to do with words.

What works for you? How can you make your brand seen, heard, felt, smelled, and infinitely more memorable? Do you play the right music in your lobby? What music do you play when a caller is put on hold? What about at your meetings? Can you start them with music? When you pick up clients in the car, do you use this as an opportu-nity to set the right mood for business with the music you play in the car? How are you making yourself heard?

Advertising versus Publicity

Advertising is different than publicity and visibility. Publicity exposes your brand with visibility, and advertising promotes your brand. The goal of all three should be to promote a response. A brand should ask for or, at the very least, encourage a response.

Here are nine common ingredients of effective publicity and ad-vertising for your brand:

1. They have a definite and clear call for action.
2. They influence by creating feelings of collaboration rather than telling people what do.
3. They create responses that you can track.
4. They anticipate and intercept the most common objections.
5. Good ads and good publicity make the audience go back again and again to reread and to reexperience what they felt when they first read the ad.

6. They communicate with words, graphics, and feelings that clearly tell the audience what the brand means.

7. They make the response easy because they are clear and convey trustworthiness.

8. They follow scientific research regarding perception and absorption:

   • We read the top left of everything first, and then we quickly surf to the very bottom of what we are scanning to see if we want to read what's in the middle.
   • Taglines and slogans should be short, never longer than 14 words.
   • A postscript should usually be added, since this is what the eye drops down to read before reading the main message. The P.S. must engage and convince the reader to go back and read the whole piece.

9. They follow color research. There is a large amount of color research available when building your brand to advertise. If you identify with certain colors, use them. If they do not reflect who you are, then don't. But do ask yourself, "What color is my brand?" and use it over and over and over.

   • The color blue-green indicates (and appeals to people with) financial prestige.
   • Deep red and plum colors get strong positive responses from both men and women in upper socioeconomic classes.
   • Bright sky blue is the number one color preference in the United States.[11]

I was honored to work with businessmen and women who were launching a new community bank with impeccable ethics, purpose, and morals. One of the favorite colors of the group was a beautiful, deep red. The first step to develop a new logo and tagline was to put them through the first few brand building steps we've identified so far in this book:

1. Examine your true experiences that no one else can copy.

2. What did these experiences cause you to value and believe?

3. How do those experiences relate to your audience's wants and needs?

4. In capturing those beliefs in a logo and tagline, what would it look like, sound like, and feel like?

I challenged them to examine their true story, subsequent values, and the best way to translate those values to relate to their audience. Think about it. These were people who all had great financial success. Their true stories all reflected success that shaped their values of growth and opportunity. They wanted the brand they were building to relate to those who shared those values. How do you translate that into a color for their logo? Not with the color red. In banking, the color red means losses and a lack of profits. The story they needed to tell was all about growth and life and financial success. What color is that? Probably green and gold. These colors made their audience feel like their money would grow.

The fact is we send a million silent signals with our brand by the way it is made visible via advertising, publicity, or its mere presence. Some of the signals are roadblocks to action.

All of us carry around a bundle of opinions, and when we see something, we immediately attach a positive or negative opinion to it without knowing anything more than our first impression.

We have a scoring system of sorts. We evaluate the color, size, sound, and feel of a brand as we approach it or as it finds its way into our path. When we experience the brand we hit the "total" button. If the total is 100, we buy. If it's 40, we don't. If it's around 70, we pause. You have to figure out what will move the response over the edge to the action you want for your brand. This is true for individual personal brands and large corporate brands. How do you score?

> *If your success is not on your own terms,*
> *if it looks good to the world but does not*
> *feel good in your heart, it is not success at all.*
> —Anna Quindlen (b. 1952)

Basic Brand Belief VI

I will do what it takes to be true to my brand with the way I sound, look, and align myself with others.

Brand Builders

1. What experiences have you had that you believe others can relate to? How will you incorporate those experiences into your brand?

2. What alliances do you have that help build your brand? That dilute or harm it? What evidence do you have of the power of either type of alliance?

3. In what ways do you make your brand seen and heard currently? Do these ways make you more or less credible?

4. How do you rate on a scale of 1 to 100? Would others give you the same rating as you give yourself? (A 1 is a low score and means your brand doesn't score.) What can you do to bring your score up by at least 10 points?

Chapter SEVEN

Planning for Your Brand

Many of life's failures are people who did not realize
how close they were to success when they gave up.
—Thomas A. Edison (1847–1931)[1]

Remember Your Story

Here's a simple little character story from which we can learn about brands without any pressure or intimidation. It's about Rudolph. Not Guiliani—Rudolph the reindeer. When Rudolph the red-nosed reindeer first burst onto the scene, he was a bashful and awkward deer with a secret. His nose was red and it glowed. This characteristic defined him more than any other. It was the essence of his existence. Filled with embarrassment and afraid of being different, his parents tried to cover his nose up with mud. Now he sounded a little funny and looked a little strange, but at least no one knew his secret. Soon all that changed when the dirty mud cap covering his nose was knocked off while playing reindeer games. Sadly, he was mocked and became an outcast.

This is a great example of how hard it is to be ourselves. It seems much easier to be like all the others and fit in. This is an example of our worst fear: "What if they don't like me?"

What did Rudolph learn? What can we learn?

First of all, secrets want out! It's easy to make them up but impossible to keep them in.

Second, trying to be like the other guy won't get you far. Covering up your true story creates discomfort, isolation, and, in many cases, depression. What are you or your business covering up?

Third and most important, keeping some secrets will dilute your ability to relate to others with the one thing you can do the best, namely being yourself. You can be an expert at being yourself. Many of us, in our personal lives and our professional lives, don't even try. But when we become living experts at this, we will attract the audiences who need the very thing we can uniquely offer. Success must follow.

When Rudolph was forced to expose himself, he was forced to rely on what he had thought was his weakest trait. He found out that his red nose that glowed in the dark didn't hold him back at all. What held him back were all the ideas he had chosen to believe about himself. We all know how his story ends. What made him different made him the best. Christmas was saved that year because Santa chose Rudolph above all the other (generic) reindeer. Rudolph was different. Rudolph was special.

Rudolph initially got attention for all the wrong reasons and success eluded him. Then he got attention for the right reasons and the rest, as you know, happily went down in history. And his nose wasn't just a special feature that could be copied. It was the outward physical characteristic that represented his desire to light up others' lives. It was a tool that he used to fulfill his desire to save friends and family. His true story is about his values of family and friendship and compassion. When he built his identity on those experiences, he was able to enjoy what made him different. He realized that this was his best strategy toward building a successful and satisfying future. He should never forget his identity but remember how it led him to real success. It's not enough to know your stories and reveal your secrets; you must remember them and use them for the greatest competitive edge.

What a great brand. Today, all you have to do is call someone Rudolph and you know they are referring to a bright red nose.

We know now that the first step in building your brand is to remember your stories. Think about all the experiences you have had in your life. Think about the life of the organization you are trying to brand. How did it start? Where was life created and born? Who was there? How were you supported financially, emotionally, and spiritually? What were the highlights and the challenges?

What did you come to value because of those experiences? Some values include success, security, adventure, love, competition, attention, family, and friendship. What do you believe has to happen to have security or success or friendship in your life? Write the answers to these questions down, because when you look at the answers on paper, they may surprise you. You may find that you are holding yourself back by believing something that is negative and counterproductive.

Because I had cancer and was attacked in New York, I value security. I had been subconsciously telling myself that it was better to be safe than sorry and that the world was a dangerous place. These beliefs were holding me back from obtaining the other things I valued, such as success and competition and adventure. I have since rewritten those beliefs. Now I trust that, although the world may be dangerous, help is all around. I tell myself, "Be careful but don't hide. And never give up." Today, success is mine. I have spent time remembering my true experiences and putting them in the right context.

Now I know that my experiences have made me an expert in certain areas that uniquely connect to audiences. I know what features to use in my personal brand and my professional brand to optimize my credibility from my true-life experiences. People know when they work with me that I can bring them something no one else can: not just experience but *my* experiences.

I stopped believing that I wasn't good enough, smart enough, and old enough. I've got proof of success in my results. My scientific analytical skills are uniquely superior in a creative children's book business because I imagine all the creative possibilities and also analyze all the business probabilities.

How many of you believe that your business isn't old enough, big enough, rich enough, or famous enough to enjoy massive success? Rewrite those thoughts and tell your true story—the story that no one else can tell and the one that has the happy ending.

Use the same strategy when you analyze any organization. Start with the founder of the company and learn why the company was started, how, where, and with what support. Learn about the company's good times and any hard times. Find out how the dynamics changed because of external or internal pressure.

When I spoke at a national conference for Health Education Centers, each director had a chance to tell a little about their center to familiarize each other with their challenges and opportunities. As you can imagine, it is difficult to hear so many names, titles, and operating structures with any real hope of remembering them. But one director talked about the center's early founder and her purpose for donating the seed money. She had a moving story about preventing health emergencies that could have been averted. She talked about the spirit and heart of the founder and how her words and motto were incorporated into every aspect of the current operation.

It touched us all. I guarantee you this was one of the centers that will be remembered by everyone in attendance. And when you are competing for funds and grants, being remembered is what counts. It's no different in any other business.

Learn to Tell It

If you refuse to brand yourself either professionally or personally, you will increase your chances for isolation and remoteness rather than prevent it. Your brand message will make you or break you—and you're in control of it. You are in control of the emotional message. Because even though you can't always control your audience, you can always control the smile on your face and the tone of your voice. After we remember or acknowledge that we can control the look and sound of our experiences, we can move on to the next step with what I call brand lessons.

If you want to graduate from "Brand Academy," you have to really dig into these lessons and put into practice your goals with the results you have in mind. As we've discussed, that means deeply learning and absorbing the lessons about your true self.

This branding process is easy because you already have everything you need to get started. It's difficult because it will take some painful self-examination to proceed.

There are many ways to get yourself branded, many of them highly enlightening. You can learn about the logos and slogans of branding and discuss how brands look. You can study a lot of successful brands and be tempted to copycat-brand. But wait. This is not a book about the advantages and disadvantages of copycat branding. It is the course of action. In fact, when you get deeply involved with your brand, you may find out it's not working and have to crawl back out.

If you have not yet developed a successful brand, then you must admit your brand efforts aren't working. You need Brand-Aid. You have a brand whether you mean to or not. Take control of it and build it for the results you want. If you do have a brand but have not built it on your authentic, true-life experiences, then it is time to face the fact that it is not working like it should.

Outline Your Future

Writing your brand plan means writing your results plan. Too often we simply write out our goals and objectives, and we think we have a plan for success. But goals are just that: merely goals. A goal is something that you shoot for or aim at. It is a target. A goal is not what *will* happen but only what you *hope* will happen. It is true that we should have goals and hopes. But a successful brand plan should be based on the *identification of what will happen*, not what we hope will happen.

Many professional and personal success coaches advise us to use the word *outcome* instead of the word *goal*. You will *always* reach an outcome. You will not always reach your goal. So identify your results in terms of an outcome. When developing your brand, use the words *conclusion* and *completion*. Plan and imagine with your mind and in your heart, on paper and in your thoughts.

Remember that whatever you do, it will get results. What kind of results do you plan for your branding?

I have been fortunate enough to work with a New York business coach, Scott Jeffrey, who gave me this exercise: If you had only 24 hours to live, what would your message be to the world and who would your audience be? He challenged me with this question because I had become a professional jack of all trades. I could have coined the phrase, "Been there, done that." And that is part of who I am. It is part of my story, and I connect with a wide variety of audiences when I describe my background and areas of expertise. But now I needed to focus on what mattered most. I needed to gather up the fragments of my life and focus on my results. I wanted to be known as an expert and not a brand of many faces.

This important exercise will change everything. When you choose your message as if you only had 24 hours to live, the most amazing thing happens. You will stop thinking about yourself and your ego and begin to think about your audience and their needs and desires. If you only have 24 hours to live, it has to be spent trying to add the most value to everyone else's life. This is the essence of brands. Remember, it's not about you and your needs, it's about them and their needs.

Your ego will get in the way of building the best brand. Not the ego that is indispensable to negotiating your true brand. The ego that gets in the way is the self-obsessed "me" that isolates us and strips us of connection to others. Don't let your pride cancel out your gut intuition and proven research.

Now, what is the most important message that the world can't live without and that only you have the unique experience to give? That's real power. This will be the defining moment of your brand.

We've now come to the part of the brand construction where you must have a kind of blueprint or outline for your strategy. You have learned your stories and realized how unique they make you. You now know that you have the ultimate brand advantage in that no one can copy what you've discovered about yourself.

You've begun to see how your true essence takes shape and form. What does the true you sound like and look like on paper, on the phone, or in a promise?

Elizabeth Dole has a biography filled with experiences that illustrate her sincere gift for person-to-person contact. Today we see her as being approachable and connecting with her audience. Her personal brand based on these unique characteristics extended to her professional brand. She was a natural choice to lead the American Red Cross, an organization defined by caring for people. All of her life's stories prepared her to personify everything this organization stands for. There was consistency between who she is and what she does.

And who can forget the incredible speech she gave to Americans when her husband, Bob Dole, ran for president against Bill Clinton? As his partner, she spoke in a format that no one had ever seen. She spoke to the studio audience not from behind a lectern but while she walked up and down among them, touching shoulders and making close, personal eye contact. It was exactly what we expected from her. When Hillary Clinton tried a similar speaking approach, it didn't connect with us. Hillary's personal brand is less approachable and more distant. She feels right when she speaks from behind a lectern or sitting still in a chair. This is what I'm talking about when I ask, what do your unique character traits look like in action?

Barbara Walters is a personal hero of mine. Forced to compete in professional broadcasting when woman were dismissed as inconsequential, she never pretended to be something she wasn't. She competed in a man's world, but she didn't act like a man or look like a man. That may sound silly, but many a woman has adopted false mannerisms, from cigar smoking to suit wearing, in order to fit in. Barbara Walters stood out because she stayed true to her values of professionalism based on the job, not the gender. She is one of the classiest businesswomen I've seen. Her experiences with financial struggles while she supported her family at a very young age gave her a determination that you could see and hear and feel in her personal and professional life. Her brand is authentic and she is an icon because of how her unique life has been woven into her valuable brand. There is consistency between who she truly is and how she looks, sounds, and makes us feel. I believe she is so successful at getting the people she interviews to open up about their true experiences because she is in touch with her own true identity. She knows exactly what to ask because she has gone there before them and asked herself the same hard questions.

New stories are being written every day in your life, about your life. Your brand has to be able to stretch beyond the plan to meet everyone where they are. If your brand lives only by today's plan, it will eventually die by this plan. A plan needs room for expansion. A plan needs room to grow, like a great house that can be seamlessly added on to. You're not changing the foundation but adding a new room. We truly do not know at the beginning of our brand what the end of it will hold for us.

A true brand will mirror the changes in our own true stories.

And as long as we know our true essence and incorporate the growth and changes bravely, we will strengthen our own brand.

Sometimes when we struggle over the particulars of the brand, it is to avoid discussing the real issues of the meaning behind the brand. When we discuss and dispute the specifics about the brand's logo, color, how it is used, and where it is placed, we might be sidestepping the essentials of the brand itself. It is much easier to debate where the brand logo should be placed on each product and insist that it be moved from the front to the back than it is to question, "What is the meaning and purpose behind this logo and has it changed over time?"

It causes less trouble to question the color of the logo or the choice of one word in the ad copy than to probe the real meaning of the company motto to see if you still believe in it. Such questions and answers might require painful action. Or, worse yet, they may result in the choice between getting on board and supporting the true story or leaving the company in order to be true to yourself. Of course, the worst choice would be to fake it and pretend you can represent the brand as an extension of your true story.

When Dalmatian Press expanded its product line from coloring books and activity books into storybooks, there was a lot of discussion between me, as the founder, and every other department manager. The conversations and debates centered on where to put the logo of the Dalmatian Press puppy dog. We had always put it on the front top left corner of each book. It was easily seen and "spotted." Some employees and associates felt that it was too noticeable and that it made the books look less sophisticated. Imagine my distress, when confronted by my own employees about the worthiness of my brand logo for the front cover of our books. In essence I was being told that our logo was not sophisticated enough. If these books were to be cherished and kept as treasures, passed down through the generations, then the emphasis should be on the content and the beautiful cover illustration.

As they showed me example after example of other precious books in the industry, they pointed out that they rarely had the publisher's logo or brand imprint on the cover. These employees had not been with our company from the start. They didn't understand that the original story of Dalmatian Press was to bring attention to the publisher and create loyalty to the publisher as opposed to the book's character and story. They didn't understand that I wanted to be associated with precious stories as much as I wanted our brand to have intrinsic value. The discussions focused on the size of the logo, the position of it, and how to combine it with the company name. But we never faced the real question: Should we change our "story" and begin to separate the book's cover and content from the publisher?

The employees and I had three choices:

1. Adopt the original Dalmatian Press mission and stay true to its essence, which sought brand loyalty to the publisher as much as the author or cover art.

2. Join a different company that held publishing views consistent with their beliefs.

3. Reexamine our past experiences and question how our new ones have expanded our story and therefore our brand. Then define

how to share this evolved brand so that it continues to represent our present identity while not abandoning our past ideals, having already achieved brand equity. Bingo—this was our choice.

Mirror, Mirror, on the Wall

The best brands mirror the changes in your life. At the inception of Dalmatian Press I didn't foresee this stage of its life. A brand has to keep in mind its audience's changing wants and needs, and stretch to accommodate them. This doesn't mean that it becomes what it isn't. Our solution at Dalmatian Press was to create a revised logo and trade dress for a more expensive line of books while continuing to build loyalty. The new trade dress incorporated a pawprint so there is an obvious connection to our Dalmation logo. But it now made the customer feel different and more sophisticated, with a more sophisticated art treatment. But first, we had to stop hiding behind conversations about the logo position and get to the difficult heart of the matter.

I don't blame the employees for sidestepping this issue, because I had pounded it into their heads for seven years that only through consistency could we build a brand. I blame myself for not doing the work of constant self-examination. Who the company is today is not who it was in 1995. It has grown, and the brand needs to reflect that growth. It needs to examine the new stories of the company and reflect them with the brand strategy. The best brands must constantly examine themselves and see if they continue to reflect the true story, past and present.

Kentucky Fried Chicken uses its acronym KFC. Its story is the same, but it appeals to the changing wants and needs of its audience. Supposedly, Americans want to eat healthier. Deemphasizing the word *fried* and replacing it with an acronym lets customers feel better about choosing to eat its chicken. Same food, but different feeling. Today, the Colonel's spirit and heritage are reflected in KFC's brand identity—the logo features Colonel Harland Sanders, one of the most recognized icons in the world. Every day, nearly eight million customers are served in terms of their wants and their needs.

Madonna is brilliant at brand alteration. One could argue that her brand is constantly changing. But it's not at all. Her brand *is* change. If she didn't change her look and sound, she would not be true to herself or her audience.

Midwest Airlines, one of my favorite airlines in the country, changed its name in 2004 from Midwest Express to Midwest Airlines. They correctly expected that their new name would increase bookings as potential passengers came to realize that they are a full-service national airline, not a regional carrier like the old name seemed to convey. Their slogan is "The best care in the air," and it makes a promise to their customers that you'll feel more cared for when you fly with them. Like many in their industry they have endured financial difficulties and they will have to decide which corners to cut and which services they must keep to fulfill their promise. A great brand eventually fails if its products and features don't deliver. Midwest is now using smaller planes that do not have their signature big leather seats. They don't always serve their famous warm gooey chocolate chip cookies. They also do not allow disabled passengers needing oxygen to fly with them whereas most other airlines do. So, although their brand name is expanding its reach, their pledge to give the best care in the air has room to grow. If your brand evolves, it must be based on true experiences and not on goals yet to be reached.

I interviewed the president of the Milwaukee Metropolitan Association of Commerce, Tim Sheehy, to discuss one of Milwaukee's most important jewels—Midwest Airlines. Headquartered in Milwaukee, it employs over 2,800 people. In addition to Midwest having a strong brand, Tim knows its alliance with Milwaukee can strengthen the Milwaukee brand. Tim Sheehy is one of Milwaukee's most important spokespeople as an advocate for encouraging businesses that build Milwaukee's brand as a great place to live. Tim gets branding. He summed up his discussion about Midwest Airlines by saying, "Everything from the chocolate chip cookies to the best service makes you feel special. There couldn't be a better way to welcome people into Milwaukee than via a Midwest Airlines flight. Their brand tells a great story."[2]

Go ahead. Live your best brand!

Here's what a dog can teach us about building brands:

- Never pretend to be something you're not.
- If it itches, scratch it.
- Be loyal. Jump up and down. Beg if you have to.

- If what you want is buried, keep digging until you find it.
- No matter how often you're criticized, don't buy into the guilt. Run right back and make friends.

Envision Your Best Brand Moments

Each time you imagine the future, put it into the context of the following questions.

How does my brand make me feel connected to an earlier time in my life?

Most often people will develop personal or professional brands that unknowingly are rooted in their meaningful life experiences. We tend to create two kinds of scenarios. Either we try to repair difficult situations or we recreate wonderful situations. Perhaps we have lived through times when we didn't get sufficient attention or recognition. Building a conspicuous brand may be a way that we unknowingly deal with that experience! Or perhaps we had a memorable adolescence during which we were recognized for the way we looked or acted. Building a brand may be a subconscious attempt to recreate that situation.

If you ask yourself what memories your brand stirs up from your earlier personal life, you'll probably be surprised by your answer. Keep asking this question, because acknowledging that connection is absolutely essential to your brand building success. Then, as you envision the future, ask what feelings your brand will stir up in others. Is that what you had hoped for? It is your audience's feelings that count. If they don't connect with you and feel like they can relate to your brand, then you are meaningless to them. Is that what you want?

What does your brand development help you to believe about yourself and your future?

Brands are what we feel about the product or the service, but they are more than that. They are what they can make us feel about ourselves.

The really potent part of a brand is that it allows you to carry around beliefs about yourself that make you feel special, precious, valuable, worth your weight in gold. But the truth is that your brand does not give you these attributes.

The fact that your brand now puts you on people's radar screens and therefore makes you feel valuable from the resulting recognition doesn't mean that the brand is responsible for you being valuable. You were always valuable, and your brand gave your value a forum to be seen. Said more simply, you define your brand. Your brand does not define who you are or how you feel.

Phil Vischer has been called one of the twenty-first century's most influential men. He is the creator of the Christian phenomenon VeggieTales, to which millions of children give their love and attention. We spoke for hours one hot summer day about the heat he was taking for his brand protection. Even though Phil grew up in the church with his dad the Sunday school superintendent and his mom the choir director, he went through the same problems and issues that any kid does. When his parents divorced, he moved into the basement of his house and, metaphorically, of his life. Deep in introspection, he realized that God had filled his head with stories and the ability to make people laugh. Yet he was also filled with moral outrage, even as a teen, that the world was in trouble when it came to values.

Phil is one incredibly hard worker, but he said, "I'm driven by need. If people took better care of their kids I could slow down. I'm not a type A." Did he feel like he wasn't taken care of growing up? He admitted that the VeggieTales brand is "me." He also confessed, "I have no desire to run a company." What an admission! He was running a multimillion-dollar company when corporate management wasn't his true story. His constant self-examination helped him remain true to his brand protection. He knows who he is and what his brand means to people. Because of his childhood experiences, he wanted to help parents raise their kids with the message of God. Therefore he kept his brand from expanding into product lines that could carry the logo but not actually spread God's word. For example, he expanded into books but not bicycles. He protected what his brand promised at the expense of new revenues. One can see how his true experiences are reflected in his business, including a succession of three unsuccessful presidents. Was he looking for a father figure, perhaps? Phil says, "Maybe."[3]

In 2004 Big Idea, parent company of VeggieTales, was sold to Classic Media. But Phil's brand story is a great and successful example of building a brand to connect to earlier times in your life in such a way that it perpetuates your beliefs and plans for your successful future—no matter how you define success.

If you were to make a list of all the things your brand makes you believe, you might find words like *powerful, important,* and *fascinating* on your list. If you believe in these qualities associated with your brand, would they disappear if your brand dissolved? No. These are the qualities that you give to your brand. Your brand does not give them to you. However, when envisioning your future, you must ask what your brand helps your audience to believe about themselves.

- Does it make them feel good?
- Does it make promises that they need to hear?
- Do they feel more important and worthy?
- Does your brand make them feel better or worse?

If you can't answer "better" to the last question, your brand is in trouble. Write the most exciting conclusion you can imagine for your brand. And learn to rewrite it and rewrite it and rewrite it. The improvement of your brand reflects the improvements in your life and its telling.

> *It may be hard for an egg to turn into a bird: It would be a jolly sight harder for it to learn how to fly while remaining an egg. We are like eggs at present. And you can not go on indefinitely being just an ordinary decent egg. We must hatch or go bad.*
> —C. S. Lewis (1898–1963)[4]

Brand Building Belief VII

I will think of my brand in terms of the results it can bring today, and as a vehicle to mirror change, while connecting me to past ideals.

Brand Builders

1. What is a "Rudolph" characteristic in your life?

2. If you had 24 hours left, what would you want your brand to communicate to those important to you?

3. How will your brand mirror the changes in your life? If your brand is the reflection of your true experiences, what images do you see?

4. What does your brand help you believe about yourself?

Chapter EIGHT

Getting Results from Your Brand

*Singleness of purpose is one of the chief essentials for
success in life, no matter what may be one's aim.*
—John D. Rockefeller, Jr. (1874–1960)[1]

The Map

We're all trying to deal with different kinds of maps in life. Personally I hate maps. I can follow directions so long as they include landmarks. "Turn left at the Holiday Inn, go straight until the road becomes a one-way street, and immediately turn right into Wal-Mart." But give me directions that start with the word *southeasterly* and I am lost. It's not that I won't ask for directions. I love directions. I just don't want to read them off of a map. In fact, when my husband hollered to me that Toronto was nowhere near Niagara Falls on our way there from Buffalo, New York, I snapped. I wadded the paper map in my lap into a ball and threw it out the window while we were speeding down the highway. That would show him.

Well, back to maps. Not only do I want to be able to read maps but I want to *be on* the map. You've heard the expression "She put him on the map," or, "She's his due north," or, "He's on the map now!" Remember the free-standing map in shopping malls or theme parks where we search for the "You Are Here" icon? Think about the Internet sites that assist you with direction, reservations, and travel plans. They all begin with the word *Start*. Go to the map. Get on the map. Figure out where you are starting from and who you really are. Then and only then can you get to where you want to go.

If you think of yourself as a kind of a map marker for other people or businesses, then you'll understand that we need to be that which others look for or look to. Success is a huge map marker. It's like a flare sent up demanding attention. It acts as a compass, and people will want to follow it and be directed by it. It's okay to emulate patterns of success. That doesn't make you any less authentic, as long as you use the compass of success to discover your characteristic behaviors you haven't owned yet. Start by defining yourself as a success to which people can relate. We are all like road signs or landmarks of some kind. We are a key word that others are searching for. To get results with your brand, you have to know that you are consistently and correctly communicating your brand. If you were a key word on a search engine, what would it be?

Let's use the word *American* as an example of a key word. This is a word that is frequently used to describe those born in the United States, including African American, Native American, Asian American. Once while watching Kelly Ripa on the ABC show *Regis and Kelly*, I saw an interview of a new television character that happened to be a puppet. She asked him what it felt like to be a sock. He replied, "My dear, I'm no sock, I'm a Fabricated American."

It seems that many people born in the United States want to be defined as some type of an American. When Bruce Springsteen sings "Born in the USA," the crowd goes wild. For many reasons people have decided that this suffix increases one's respect, value, credibility, and ownership of various rights. The brand "America" is powerful. It is influential. Its logos and brand images make people feel a wide range of emotions, regardless of political affiliations. Liberal Americans tear up when the American flag is presented. Stoic citizens will stand to sing the national anthem. The American soldier in uniform stirs up feelings of loyalty no matter whether we support the war effort or not.

In 2003 when the George W. Bush administration led the U.S. into war against Iraq, one of the most popular country music groups of the time spoke out against the president. At that time, Bush's approval ratings were extremely high. Lead singer Natalie Maines of the Dixie Chicks said that she was ashamed that George Bush was from her native state, Texas. Many people who had aligned themselves with the "America" brand took this as a personal insult of their brand. Record sales plummeted. Radio stations refused to play the group's singles. Other music stars criticized the Dixie Chicks and distanced themselves from them.

No one likes to be told that they have made the wrong choice. And when the Chicks criticized the president it was as if they were saying, "Bush is no good so America is no good, either."

We don't just choose brands because they make life more convenient. We choose brands to affirm our values and align ourselves with what we believe in. Our choices say a lot about who we are. It's one thing to be told that our choice of music is wrong. It's quite another thing to be told that your alignment with your country, and all it represents, is wrong. Some products and services matter more and, therefore, so do their brands.

Many Americans never watch hockey or even care much for the game. But in 1980 when the American team won the Olympic gold medal in hockey, people were proud to be an American. I felt the pride bursting through me as I watched the games from the campus brew house along with hundreds of other screaming, excited college kids. Part of America's brand is the feeling of being winners, whether on the ice or on the battlefield. If you attack the America brand then you make Americans feel like losers. People don't like to be called losers. When Russia, France, or any other country wins, it makes everyone who aligns themselves with the country's brand feel like a winner no matter what the competition is.

When J. B. "Van" VanCronkhite was an American soldier it was the early 1950s. As a young enlisted man he was taught the art of psychological warfare as the cold war heated up. His training was for the express purpose of building or maintaining brand loyalty to America with the armed troops. Van tells the story of his days as an information and education specialist in western Germany during the 1950s. Having been trained in psychological warfare methodology, he was asked to develop a program that would negate the effect of Russian propaganda that was wooing American soldiers to embrace Communism.

With the assistance of one female and two male soldiers, he developed a team that visited Army units along the Russian-American checkpoint during the notoriously hated Saturday morning information and education training sessions. After announcing that the four-team members were card-carrying Communists (during the tag end of the McCarthy Communism hearings), the four extolled the supposed virtues of Communism as their audiences sat quietly in disbelief over what they were hearing.

Van anticipated that at least one older master sergeant would have his fill of the talk, and he was never wrong. Inevitably, the intolerant older sergeant would stand and tear apart the team's message by bringing up the virtues of being an advocate of American freedom. Soon the others would join in and cite examples they probably had not consciously thought about. There were times, Van reflects, that the team had to admit to the hoax before leaving the session, for fear of not making it to their vehicle in safety, so heated did the arguments become.[2]

Before the session, the soldiers believed that the United States had an authoritative brand that was also shorthand for restrictive and limiting. But when the brand that they had sworn allegiance to was being attacked, it made them feel like they were being personally attacked. This was about more than loyalty to their country; it was about their egos, too. By noon, the brand had changed from something slightly negative to one that was powerful and positive, standing for a wide range of freedom protected by a disciplined military and personal sacrifice. The military had become a map marker for others looking for freedom and opportunity.

What other defining adjectives are on your brand map? To get the powerful results you want from your brand, your brand map must be clear. Not only must you identify your starting point, but the road behind you must be as clear as the road ahead. Can you trace your way back home? Can others looking at your brand connect with the foundation of the brand? I guarantee that if your brand's beginning, humble or otherwise, is kept out in front, your audience will better relate, connect, and remember your brand. There is a common expression, "Don't forget who you are and where you came from." Never is that truer then when you're growing your brand identity.

How Does Your Brand Travel?

Next let's look at your map for diversity. When plotting a course to success there are many pathways to take. You can go the most direct route. You can take a few side trips to enjoy the scenery. You might make a stopover to pick up another passenger. We base our travel plans on what kind of traveler we are. Do you travel well? Do you like to conquer and get to your destination as quickly as possible? Do you drive with a phone in one hand and a super-sized slurpie in the other? Once again, you have to look at yourself to know not just where you are starting from but what characteristics you have as tools to use for the journey to greater brand success. It's not enough to know the road; you have to know what kind of a driver you are.

I have a science background, and I build analytically and with organization. I must be able to accurately and systematically trace my results back to their definitive origination. I felt like I lived my early life in a world of chaos and upheaval, so order and logic became very important to me. I learned to believe that only by taking control of everything could I control my success. These tapes that constantly played in my mind kept me from reflecting on more recent experiences I'd had, including whirlwinds of spontaneous achievement and artistic accomplishment. Only when I examined my whole life and not just my old self-concept did I build a more successful personal brand, which extended to my business success and corporate brand at Dalmatian Press. Dalmatian Press is in a constant state of commotion that makes people feel like anything can happen.

Follow this example of my personal and professional branding pathway: My early experiences of chaos led to values and beliefs of extreme organization. These values were translated into a brand that looked and sounded precise and controlled. I became a scientist. My brand felt logical and scientific and made my audience feel safe and sensible. My brand at home and at work could be traced back to my authentic and unique experiences in life. More recent experiences allowed me to value spontaneity, which when incorporated made my expanded brand identity look more colorful and fanciful, and excited and intrigued my audience. Now I expanded my brand to a kind of scientific, creative children's publisher. The combination of past and present experiences expresses the kind of diversity that connects with a wider audience but still has a focus and purpose based on my authentic story.

Develop a passion for helping yourself look for what you typically overlook in yourself. Get connected to you. Specialize in finding what you have buried and what, for practical purposes, you have lost, regarding yourself. Next, remember to incorporate each new day's experiences and what they teach you instead of remaining in the past and in the past brand. When you know your heart, wear it on your sleeve, put it on buttons, send out fliers, and wear it for all to see until it becomes written on the hearts of those you care about.

Sharing your new and current true story prevents the growth of disparity between who you say you are and who you really are. Stay connected to your truth or you're in danger of creating a false relationship with your business associates, your friends, and yourself.

Labels and Map Markers

As much as we love brands in this world, we love their labels even more. If a brand makes our life a little easier, then putting a label on a brand would seem to make it even easier! When we label something, we can file our knowledge away in a little mental file to be accessed whenever we need it.

Labels shouldn't be taken lightly when we are building a brand or analyzing brands. They are limited by their very nature and they can erode your authenticity. They can hold you back from developing your brand. Remember that a brand is how you feel about something, and a label can cover up what you're really feeling deep inside. The labels tend to be stuck on the surface of companies or people and can actually put up a barrier to getting down underneath them. They can become convenient works of fiction that influence everyone who uses them.

Our businesses have labels and we each have personal labels. Sometimes we inherit them and sometimes we make them up ourselves. But as long as they remain unchallenged we will never sustain the success that depends on constant self-evaluation and incorporation of our daily new and unique experiences. You'll never become your real brand. You'll only be yesterday's brand. If you don't keep up with your work of ongoing discovery and define your new self every day, then the label you've put on your brand will be its limiting factor.

This limitation will result in a box of judgments from which you can't escape. It may be a comfortable box. In fact it might be so comfortable that you start putting all of your energy into supporting the falsehoods of how you've labeled yourself.

That's when companies and the people who run them lose the success that they had—because *who you were yesterday is rarely who you are completely today.* Dalmation Press was labeled as a Wal-Mart supplier at first and then as a mass market publisher. Those are limiting labels; they are not what we are but just things that we did. The true experiences that each day has brought continue to shape you, resulting in your better, more successful brand. You may not notice much change, but your brand can't help but continue to grow if you absorb each day's new experiences, think about them, and use them.

I'll never understand how people can go through major crises in their life and not change. Cancer, death, and divorce happen, yet they live in denial of what that means for their lives and how it should shape their identities. They tell a story of shallow indifference when the truth is more about pain and fear, which could be about survival and perseverance if they did the work of self-examination.

I'll never know completely why I went through the pain and trials I did, much less why others do. But if a child goes through sickness, chemotherapy, radiation, pain, needles, tears, or death, let it not be for nothing. If an organization goes through layoffs, downsizing, bankruptcy, scandal, and despair, let it tell a story to learn from. *Let the pain serve the brand.*

Corporations and businesses live lives that are sometimes filled with crisis. Do we analyze them or do we just try to forget them because they embarrass us or hurt us? Remember the earlier discussion we had about hidden treasures? These crises are valuable to the extent that we study them and figure out how they make us different from everyone else. No one else has had that experience, even if it is a bad experience. These unique experiences are the true stories that should be shared via the new and changed values we've developed from what has happened. Too often we stay stuck in an old, comfortable definition of who we think we are or who we think we should be.

Brand Boxes

As a student of corporate brands, I have seen how companies not only try to be like certain other companies but they even try to fit into a category or type of company. They build a brand and then they build a box around the brand by deciding what kind of a brand they are! Here are six examples:

1. The *informational company* is typified by a big building or lots of buildings housing conference rooms for education, auditoriums for seminars, management training rooms, and human resource departments. It emphasizes knowledge, information, huge product lines, and data as much as profits. Universities and hospitals fall into this category. Johnson Control and Johnson Wax do also.

2. The *artistic company* emphasizes feelings, beliefs and, emotional output resulting in great works. Sometimes the means to success

are anything but logical. Five-year plans with spreadsheets and system queries have at their core the desire to be true to the company philosophy as the end result. Great achievement and successful results come from gut feelings, intuition, and artistic expression layered on top of P&L analysis. Some film studios, such as Dreamworks and Sundance, wear this kind of a brand.

3. The *corporate* or *institutional company* emphasizes the corporate experience. There is even an unofficial uniform that everybody wears. Remember the joke about IBM's mandatory blue pinstripe suit? Here everyone's office decor is similar. Corporate assembly is important and the term, *company man* gets used as a compliment. Conformity is important. The IRS and other federal institutions are like this. Wal-Mart shares some of these brand traits.

4. The *nonprofit* or *community company* emphasizes social importance. Profits are important but not if the cause isn't met. Benefiting the cause is often used as an excuse for not being profitable! The community company doesn't need a building. It operates house-to-house, moving within the community, meeting the needs of the world without set hours or days of operation. Museums, the Red Cross, Girl Scouts of America, Planned Parenthood, and Campus Crusade for Christ share this look and feel.

5. The *healing company* emphasizes the employees' benefits as much as the company's success. Healing companies value the growth and improvement of individuals. They believe that one of the most important roles of the company is to mentor the employee. The work of the company is as much about growing strong individuals to send out into the world as it is to serve the outside world. Every year a variety of business magazines rank the nation's best places for people to work, based on the benefits, opportunities, and personal growth potential. Some companies simply care more about this. Some companies define themselves by how good the work experience is for the employee. A consultant for Boston Market once taught, "Happy employees sell more chicken." Either way, companies that pay as much attention to the employee as they do the customer have a different type of brand. Examples are Focus on the Family and some family-owned businesses.

6. The *entrepreneurial company* is characterized by energy, individuality, and a never-give-up attitude. Such a company emphasizes the

vision of its founder. Usually privately owned, it has a brand that makes people feel both invigorated by possibilities and frustrated by constant change. Sometimes corporate organizations want to be seen as entrepreneurial to hide from their true identity. Dalmatian Press wears this brand, but so does the conglomerate of Oprah's Harpo Productions.

Every company is probably a mixture of brand traits.

However, when you know who you are and define your true brand, don't disregard that which you are not.

For if you center all your thoughts on only what you are, you can become arrogant and unbalanced in your approach to the business you are building. If we focus only on who we are, we can begin to believe that we're better than others. Plus we will become weaker and weaker in our undeveloped areas. If you realize that your strengths lie in one area or another, it's only natural to put all your energy there. It is certainly more comfortable to operate in that zone. But you do so at the risk of losing perspective about others and about the changes you are likely going through. Don't stop working to discover who you are and what your authentic brand is. Change doesn't mean that you are abandoning your brand, it means you are making use of the experiences you have day after day. What did you learn today?

Well-intentioned businesspeople can be heard saying, "I'd use all my talents and I would incorporate all my good qualities and gifts—but I can't find them." Sometimes this is just dodging the work, and sometimes it is a genuine concern. But we need to talk about the word *can't*.

If you want to find those qualities to better yourself and your company, you need to make it a priority.

Get serious about searching out your diverse self, as it contains the essence of your uniqueness. Do this not only because it is good for you but because it is a smart business decision. In today's market, with increasingly diverse backgrounds of customers and customer needs, satisfaction depends on your being able to harness your diverse characteristics to meet those needs. The more you understand yourself, the more you are likely to understand your customers.

I'm not talking about some cozy management meeting where we all hug each other and sit around talking about our grandchildren. This is really about improving our company performance by knowing how to connect with people and instituting a feeling of inclusion.

The Journey and the Search

When we choose our map we can wholeheartedly begin the journey toward who or what we envision as the best person or place to be. This journey or search for your brand must be consistent and flexible at the same time. How is that possible?

When I was a scientist I wore a white lab coat. I thought it was cool. Actually, I'm sure I looked like a nerd. But it made me feel smart every time I put it on. Can clothes affect who you are? Of course they can. There's a well-known expression, however erroneous, that "The clothes make the man." If clothes affect how you act, do they affect your brand image? Does your organization's or corporation's packaging affect your brand?

Certainly if Barney, the famous purple dinosaur on PBS, changed his color and became a red dinosaur, his brand would be noticeably changed.

Is it a contradiction to have a true brand identity and the need to reformulate yourself at the same time? A friend of mine, Pete Fisher, has one of the coolest jobs: He's the general manager of the Grand Ole Opry. Last March he divulged that he constantly assesses the status of the Opry's brand and the strategic plan to further develop it. He confessed, "We're all just creatures of habit. We have to challenge our natural tendencies to fall into routine."[3]

Pete manages the business of one of America's best-known brands by protecting its authenticity. I had the chance to be backstage during a few fabulous performances at the Opry. The genuine excitement that pours out of the performers night after night is unmistakable. To quote Pete, it is the feeling of Americana, patriotism, heritage, and legacy translated into music and lyrics that make every listener validate who they are meant to be. The Grand Ole Opry has 83 percent unaided awareness. Pete's vision is to increase that awareness to 100 percent. I interviewed him in his cozy office, filled with historic memorabilia from the likes of Minnie Pearl and Johnny Cash. His message was delivered softly, smoothly. He's a smart man with a meaningful past of his own.

"I have to love what I do or I don't do it well," he said. I asked him what the word *brand* meant to him, and he explained, "It is dialing up the thoughts and feelings of the true essence of something." I asked him how he was managing this brand that was in a time of transition. It's cool to be country now. How does one stay true to one's essence and also stay in touch with today's audience? "It means knowing the right ingredients and staying true to them." Pete smiled, "I'm not trying to make the Opry something it's not. We are telling the same message of Americana and family, only we package the message differently. We used to tell the story with Minnie Pearl and Roy Acuff. Now we tell it with artists like Brad Paisley and Vince Gill."

Pete talked a bit about his childhood and the values he developed based on his experiences. His passions are his family, music, God, and the people whose lives he touches. What a perfect fit that makes him for his position at the Grand Ole Opry, which is the one that can most affect the brand. His personal passions permeate his professional life. When he looks around the place he thinks, "Let me make a difference here. Let me make a difference so that the people who have worked here for 40 years have not done so in vain."

While growing up, he had a dog named Lucky. Maybe that name was evidence that he could believe in the impossible. He told me that, when building a brand, you simply must see the impossible. "Dream, dream, dream," he said. "Dreams feed the vision." Making dreams come true takes more than luck, but sometimes luck doesn't hurt.

Pete Fisher has studied the map for building his personal and professional brand, and now he is on the journey. He is focused and yet flexible. His story illustrates how important it is to know what your audience wants and how that evolves over time. He has been successful in giving the fans what they want without changing the true identity of this national treasure. He knows exactly who he is and who the Opry is. We can depend on him to weave his experiences into his work so that both his personal life and professional life are enriched. He uses the key ingredient—the truth—to enrich his personal brand and the brand of the Opry. What a great example of evolving in place! The Grand Ole Opry has never been more popular and more connected to its audience than it is today. Building on truth has certainly made the journey for the Opry rewarding.

The most critical principle that a leader must embrace for success is to know the objective. Military leaders, corporate CEOs, football coaches and *you* must all follow this principle. "Everywhere in life, lack of clarity with regard to goals is 89 percent of failure, and clarity is 89 percent of success," says success coach Brian Tracy in his book *Victory!*[4] Make sure that as you develop your brand, your goal is a crystal clear reflection of who you *are*, more than who you want to be. Furthermore, your brand objective must be absolutely clear to everyone who is likely to help you achieve it.

The Grand Ole Opry's parent company is Gaylord Entertainment. Its chief, Colin Reed, approaches branding from the opposite end of the equation. In a 2003 interview with a Nashville newspaper, *City Limits*, he was quoted as saying, "What we have to do is define what we want people to say about us, and then we have to develop a plan to market that."[5]

This strategy needs further clarity. It's okay to identify the results you want from your brand, such as wanting your audience to think you're smart and to tell others that you're sharp. But if this isn't your true identity and you manipulate your market to feel something that is phony and bogus, than disaster is waiting. Rather than defining what you want people to say about you, define yourself and get people to tell your true story.

Focus

What is the brand's goal? What is the company's brand? What is the individual's image? The clearer you are about these things, the more likely you will have success. This is the only way to continue building your brand and get incredible results. Imagine looking through a telescope and finding the optimal focus, but it keeps slipping. You must keep refocusing constantly, or look away from the blurry picture. How would it be if you got new eyeglasses that gave you perfect focus, but the focus gradually slipped?

Objectives are meaningless unless you focus on them. Whatever you focus on will surely manifest. In these days of multitasking, there seems to be less emphasis on focus. This is a mistake. We laugh at how juvenile news reports, books, movies, and music are nowadays, but in fact writers must write at a low level of comprehension, not because we are stupid but because we have split our concentration into so many places at the same time that there is no one part of the brain available to summon up enough focus for an intelligent study.

Yes, we must do more and more at the same time, but it is more important than ever to focus, precisely because we have so much to do and only limited resources. Imagine how, looking through the small lens of a telescope, we can make what we're looking at bigger! *Sometimes, only by looking at less can we see more.*

We can no longer afford to scatter our efforts. We have to fall back on our core abilities, our core products, and our core services. And these are precisely related to our core identity, which I call our essence or unique fingerprint. Focus single-mindedly on this.

Maneuver

Charles Darwin is remembered for teaching, "It is not the strongest of the species that survive, nor the most intelligent, but the ones most responsive to change."[6]

The ability to maneuver is the result of remaining flexible. This does not mean that we are tossed to and fro in the wind with change. It means that we can take our objective and our focus on it and think outside the box regarding how to reach that outcome. Progress comes from originality and from knowing when you have to do things differently. Sometimes a makeover accomplishes uncovering the true you that wasn't being seen.

According to an article in *USA Today Weekend* in July 2003, it wasn't age but necessity that led Betty Crocker, the grand dame of baking, to seek a superstar makeover. General Mills of Minneapolis devoted more than a year and more than a million dollars to making over its packaging to appeal to today's bakers. Audrey Guskey, marketing professor at Duquesne University in Pittsburgh, said, "It's a manufacturer's silent salesman and has to have a 'wow' effect. The average shopper spends 27 minutes in the supermarket, and the average store has 30,000 items. So consumers spend a fraction of a second looking at a package."[7]

The package is the business's way of telling the brand story. A package can be almost anything. For Betty Crocker, it is the cake box. The marketing firm Lipson Alport Glass & Associates sketched 800 versions of new packaging ideas, and handwriting analysts evaluated over 100 versions of the Betty signature, to get the look and feel of the famous homemaker. The branding efforts' target was to make consumers feel like they wanted to eat that piece of cake on the package right *now*.

Since 1921 Betty Crocker has been turning out dessert mixes. Since then Betty herself has had several hairstyle changes to relate to her audience. One thing that has not changed is her signature hot red-orange cookbook. Back in the 1980s her cookbook was on everybody's must-have list. Western Publishing (later known as Golden Books) had the honor of printing this tome. Year after year, book after book came off the press line until one year "Big Red," as we affectionately called the book, printed up an awful orange color. Taking care of the brand has to start at the top of a corporation, and it must be cherished and cared for at every touch point along the way. In this case the pressmen didn't take very good care of the brand. They didn't honor the trademark color that generations had come to recognize. It became a publishing nightmare, costing the company hundreds of thousands of dollars, their reputation, and a few people's jobs. Had the orange book been allowed to get out in the market it would have opened up the floodgates for other manufacturers of Betty Crocker products to get sloppy with Betty's brand. Every time Dalmatian Press doesn't protect its brand by using either its spots, name, or logo, it dilutes the long-term brand for short-term gain.

What is your signature packaging? Is it protected? Is it working? Is it going to work tomorrow? Between focus and maneuver, you'll find the balance for success. Insanity is doing things the same way and expecting a different result.

When at first you don't succeed, try, try again. But don't keep trying the same way. Keep changing your method or your model until you get results. This is how business executives and leaders succeed. Thomas Edison said, "I have not failed, I have only found 10,000 ways that don't work."[8]

If you want different results, you have to do it differently. Not *be* different—*do* different. The only way to show your whole, true self is to present yourself from different angles and perspectives. This is the only way to be fully appreciated.

More specifically, this book has discussed focusing on you and your true story such that you know how to define it and then use it to define your brand. When we look at corporations or significant individuals, we rarely see them as who they really are. We see them as similes, metaphors, allegories. We put them in context with comparisons and references. When people see us, whether it's ourself or our company, they see what they came to see. Their viewpoint is enhanced or obstructed by so much subjectivity that they really see more of themselves than the reality.

Imagine

Imagine that you could create and transform your brand into anything you want it to be. Imagine this in terms of your own personal brand identity, your corporate brand, or some combination of the two. But think about what you could do, or would do, if you had a magic wand to zap your real and your perceived image into anything you wished.

If I had been given the proverbial three wishes in the past, I might have mistakenly wished to have the following:

1. The best-known brand.
2. The brand best known as successful.
3. The brand that makes me a lot of money.

Some people probably would have begun by wishing for more wishes. I don't know what your dreams are and what results you are seeking, but today, I would be wishing differently.

The "-est" Brand

This is what I've learned about best-known brands: Sometimes they are well known because they are bad brands. Some brands have made their reputation on careless mistakes and breaking trust, hurting their customers with poor quality, empty promises, and even damaged lives. Just because we want attention, we don't have to behave like puppies acting out for any kind of attention based on good or bad performance.

What Dalmatian Press has evolved into is the type of attention-seeking company whose honor it is to acknowledge attention, say thank you, and turn it right back towards the customer, partner, or whoever it is that gave it to us.

Some people will strike out on their own and make a name for themselves, as individuals or within organizations, in an attempt to be the "-est" of something. The "-est" symptom comes from wanting to be known. They want to be known for something, *anything*. So we become the biggest, loudest, rudest, fastest, whiniest. They shock people into listening. They get attention for exaggerations, bad behavior, or for making statements that are controversial. And once done, they're too afraid to change their ways since they are now being watched (isn't that what they wanted?). There are a dozen bad-boy CEOs out there who live this way. Howard Stern, Rush Limbaugh, and Bill O'Reilly have personal "-est" brands. New York City, Wal-Mart, and General Electric have corporate "-est" brands.

There are many brands that "have a reputation"—a bad reputation. They're like the kids in high school who your parents didn't want you to hang out with. Some companies have the same buzz about them because they have shocked the world or hurt the customer or have been deceitful to the culture and society.

Calvin Klein was a company that shocked the world with its advertising campaigns. On billboards, television, and magazine ads, one could see the brand associated with scantily clad models or partially nude children. It certainly got attention. Its corporate spokespeople were whisked onto major news networks to talk about those campaigns and defend their use of nudity to sell clothing. Did it become a better-known brand? Yes. Did it create both positive and negative perceptions of its brand? Probably. Is this a brand strategy that can be copied and take away from the unique position that Calvin Klein was attempting to create? Of course.

Tylenol, Firestone, and Kathie Lee Gifford were companies that acquired more brand awareness at one time by hurting people. It wasn't their intention, but it was the result of some of their business operations. These companies had associations with arsenic, poor safety performance, and the frightening use of child labor. These brand builders had no intention of connecting to these problems that brought them so much attention. Once the spotlight was on them, they had to put their valuable time, energy, focus, and money into changing their tarnished brand image. Instead of being able to focus on building their companies, they had to focus and maneuver to keep their companies alive.

In some cases, a company's reaction to bad publicity will help create an even better brand. For instance, the way Tylenol put the public's safety first, no matter the cost of business, made customers believe that it did indeed really care about them, and that they could trust it again. Likewise, Kathie Lee Gifford put all her effort into eliminating child labor from her clothing line's production as well as fighting against it in the rest of the world's consumer products. She testified before Congress at the request of President Clinton and used a painful personal experience, her values, and her professional brand identity to help get the "hot goods" act passed. She built a greater reputation for her brand by appealing to our values of righteousness and defense of the weak and vulnerable.

Most recently, companies have created incredible brands labeled as greedy, untrustworthy, and unscrupulous when they were shown to have unethical accounting practices. In 2001 few people talked about big accounting firms like Arthur Andersen or Strong Financial. They were in the background of society. But by 2002, whether your business was managed by these firms or not, you saw them everywhere on television and in newspapers, exposed for their questionable profit reporting that misrepresented the facts. As the SEC got involved and founders resigned or were fired, so did the brands fall. These company names became shorthand for corrupt, insincere, and fraudulent. To some people, they even become synonymous with the single thing that stole their secure retirement from them.

Being the best-known brand is meaningless. I would rather be the best-kept secret of a few who know me as trustworthy, a quality company, and a brand that makes a positive difference in the world. Being little known is one of the hardest things for some people to reconcile in their lives, especially if they have something that they are proud of, something that they believe is the kind of good news everyone *should* know.

There is a huge difference between pride and humility. Sometimes it is just a matter of timing. Sometimes it is a matter of your true intentions. But as you seek publicity for your brand, remember: Go in with good intention and you'll come out with the right attention.

The Most Successful Brand

If I wished to be the brand best known as successful, I believe I could build this several ways. The key is acknowledging that there are many, *many* different definitions of success, not only among different people but also within one's own way of thinking. What you think of as successful may not be perceived as successful by your audience.

Dalmatian Press was often in negotiations to acquire important licensing deals with big Hollywood entertainment studios. We typically defined the potential success of our licensing acquisitions based on financial projections. Would the licensed children's books sell sufficiently that we would earn out the royalties guaranteed? Would the product be profitable after the percentage of its price received was paid to the licensor? One opportunity in particular was a risky business because of the magnitude of its financial guarantee. I asked, "How are we going to measure the success of this business?"

I knew that if it was based on our previous standards of surpassing financial guarantees I was in trouble, or would be three years down the road. I suggested that our success be measured by new product introductions, a greater presence on retail shelves, and much greater brand awareness for Dalmatian Press via this pressworthy alignment. In fact we accomplished all of that with 80 new books, huge retail promotional space, and photos of our product line in the *New York Times* and on the cover of *Publisher's Weekly*.

But what was the cost? In dollars and cents it made calculated, but risky $ense; however, we definitely got on the publishing industry's radar screen when we built the intangible value of our brand, too. Now it is a matter of time to see how that intangible value translates to concrete bankable value. I believe that as a result of that successful book launch, other cartoon character licensors have seen greater potential with a Dalmatian Press partnership. We have their attention and have been pursued by the some of the biggest and best Hollywood studios to publish their characters in the children's books business.

We have a brand that has proven itself to be fast, innovative, and easy to work with, based on these particular cases. Our spotted spine is everywhere, building the recognizable moment of, "Oh, they're the books with the puppy spots on the spine, aren't they?" I hope that 80 years from now grandparents will be buying our books for their great-grandchildren and saying, "I had the spotted books when I was your age. I remember them fondly."

Success means something different to different people. If I had become known for my participation in a social cause, such as building literacy, I would be successful in some people's minds but not everyone's. If I had become known for constant growth in my company's revenues and profits, I would be successful in other people's minds.

Now is the time to check in with your original true story. Your definition of brand success should be an extension of how you define your own true success story. What were you intended for? What was your company created for? When you copy other company brands, you make the mistake of chasing after *their* definition of success.

The most obvious example of this is when people decide that their company is only successful if it is called so on a profiler list of who's who. *Forbes, Inc., Fortune,* even *People* magazine all have an "-est" list and the most successful list. The idea of making it onto those lists can become more important than remaining true to your original plan. Making their lists can detour you from your true identity.

I know several companies that are tricked into thinking that if they are on a "future 50" list or a "top 100" list, they really are successful. They may fool themselves into false importance and perhaps are trying to fool others, too. It's so easy to get caught up in the name game of who's who. Sometimes our benchmarks change because we are growing and stretching our abilities, but too often they change because we think that to be successful we have to use someone else's definition. Are we really trying to be successful or just to get approval?

My true success comes from making people happy. I try to connect with people and make them feel better about their circumstances, be they personal situations or a corporate state of business. I have lived through experiences that I can now use to help others improve their personal and professional lives. When I have the opportunity and honor to do this, I feel successful if I help others become more successful. This doesn't impress those who judge success by financial standards. But for me, making people happy has usually resulted in financial success as well.

I may not become well known for this, though, unless I proceed to let everyone know that I thought I was largely responsible for their success. Again, there's the bad type of notoriety. Building others' success doesn't necessarily put you on the lists of America's top 50 entrepreneurs, or *Inc.*'s 500 fastest growing, or *Entertainment*'s 50 most powerful people. About all you get is a ballad recorded by Bette Midler, singing "You are the wind beneath my wings." Nice song, but not enough to keep me going. If I wanted to get on those lists to feel successful and become well known, it may mean abandoning what I do best and neglecting my true gifts. Ultimately this will backfire, because if I am not doing that which is an extension of my true essence, then it will not be that which I can do best, for the long term. What I can do best for the long term is what will make me happy and make me a pleasure to do business with! That's the success cycle.

If building other people's success makes you feel successful, be prepared to be frustrated. Consultants know all too well that sharing your experiences via business plans and strategic consultations doesn't ensure that people will use or implement what you have shared. But when you are the best at what you do, no one can ever say that you didn't do what was right, but only that they didn't follow what was best. There are some great recognizable business leaders whose business it is to help others succeed: Tom Peters, Brian Tracy, Peter Drucker, John Maxwell. So take heart. You can help yourself by helping others.

The second wish I would have made in the past I would still wish for today. I would like to build a brand that makes people think and feel that it is successful. I would wish to be known as successful in a variety of ways and to a variety of people. But rather than starting with the question, "How do *they* define success?" and then trying to become that, I would ask myself the question, "What can I do better than anyone else? What can I do that no one else can do because of the experiences only I have had?"

Then I would market myself to those who define and admire my kind of success. You've heard the expression or read the book, *Do What You Love, the Money Will Follow*. My rewording of that is, "Do what you like, and you'll be good at it. Do what you're good at and you'll attract the customers that you are meant to have." You will be the best at it. People will be drawn to your type of success. You will have the inherent ability to define your strategy and set your course because you have studied your brand map from the vantage point of where only you have been. When you control the map and your audience sees your expertise, they will follow you. They want a leader, and you're it.

> *I honestly think it's better to be a failure at something*
> *you love than to be a success at something you hate.*
> —George Burns (1896–1996)[9]

Retail giant Target reported sales of over 45 billion in 2003. They made Forbes Top Company list that year. Compared to Wal-Mart's sales of over 250 billion, they have room for growth. But how will they grow? The Target brand tries to make its customers feel a little more sophisticated than Wal-Mart or KMart. The way the store is laid out, lighting, designer brands, and overall product offering is a little more upscale than Dollar General. People told me they think the store is a little classier than Wal-Mart and that's why they register for their wedding gifts there. It makes them feel classier.

In late 2004 Target embarked on a dollar item promotional area. To be certain, the competition from dollar stores is increasing and taking a bite out of everyone's business. But if Target becomes known as a player in dollar products, how will that affect its brand? Will its loyal customers be confused about the Target identity? Will they feel like the promise of higher quality and a nicer shopping experience is at risk? Is Target maneuvering its brand because it has changed its philosophy and true identity? Or is it chasing dollars and trying to attract customers to someone else's success that it is trying to make its own? If its true identity is a better shopping experience and product selection, than why not make that more visible and attract the customers that it is meant to have? I don't know if Target management has done the hard work of self-examination. I don't know if they have a brand manager at the highest level to protect its value. But this change in product offering will result in a change of the brand, possibly for better, perhaps for worse. Time will tell.

Brand Bling-Bling

I suppose I will always wish to be the brand that makes a lot of money. Once again, this goes back to my true story that defines me personally. Because I have struggled for money throughout much of my life and have seen my family fight the money game and suffer for lack of money, it will always be important to me as a tool that creates security and a vehicle to help myself and others. Let's face it, money means something different to everyone, but it is almost always associated with opportunities and possibilities.

So imagine exactly what you want your brand to look like, sound like, and feel like. Imagine exactly how you want people to feel when they encounter your brand. You've made the connection between who you really are and what you really want from your brand. Now, live your best brand.

Living this way to success isn't pretending. It is identifying through visualization—imagining and believing a set of behaviors and actions that get you the results you want.

Brand Building Belief VIII

I will focus on my brand to get results and make its evolution possible for the greatest possibilities of success. I will set clear, achievable goals and take action to reach my objectives.

Brand Builders

1. How much energy do you put into protecting your comfort zone? How much is this helping you and how does this hold you back?

2. Think of some of your personal and professional painful experiences. How have they served you in the past? How can you make them serve you in the future?

3. Do you focus on what you are and disregard what you are not? How can you pay attention to what you are not, so that you can relate to others?

4. What are the "-est" qualities that you wish for? Are these features or truly brand results you seek?

Chapter NINE

Sustaining the Results
You Get from Your Brand

Success isn't permanent, and failure isn't fatal.
—Mike Ditka (b. 1939)[1]

D r. Phil has a great line that the pop culture has adopted: "How's that working for you?" When building your brand from the beginning with your past and present true experiences, you have to come to the point of looking at the results. You've identified them, visualized them, and planned for them. Now ask yourself, how is it working for you?

Some people have better experiences than others. Does that mean that they will have a better brand than others? Many intelligent people believe that isolation from customers in business is the absence of enough or the right customers. This is a mistake. The same can be said for individuals who think that they aren't connecting with other people *because of* the other people. They believe that their isolation is a by-product of another person's absence.

Read this again. Your brand disconnect is not about the other people. If that's so, then what is it about? Your connection to your audience doesn't come from them. Nor does your detachment. It comes from you. If your brand is emotionally detached, you alone have the power to push it out of solitude. Your brand development doesn't belong to any other person. It is yours and only yours.

This is the most important realization for your success. Realizing that any failures you have are not the product of anyone else or even any other condition in the marketplace brings the failure into a place where you can work with it instead of diverting your attention to some temporary fix.

Distinguishing Characteristics

One of the biggest differences I advocate in today's business world is to bring your whole self to the workplace. Whereas it's usually best not to bring your work home, the old adage, "Leave your personal life at home," just doesn't apply anymore. Now I'm not talking about carrying your personal problems and household gossip into your lobby and through the workday. But I am talking about the essence of how you might solve those problems. I'm talking about the joy or hilarity that you are composed of that would give rise to amusing gossip.

You are a composite of joys, sorrows, deep thinking skills, and so many other emotions and abilities. These are the traits that are both innate and the direct result of all the experiences that you and only you experienced in life. These have given rise to your unique fingerprint of hope and dreams and, yes, even your coping mechanisms.

Whatever is rare, whatever is different about you—this is your value.

That is your brand. And when you bring those elements to the workplace, you have added something that no one else can contribute. Work with and build with those truths. Those are the things that have created your true story.

I'm not talking about your sad stories or your bad stories. Remember that the things that happen *to* you happen *for* you. I know how hard it is to define and use those distinguishing characteristics.

Forty-five percent of singles say that the worst conversation killer is the discussion of past relationships.[2] There's a great line delivered by Renée Zellweger to Tom Cruise in the movie *Jerry Maguire*. The two are on their first date and Jerry (Tom Cruise) begins the typical sob story about his past broken relationships. Renée leans across the table and says softly, "Jerry, let's not tell our sad stories."

Similarly, in business, people don't want to hear about how you hate your old boss or the company you're leaving. They don't need to hear about how some client screwed you or your plan for revenge. These are not the secrets to tell. These are things that develop a belief system that will hold you back and keep your brand down.

Nip/Tuck

In the physical sense, there are few distinguishing characteristics that cannot be easily altered without plastic surgery. Police officers will train people to look for these physical traits as a way to identify them later. Whereas hair can be quickly cut or dyed, a person's earlobes can be identified as attached or hanging. The amount of eyelid crease cannot be changed without the knife. The tip of a nose displays the amount of the nostrils' opening. These are lasting physical characteristics that distinguish one person from another.

What are the characteristics that cannot be altered about you, and hence about your brand? We haven't really discussed the difference between the traits that people can change and those they can't. The expression "You can't change a leopard's spots" reminds us that some things just never change, no matter how much a spouse nags or a counselor counsels.

Women need to like the job that the man in their love life has. Men know that. That's why men create names for their jobs that will impress women. They're managers or supervisors of recycled engineering (garbage man). They're directors of human resources (mall information booth). In a *Seinfeld* episode, a woman with whom Jerry has been involved dumps him because she sees his comedy act and doesn't like it. She can't be involved with him if she doesn't respect his work. A man has to brand himself to get the results he wants. People look at other people's jobs as an outward display of their true identity. It's part of their brand. So we all nip and tuck at ourselves to make permanent what might not have once been.

Price versus Cost (What Price Will You Pay?)

It is one thing to establish and grow a brand in a marketplace that has a need for you or where there is a void in the landscape. Additionally, it is easy to put your brand in the face of your consumers in a robust marketplace because there is ample opportunity to do business. It is quite another thing to be recognized, become memorable, and gain loyalty in a flat or oversaturated industry.

Brands that have gotten worldwide results have done so with skill and luck. Here are some of the ways you can skillfully get the results your brand deserves.

Get in Their Face

I had ordered a special bed—half for medical reasons and half for luxury—that was more of an amusement park ride than a mattress. The order was written wrong and the delivery was fouled up. I had repeatedly done business with this particular large, upscale furniture store, Sprintz, for its service. Good service doled out by great personnel was their brand when you could find the less expensive product in many other locations. I needed this bed. I had counted on its delivery. I had a moment of doubt that the company had let me down when the busy owner, Mr. Charles Sprintz—alerted by my salesperson, Denise—called me himself to apologize and promise to do everything he could to make me feel good about being a customer with them. He did more than fulfill that promise. He fulfilled the promise of his brand, making me feel special. Many of us feel special when the president of a company makes a guest appearance at a meeting. We should. Everyone has many places to spend their time and when they spend it with you they are saying, "I respect you and you're important."

Remember that the prize in our brand competition is attention. We have realized that we need and want brand attention and that our businesses depend on getting attention—as long as it is for all the right reasons. Conversely, *no amount of attention is too much for your customers*. There is no substitute for face-to-face business to establish, build, and protect a brand. Go ahead, make it personal. Defy the trend toward electronic communication. Remember one of the most important branding rules: Be human. Good branding incorporates as many human senses as possible. And there is no replacement for the touch of a handshake, the smell of human contact, and the feedback that all the senses can give immediately during person-to-person interactions. The nonverbal cues noticed in personal contact are enormous and have enormous possibilities for the growth of a company and your brand.

I believe in constant contact. If the goal of branding is making a connection to your audience (and it is), then there is no better way to do so than in person. A radio ad campaign playing at the start of 2004 featured a recorded voice saying, "This is Gigantic Medical Offices. To schedule an appointment, press 1. To schedule an appointment this year, please call back next year." Another medical ad campaign goes, "Here is your new doctor, X19." Then a robot voice proceeds to misdiagnose the patient with appendicitis and try to anesthetize him although he has come in for cold medication. Both ads are exaggerating how impersonal many companies can be and are branding their business as one that is extremely human and personal. They are building brand power based on the power of human contact.

A classic example is Sam Johnson's company, SC Johnson Wax. In addition to advertising their myriad of home-care products, from Pledge furniture wax to Off! insect repellent, they now display and voice the tagline, "Johnson Wax, a family company" at the end of every commercial. They are trying to touch the consumer by portraying a human dimension to their product. As one person in the company's hometown put it, "They are really in the business of manufacturing poison, so they need to show their better side." In fact the Johnson family is responsible for too many works of charity and philanthropic acts to mention. Their generosity is unparalleled. By connecting their name to the already successful product line they offer, they will effectively compete with their growing competition. In the summer of 2004, the legendary CEO, Sam Johnson, died; but his company's brand will outlive him—a huge accomplishment for a company founded and named for an entrepreneurial individual.

They have what no other competitor has: the Johnson family and the Johnson tradition of giving back to the community. Even if they can't actually meet every customer, they can at least remind us that a real family is at the heart of the business that cares about our family.

It is much harder to forget someone with whom you have shared a laugh—not just heard it over the phone or, worse, seen it on an e-mail smiley face. When you are with someone in person, you can overlap all the senses at once for maximum impact and brand building. It stands to reason that since *you* are human, the best way to represent you is with all the human qualities and characteristics that you can muster.

We have discussed building your brand with the essence of *you*, so stop and think about the advantage you bring when you arrive in person. Only *you* have your tone of voice, your touch, your smell, and your look that cannot be copied. Who better to build your brand then? Whether this is actually you or your company carefully grown to represent your brand, the purpose is the same: Your much-visited clients will respond with greater loyalty and more business.

Obviously we cannot be everywhere all the time. Nor can we always afford the time or expense of traveling to our audience and clients. But still the same rule applies: Use as many human character-istics as possible to communicate the essence of you—which is the essence of your brand.

I was happily surprised one day when I received a note from the president of a children's entertainment company, expressing his plea-sure and astonishment over my handwritten thank you note to him for awarding Dalmatian Press an important contract. I had made a small impact on him. I had extended the very essence of our com-pany philosophy, "Let's make a difference in people's lives," by mak-ing my note personal so that he could see my handwriting, with its suggestions of thoughtfulness and care. These were some of the very reasons his company had chosen to work with us over our bigger and less personal competitors. He was just *e-mailing* me his acknowledg-ment that we were special.

Show No Mercy—Audit Your Relationships

This is a hard but fast rule to observe—hard in the sense that we want to live by the golden rule, which tells us not to be cruel, but fast in that cutting off contact and business with damaging clients must be swift (and possibly painful). When associations are more about dam-age control than they are about growth and development, we need to ask again, "How is that working for you?"

There's an old fable in which a wise father tells his son to pound a nail in a fence for every wrong he committed. After apolo-gizing for each misdeed, the boy is allowed to remove the nail that represented the wrongdoing. At the end of the lesson, when all the nails have been removed, the father reminds his young son that al-though the nails have been taken out, the holes caused by his un-kind words and deeds will never go away. That is the tale of brand bashing.

Now that you have defined who you are and the essence of your character, put the spotlight on what you want to become rather than on what you are trying to not to be, or rather not be called. Con-stantly rethink your clients and customer base in terms of their drain on your time, energy, and brand. Rethink your associations as to whether they enhance your true story and retell it in their own value-adding way, or detract from and destroy it. If they aren't adding to the sum then they are subtracting from it. There is no such thing as a static relationship in business.

All the revenues and profits in your world cannot offset the losses of brand damage. Your net value will be greatly influenced and will again be the sum of your financial and intangible worth.

Reconsider Bonding

We all tease each other about bonding opportunities and bonding exercises. We know the importance of father-son bonding and many other types of bonding. So, in light of the preceding caution about relationships, apply this to your brand growth. You don't always have to go it alone. The right alliances can definitely help build your brand. Good strategic partnerships can catapult your brand onto the radar screen. The price you pay can be anywhere from an equity position in your company to the purchase price of licensing deals to the distribution margin points in the sale. But the real cost is the risk of not being able to control that company's brand equity. Imagine partnering with a strong company that soon becomes riddled with a scandal or liability.

Tim Welu, CEO of Paisley Consulting, had just that experience. In 1998 he began what seemed to be a fortuitous relationship with one of the biggest of the big five accounting firms. Yep, Arthur Andersen. The Arthur Andersen name became something of a joke when its 2001 meltdown occurred in the wake of scandal and legal battles. Tim Welu can, however, call the whole of the experience a positive relationship. He himself should be congratulated for making one of *Inc.*'s lists as one of the country's 500 fastest growing companies. But he also defines the ordeal as being a double-edged sword. His experience illustrates that even the most promising relationships have unforeseen risks.

Another cost of bonding is that your brand has the potential for getting diluted or even covered up by a strong brand. Dalmatian Press was sometimes initially mistaken for a Disney company. The association with Disney's movie *101 Dalmatians* was natural. And although Dalmatian Press was happy to have the halo effect of kids being inundated with Dalmatian puppies, we were also quick to differentiate ourselves distinctly, quickly, and meaningfully.

Bonding with another strong brand should never be substituted for building your own brand. Its purpose is not to copy someone's brand or be something that you really are not. Bonding is just that: combining your very real and valuable brand with someone else's by association. There must always be a clear division between the two. It must always be understood where one leaves off and another begins. If you don't maintain that distinction then you have really sold your identity—and nothing should cost you that much unless you are in fact intending to sell out.

Think "Pretty Woman"—Kiss Up to Your Customers

Who can forget the wonderful and enviable Rodeo Drive scene in the movie *Pretty Woman*, starring Richard Gere and Julia Roberts? When they were prepared to spend an obscene amount of money they required only one thing: a lot of sucking up from the store. And the store was only too happy to oblige. Were they remembered by the pretty woman? Most certainly. She made a point of going into the store that had snubbed her the day before and pointed out their costly mistake in not paying her attention.

Here's the rule: To get attention you must give attention.

Now I am really not suggesting that you give meaningless and insincere attention to your customers. That is a price not worth paying. But the right kind of service will be remembered. And the only thing you have to offer that your competitor doesn't is *you*—you, given in a timely manner over time. Happy customers may not exactly remember everything about your business, but what they will remember, and what will stay with them, is the feeling.

You want them to have a good feeling! Unhappy customers quickly turn into brand bashing and lost business. Happy customers become your best salespeople. If a customer is unhappy with your company, they lose trust and loyalty to your brand. Everyone has to be in charge of the brand.

Make them happy. Get in their face and make it personal. If they are not happy, get in their face and get a quick and meaningful resolution to the problem.

I once had a colleague who accused me of being the ultimate schmoozer in business. She was implying that I was a phony because I was so friendly with all my business contacts. In truth, I told her that I did try to make friends with my business associates. I did this for two reasons.

One, I genuinely believe that there is something about everyone to like or at least some common interest we can share. So I am always searching for clues about activities or associations that I can use to launch a conversation. When we have a common denominator, we have a basis for remembering each other. This leads to my second reason: There are so many people to do business with in our marketplace, we might as well do business with people we like. So be nice. Be sincerely nice.

When building a brand you must think of yourself as the consummate public relations department. Relentlessly pursue the resulting referrals. Relentlessly be nice to your customers and contacts. It will come back to you, directly or indirectly. It will be a crucial component to your brand identity.

> *The most important single ingredient in the formula*
> *of success is knowing how to get along with people.*
> —Theodore Roosevelt (1858–1919)[3]

Stay in School, Do Your Homework, Stay the Course of Your Map

The problem with the execution of plans is that it just isn't as much fun as it was to come up with the ideas. Execution is the stuff that visionaries and leaders delegate to others to do, right? Wait a minute. Do great CEOs and Nobel Peace Prize winners execute their own visions? Yes!

Great brands are inherently about executing the promise. They are built by leaders who realize that unless I can make it happen, my brand is just an unfulfilled promise. Doing homework has nothing to do with luck and everything to do with work. In a flat or saturated business field, a brand is all you have to build on. In this type of environment it is even more frustrating to compete with price or features as the motive for sales and attention. Build the brand. Greatness is beyond the plan. Don't break the promise.

Build the brand by doing the work required to "know thyself." Don't even think about serious brand building until you know everything there is to know about your character and what you are made of. Then, study everything there is to know about your clients, your audience, and your competition. When you are armed with that type of understanding, you will have insight and credibility and the knowledge to follow all the previously listed rules.

Being Special Isn't Special Enough

If you want to build your brand, you understand that its purpose is to say you or your company is special. But being special isn't special enough. If you want your true story to be successfully told with your brand, then it must clearly reveal its core benefits as well as the story. The story doesn't mean anything to your audience unless it has some benefit to them.

At Dalmatian Press I respond to sales, marketing, and creative presentations with the same reaction, over and over: "So what?" That's become our code for "Don't just tell me about a feature this product has, tell me what the unique benefit of that feature is." A feature is meaningless unless it is attached to a benefit for the customer, audience, or whoever comes in contact with it.

If we are developing a book with 128 pages, I ask, "So what?" Someone responds, "Well, it provides more hours of fun." So say that. If the toy has educational content I ask, "So what?" The product manager defends himself: "Parents will be getting a toy that is fun and teaches children easy counting lessons at an early age. It will help prepare them for kindergarten and give them an early sense of achievement." So find a way to say that.

Coca-Cola doesn't just advertise the fact that it is a good-tasting beverage. It ties the beverage feature to the benefit of refreshment. Their web site says, "Refreshes people across the world." In other words, Coca-Cola doesn't build their brand solely on the feature that it tastes good. They build their brand on the whole story: The good taste makes people feel refreshed.

Know how your brand benefits those who contact it. And understand that what your audience values today they may not want tomorrow. Your feature, or the essence of your brand, doesn't necessarily change, but how it meets people's wants and needs will evolve as times change. For example, bottled water companies had to change the way they communicated their brand to meet the changing desires of their customers. The bottled water brands are built on the essence of clean, pure water. At first they emphasized the benefit of safety, people felt secure when they thought of the brand. Over time the desires of bottled water consumers have evolved, and now the brands promise health and energy. The feature never changed (clean water) but a different benefit was explored and delivered.

If you manage a powerful brand, you need to keep in touch with how your audience's wants and needs are changing. You must actually anticipate how their wants will evolve. If you do not have a dominant brand right now, it is still possible that as the world's wants and needs change, your brand will be better able to offer the right benefit over another brand.

If you have a powerful personal brand, the benefit you offer your organization today may not be beneficial to them tomorrow. Should you change or try to become something you are not? No! Be yourself but find the opportunity to share how your true features provide multiple benefits based on different needs and wants.

The point here is not to make you feel that as trends change you either have to change who you are to succeed or you're out of luck. It is to remind you that you have to constantly monitor change and search your experiences to see how you can relate to the change. How can your true experiences be beneficial to others? Pay attention to others' changing wants and needs, and they will pay attention to you.

Protecting the Prize

Not everyone wants fame and fortune, but most people want to guard what is theirs and feel safe from crimes of theft and fraud. We all seek something in life. We're looking for more responsibility, reward, opportunity, and whatever else we define our personal and professional success with. We are all looking for more, or, as one game show host said, what's behind door number two. And as we accomplish our goals and reach our target, we want and need to protect what is unique and personal to our lives and achievements. Today it is becoming increasingly difficult to protect our assets in any form. When we incorporate our business and finally establish a successful corporate identity, we are in constant danger of being robbed of its value, whether it is intangible value or tangible worth.

Today we have complicated copyright and trademark laws designed to protect ideas, designs, and literary works. Our founding fathers wanted copyright terms to be only 14 years with an additional 14 years if the author was still alive. Others argued that in America, land of the free, there would never be a lack of expression and a flow of new ideas. But think about what has happened with the great works of Disney and Irving Berlin. Ideas that build our great society are limited from expression as they are restricted within the confines of today's copyright laws. Today, fierce opponents of these laws cry out, "Give up those rights you've had for too long! It's not just the right thing to do, it's a right."[4]

When is there too much government regulation and when is there too little? In 2003, the Supreme Court has made it harder for companies with famous brand names to protect their names and the value associated with them. The Court denied a claim that imitators dilute the value of a famous brand. The Court's unanimous decision involved a lawsuit brought by the owners of Victoria's Secret, the huge lingerie chain, which sued a small strip shop company called Victor's Little Secret. Victor's Little Secret, owned by Victor and Cathy Moseley in Elizabeth, Kentucky, sells lingerie, adult videos, and adult "novelties." Originally the store was named Victor's Secret, but it received complaints from Victoria's Secret, a business unit of Limited Brands Inc. When the name was changed to include the word *Little*, the big chain complained that the small store's lingerie and adult toy business "blurred and tarnished" its famous brand. The Court ruled that the use of the name Victor's Little Secret "neither confused any consumers or potential consumers, nor was likely to do so."[5]

Personally I believe that this small chain does tarnish the reputation of the big chain, Victoria's Secret, and drags it down into the realm of soft pornography. In recent years, Victoria's Secret television commercials, catalogues, and special broadcasts have become so overtly sexual that any association with the pornography businesses, intentional or not, will put the stamp of crude porn all over it. In my opinion, Victoria's Secret is riding a dangerous tide of sophisticated sexuality and crude pornography. It must protect any association that will push its reputation over the wrong edge of its goals.

In 1995, Congress amended the Trademark Act to cover "dilution of famous marks," defining *dilution* as the "lessening of the capacity of a famous mark to identify and distinguish goods and services." Congressional debate used examples such as Dupont Shoes, Buick Aspirin, and Kodak Pianos.[6] Here's my question: How does anyone prove exactly what dilution is? How can anyone calculate financial harm and measure the loss in products or services sold? This ruling will encourage people like Victor Moseley to associate themselves with successful brands and rip off famous marks because no one can prove the exact damages. How can you protect your brand?

Now let's examine why Victor's Little Secret chose to attach itself to Victoria's Secret. Obviously Victor Moseley knew that his company could quickly ride the coattails of the big chain's efforts in advertising and successful marketing. With this name they could leap past years of work that would explain what their product was. They captured the customer's attention with the built-in and unaided awareness of the words *Victoria* and *secret*. They evoked all the emotions of intrigue and sexuality that Victoria's Secret had spent years and millions of dollars building. And with the play on the words *Victor* and *Victoria*, they put a clever spin on their brand's promise. Brilliant? Or just easy?

Well, it certainly was easy. And as an angle to launch a business it was clever. But when a company so blatantly defines itself as being like the other guy, rather than as itself, it may launch a business but it will never sustain it or grow it. Now, for better or worse, Victor's Little Secret will always be associated with Victoria's Secret. In good times and through bad times, the little company will have less control over its identity than if it had been true to itself from the beginning. From now on it will struggle to define itself; instead it will be mostly defined from outside influences. Any points of differentiation will take considerably more effort, and the very thing that it hoped to build its success on could become the albatross around its neck.

It will never have the dignity and strength that comes with individuality and being special to the consumer. It will always have the reputation of being a clever copycat. Again, this may have been a good starting point for the store, but it will not be a great pathway to long-term and continual growth. Perhaps it never wanted greatness.

The Name Game

Companies that try to mimic other companies in name and in brand do themselves a disservice. Eventually they realize that they should try to outdistance and outperform the one they were copying in the first place.

The only company who successfully built a brand on being second was Avis. In the 1960s Avis, number two in the rental car market, turned their true experience into their amazingly successful brand campaign. They convinced customers that being second made them try harder, and trying harder was a brand feature more valuable than market share or being the biggest. The "We try harder" program told their true story. It touched consumers' hearts and, I believe, made us root for their success. It seemed to be a personal admission of their values, which was memorable because it was emotion over information.

Brand Building Belief IX

I can protect my brand best by building on the only thing that no one can copy: my true experiences.

Brand Builders

1. List the features of your brand.

2. What are the benefits of these features?

3. How are the benefits of your brand tied in to your true experiences?

4. As the needs and wants of your market or audience change, can you turn to other benefits that your true self can offer without changing who you are?

Chapter TEN

Conclusion—Back to You

*Getting people to like you is simply
the other side of liking other people.*
—Norman Vincent Peale (1898–1993)[1]

Your Brand and Your Competitive Edge?

There are so many ways that a brand gives you an advantage in life. We've discussed how being memorable is essential to both business and personal relationships. We've realized that we can maintain that memorable, unique identity when we feature the one feature that can never be copied, and that is our true-life experiences. Now let's look at one more edge your brand will give you.

Your brand will give you permission and approval to do the things you never allowed yourself to do before. Having a powerful brand is intoxicating. It fills our heads with thoughts of grand possibilities such that we have the boldness to step out beyond our stifling behavior that usually holds us back. When we have a strong brand that is compelling, influential, and important to other people's lives, we do things that we don't usually allow ourselves to do. We say yes to invitations that we don't usually accept. We make calls to people that we once were afraid to call. We go to sleep peacefully and wake up excited to start the day because of the confidence we now live with. A brand gives you the edge of freedom: freedom to be who you really are and all that you can be. Your competitive edge is that you hold all the keys to your brand.

More and more we see evidence that phony corporate images are dying slowly. In addition, the concept that organizations should have

196

an active social conscience is growing by leaps and bounds. Both of these telling trends point us in the direction of integrating our personal brand into our professional brand. Your professional brand will benefit from the personal experiences you have tapped into, and your personal brand will benefit because professional brands simply don't last as long.

Someone called Dr. Smith may enjoy the prestige and power that his positional brand brings. The "Doctor" brand makes people feel respectful and impressed. But after the job is done or the doctor retires, only the personal brand remains to draw strength from and sustain the results you want in your life. Combining your personal brand with your professional brand will tell a story that has the maximum impact on your success.

We see television sitcoms all the time that depict a powerful CEO who comes home, where he is henpecked and dominated by his wife. One of the most famous Christmas movies of all times, *White Christmas*, revolves around the attempt by Bob Wallace (played by Bing Crosby) to honor his retired army general, now living as a custodian of an old Vermont Inn. His sentimental song sums up the problem with positional/professional brands with the chorus, "What do you do with a retired four-star general?"

Colin Powell, the United States' sixty-fifth secretary of state, is quoted as saying, "Don't let ego get too close to your position, so that if your position gets shot down, your ego doesn't go with it."[2]

The same is true of your brand. Positions are just features that come and go. If your position goes, you don't want your brand to crash and burn with it.

A company could—and I think this is a common challenge—try to extend its corporate values or founder's values into the marketplace, assuming that its values will resonate with the market as well as they do with the employees or the founder. I founded Dalmatian Press on the values of making a difference in kid's lives by creating wholesome products that were packed with value and quality and sold for a low price. On top of that, the parent company added the values of following Sam Walton's model of business success defined as superior service and relationships with the retailers.

For years I directed product development to share those values. I know this is the source of many frustrated creative processes. I extended my values for wholesomeness onto our product line even though the marketplace showed a demand for some of the most violent and horrific cartoon characters. I had certain values—call them inspirational—that I developed from my personal experiences and wove them into the consumer product line of Dalmatian Press. These values became part of the Dalmatian Press brand. We even got letters from parents who said that when they saw the Dalmatian Press spots on the book spine, they felt they could trust the product to be squeaky clean and a great value. Sometimes it was evident that the market would bear a much higher price point, but that's not our brand. We often priced books at a dollar less than our competitor's book product.

Our competitive edge continues to be that we know who we are today, and we will continue to ask tomorrow, "Who are we today?" What are the constant values that we can bring into the future? What are the evolving values that we should incorporate into our current brand without losing focus and brand awareness? We hold the key to brand success because we can unlock the treasure chest of the real experiences that make us authentically unique. These real experiences will be our best and most powerful connection to the world. And as the world changes, we need to harness our new experiences to stay real to the world.

You'll Find Your Brand as Much as It Finds You

Who'd have thought that with all the marketing platforms we've built to create bigger brands—web sites, simulcast, computer graphic imaging, MP3 communications, 127 television stations—we'd be looking at the proverbial smoke and mirrors instead of authentic brand images? In our personal branding there are a growing number of ways to market ourselves, from plastic surgery to video dating to life coaching. But you will find your brand as much as it finds you. It's like Michelangelo told us: the sculpture is already in the stone.

Once you determine who you are through and through, you can go to the end of the mission and work backwards. Your ultimate mission is to figure out what you want your brand to stand for and what response you want to get whenever people hear or see your brand name and image.

I believe that your brand identity will find you as much as you find it. Imagine my surprise when the whole world of branding found me. There is a long list of skills that I have not mastered, a lack of skills that downright embarrasses me. But this I know, branding is as much about book knowledge and following marketing models as it is about gut instinct and an intuitive knack for getting it. Branding is something that I get. I have always been drawn to the magnetism of strong brands. I could sense when it was the image more than the substance and clearly define which was which. Branding strategies and efforts are not lost on me. I love to feel them and study them and play with them. When you find someone like that in your personal or business life, my advice is to use him or her however you can to improve your branding strategy.

But first, know that as you define your story, your true story, you can take control of the brand message that you send out. What you can be sure of is this: Every day, you are in business professionally or personally and you have a chance to exhale your very own breath of life. You breathe in and out as you live your brand and tell your true stories. For that reason, I love the expression, "Mind your own business." Get it? Mind your business! Pay attention to it, and others will pay attention to you for all of the right reasons. Breathe your brand in and out. You can either breathe deeply or gasp little shallow breaths of air.

When we are overwhelmed, unsure, or nervous we breathe differently. We breathe from the throat and with our ribcage instead of the diaphragm. This breathing is shallow and ultimately uncomfortable because we're not getting enough oxygen—we're being poisoned by CO_2! This is a physical metaphor for branding based on your true story. If you are unsure of your experiences, if you haven't analyzed them and defined what they mean to you, then you will be unsure of your brand and will be tempted to copy someone else's brand. If you are unsure of your brand, the effect will be shallow. The best branding starts from deep inside of you. It is all that you are. It is you in your best light. And it is vitally important for you to share it. If you try to be something you're not, you won't have the endurance to sustain you through good times and bad times.

Brand Maturity

A lack of maturity often accounts for bad brand decisions and strategies. It's ironic that brands are best built from the start, exactly when you don't have maturity. Consider how young people lack maturity to develop smart brand strategies. Young celebrities are good examples of young brands gone bad because they didn't have the maturity to examine themselves and know what to do with the information and emotion they turn up.

Country music sensation LeAnn Rimes was set for unprecedented success when at age 11 she first recorded her single soulful hit song "Blue" (written by Bill Mack). She was so young and innocent. Yet she admits, "It's funny, when I was young, I always wanted to be sexier than I was and now I'm so glad that no one let me do it."[3]

Young companies are often in such a hurry to be all grown up that they will focus more on their future than on their precious, previous experiences, limited as they may be. At Dalmatian Press we were tempted to hire some of the heavy hitters in the industry for vice presidential positions. We wanted instant respect and status. How silly that seems now. The very concept that brought us to the top of our retail buyers' awareness was that we were a young, innovative group of individuals. Our story is that of a small organization with the senior management doing the sales calls themselves. It was the fact that we weren't stale that was intriguing and captivating to the buyers. It's a good thing we chose not to bury that story under the hiring of people who couldn't tell our true story of a start-up.

You have the choice at this moment—and this is the only moment you have for sure—to exhale deeply and show the world who you really are. Show them the good stuff that you were born with. Show them the stuff that happened *for* you because you turned it toward your goals and purpose. And show them the real stuff that you were destined to become.

I don't want to put you on the defensive by telling you that you *need* a brand. A far more powerful motive for you is to believe that you *deserve* a brand.

In the summer of 2003 I took a young girl to see a movie called *What a Girl Wants* portrayed a teenager trying to adjust to her newly found family and environment. She tries so hard to be the type of success that her new family expects, that she forgets who she really is. I left the movie thinking this: "Why are you trying so hard to fit in when you were destined to stand out?"

If your life ended tomorrow, what would you regret not doing? Who would you regret not being? For many of us, the answer is, "I wish I could just be myself."

Even when we go to funerals we hear someone say, "They looked like themselves." What does that mean? I can't say whether they really did or not, but I can comment on what they meant. We all desire to be ourselves, the best of our selves. And even in death, what we hope for others is that they lie in peace as themselves, no longer trying to be what they were not. That's the final compliment we offer, that they look like themselves.

Anyone who has built a business of any kind can tell you that at the end of the day, the fiscal calendar, or even a liquidation, you probably don't want to be remembered for the image you were trying to fake. You want to be remembered for what lies behind your strategies, your results, and your business plans. Hopefully, you will be remembered by others for who you are. Don't quit while asking the question, "Who could I have become if only I had known who I really am?"

The gift you give yourself when you recognize who you really are is a gift that you give to every other life you touch. Whether you brand yourself or are branded by another lies in your hands. As much as you make powerful impressions on other lives, you are the single most important influence on your own life.

Don't get so wrapped up in the nonessential stuff of branding that you don't really know yourself and enjoy yourself. If you have the chance to be branded or to brand, I hope you brand.

Share Your Story

When it comes to sales and marketing, *branding* is probably the most overused term today. The problem is that most people don't really know what good branding is. Testing and evaluating your brand are essential tools for learning and growing your brand. Let's review specific communication strategies to test and build your brand. When you pass these two tests you will be on your way to enjoying a more successful and satisfying life.

1. Communicate Your Brand with Integrity

Simply stated, you've got to tell it like it is. You've got to develop and communicate your brand with absolute accuracy. No matter who writes or designs for you, you must demand accuracy. Whether your brand is boldly stated, implied, or suggested, be meticulous. Be precise.

Integrity has as much to do with intellectual information as it does with an emotional dialogue. Some companies complain that they don't think their customers understand their brand or really connect with their goals. Of course not—not if their brand lies!

Does your brand tell the truth? Does your audience believe that you are telling the truth?

2. Brands Must Be Built with the Means for Two-Way Communication

A one-way brand tells its story but never listens for the reaction. A brand that has no means to accept feedback only exists to say, "Hey, look at me!" It's all about me, me, me. It puts itself out there but doesn't care if anyone really gets it. If that's how you brand, then all you know is what you've said, and you haven't a clue about what's been seen, heard, or felt. Result: Lack of action. Brands must actively talk and listen. Does your brand have the means for two-way communication?

What Do You Know for Sure?

This chapter evolved out of my favorite question, what do you know for sure? What is the one thing you know for certain? When you are in the habit of asking yourself this question every day, then you are in the habit of constant and useful evaluation of your self. And when you do that and make choices based on your evaluation, then you can answer another question with certainty: Will you let other people define you? Or do you know yourself well enough to represent your true self with your true brand identity?

Even when people like you and love you, keep challenging your habits. Don't let people's praise keep you from constantly improving yourself with self-examination. Don't let your habits let you off the hook from continuing your constant self-examination. You must understand your story in the context of current times.

What do you know for sure? Asking this question or some form of it is a little frightening. When I started to wonder about what was true and certain, I came to an alarming conclusion. I had been playing it safe for years. I had had opportunities to start new businesses but couldn't (or wouldn't) because the timing was never right, I didn't have the money or education or something. But the truth was I had all of those things, as much as they were truly necessary. What I didn't have was the certainty that I would be successful.

What I knew then for certain was that fear was paralyzing me and holding me back. A wise friend said to me, "You can continue to be very successful doing what you're doing and play it safe. But you are like a ship in the safe harbor. And ships weren't meant to be safe. They were meant to sail across deep water, rough and wild, calm and true." I knew then that this was my truth and that I had to live from it.

Will you let others define you and your brand? As you enter this new phase of your business growth, focus on what is true for you. Examine your whole self and let it serve you and others. So what do you know for certain?

> We all want to be something special, and some of us manipulate the world around us to put ourselves in a special light. But it is really a shame if our life is going just the way we want it to go and not the way it really should.

We are all conditioned to focus on our external conditions. We learn from the earliest age that the stove is hot and the street has fast cars. The older we get, the more we concentrate on what we think others are thinking. We spend a lot of time wondering what others are thinking. When we think we know, we even conjecture about why people feel the way they do, especially when we think that others are thinking or feeling badly about us. Challenge what you think you know at every opportunity.

The Language of Your Brand

What exactly is the right language to speak in when creating the emotional dialogue with others? It has nothing to do with the words you choose and everything to do with your intent and purpose.

There is something in the human heart that wants to be moved. It is why we feel stirred when the Olympic flame ignites. It is why we tear up when we see sentimental movies. It's as if it is happening to us, if not for real then at least in our hopes and dreams.

If you have the right intentions, you can create the powerful emotional dialogue with your brand language. Then your language will be understood clearly and you will achieve the best possible results. When you are true to who you are, your communication will carry the truest intentions for a positive outcome.

I think one of the keys to building brands based on your true stories is to stop trying to change others. Change the way you express yourself. When you go to Spain, it is helpful to speak Spanish. When you go to your audience, speak their language while expressing your true identity and story.

Testing Your Brand for Effectiveness

Test how your brand is positioned with the following five sets of questions:

1. Does it incorporate both the personal and professional experiences that you have defined? If one brand erodes, does the other one shore it up? Does your company use the valuable personal experiences of the management and employees? Do the personal brand identities flow smoothly into the corporate or organization's brand identity?

2. Do you actively resist the temptation to live by old habits?

3. When you have personal or professional policies and procedures, do you challenge them and ask if they were part of the old you? Do your current brand policies reflect the stories of the current you?

4. Do you see evidence that the marketplace or your audience, friends, and associates connect with who you are and what you offer? Or are you stubbornly holding on to an identity that you defend because "I am who I am and the world will have to deal with me, like it or not!"

5. Are you paying attention to your development that ultimately pays attention to the needs and wants of others? Are you learning to speak your audience's language?

When was the last time you made a significant change in how you conduct your personal or professional business? No change probably means that you are not paying attention to yourself and your true stories. My friend thinks she shouldn't have to change because it implies some kind of a cop-out. "I am who I am," she says. I asked her, "Are you getting the results you want in life?" Silence, then "No."

You have a new plan now for developing and succeeding with any kind of brand. The four final tests of brand worth—if you are about to make the commitment—are as follows:

1. *Does your brand involve everyone?* The greatest resource we have is our true experiences. Know them. Define them. Tell them. Share them. How does your personal or professional brand create new stories in the lives it touches? We create new experiences with constant feedback and exploration that invite expression and sharing of true stories. "Words are, of course, the most powerful drug used by mankind" (Rudyard Kipling).[4]

2. *Is your brand empathetic and compassionate?* Any brand must connect with the audience's heart and soul. And then it must fulfill the promise that it can improve their lives and contribute to a better world at large. People everywhere want to know that the brands they choose share their social, ethical, and moral concerns. "No man is so poor as to have nothing worth giving. Give what you have. To someone it may be better than you dare to think" (Henry Wadsworth Longfellow).[5]

3. *Is your brand dynamic?* Does it reach, stretch, and permeate with every experience, or is it just a static image? Does it go beyond the intellectual encounter and become a human sensory experience? It's not what you say and what they hear, it is about how you say it and how they feel. "An image is one thing. A human being is another" (Elvis Presley).[6]

4. *Does your brand speak across all platforms?* Today's brands must communicate equally well across all types of media, from print to television. How will your experience translate across the telephone lines and e-mail with the same result? Is the message undeniably clear? "Be yourself and no matter where you go, there you'll be" (Chris Hilicki).

Is your brand working for you? If you examine the relationships around you and people are constantly put off by you, you need to reconsider whether the brand you are building is really one of destruction. It simply isn't truthful to go through life with the attitude and expression, "Well this is who I am. I can't change, so like me or leave me."

Change the World

Everything we do and don't do represents us. The things we buy stand in our place for who we try to be, whether it's the sports car, the house, or the style in which we furnish our home or office. We go through our country stage, our high-tech stage, our sexy stage. When we make changes we even say, "I'm not country anymore, I'm traditional now," or, "At home I'm art deco but at the office I'm contemporary." So we try to let an obviously recognized style speak for who we want others to see us as.

We let the people we hang out with define our identity. Since the day we toddled into day care, we have cared about the clique and peer group that we were seen with, knowing that we would indeed be seen as one of them. Today, in our adult years, we still pick the group we want to be known by instead of knowing who we are and choosing the appropriate group. Be careful, because who you are with is who you become.

In all these instances, what we are doing is letting someone else's brand build us instead of building our brand for others to see.

Hope

The words *hope* and *whole* sound very similar, and, they resemble each other in more than just sound. They share meaning. We can't have hope without the pain of wanting something or without the feeling that something is missing. That's why we hope. We hope for something because we know deep down inside that we want, yearn, hanker for, or desire something more. What we hope for will make us feel whole. We believe that it will fill the void and make us complete. And many times it will. I believe that what we hope for most in life is to know ourselves, love ourselves, and get the attention that makes us grow and thrive.

This is not selfishness. Selfishness is when we are interested in ourselves or our businesses at the expense of others. What I am talking about is self-interest. Self-interest is about our true purpose and ability in life to care about others the way we care about ourself. Self-interest means we think about others as we think about ourself. Self-interest allows us to share our ideas and thoughts and plans with others because it teaches us to search out what is best for us, which is always in relation to others. It is in the fullness of self-love that we have the capacity to love and care for others.

The issue as explained in this book is not our desire for attention. It's how we meet that desire for attention and who we trust to fill it. If you try to get from the attention something that it cannot give, then you will warp that desire for attention.

In other words, if we think that the attention in itself will make us feel whole, we will never get enough. The attention in itself will never make us successful or worthy or triumphant. No amount of attention can give those things. And if we think it will, then we will act out in our business and personal life to get more and more attention. We'll end up doing all kinds of crazy things to raise the level of awareness, kick it up a notch, keep people interested. Our actions will turn into shocking and extreme measures to feed the attention-getting monster. Our desire for attention becomes warped and often takes the form of addiction. We get addicted to all kinds of things in business. We get addicted to praise and we work ridiculous hours. We get addicted to power and we rant and rave to show others who is in charge. We get addicted to money and we put our business through its steps for all the wrong reasons, getting all the wrong results.

Attention is a good thing when you get it from trusted sources to use for trustworthy reasons. Don't try to get out of it what it can never give. It cannot make you or your business whole. Only by knowing who you really are will you know how to make yourself and your business best known.

What will give you the energy and endurance to keep searching for your true self? Every day you change and create more true stories to live by and to base your true brand identity on. Everyday you must ask what is true today. The thing that will give you the energy to keep searching and digging will be hope.

Why do we hope? As long as we have hope we will have a longing inside of us. Hope and aching go hand in hand. We hope for something because we feel like we are missing something. And it is that state of feeling like something is missing that makes us long for something more. Hope makes us believe that all things are possible. We don't actually live in the state of knowing. We live in the land of believing. Certainty flickers like a firefly's light. Believing is an admission of hope. Sometimes hope is a state between doubting the least and believing the most.

Hope. It is hope that propels us. It is hope that compels us to keep digging. When you keep digging you will ultimately discover what is true. And the best thing will happen: You will behold who you are and you will become what you see. This kind of hope does not disappoint. If you hope to merely be like someone else you will eventually be disappointed. It may motivate you for a while, but only the hope we have in ourselves and the creator who made us for our true purpose will satisfy us.

Our desperate desire to have our identity, our image, and our brand make a difference *now* must be put into the context of how it will make a difference *always*. If we only think of our brand identities as an immediate source of power, then we are bad examples. Many times I have worked with people who say they want a long-term, enduring brand power. But when push comes to shove and crazy, busy schedules force us into positions requiring immediate gratification, we live and work for the day. Long-term strategies go out the window. We end up with nothing more than new packaging, professional or personal. As such, we are bad examples. We must live and work for the future as much as we do for the day.

Hope makes us aware of our dissatisfaction. If we are satisfied than we will not improve. If we are satisfied then our future is empty because we are content with today's prosperity or accomplishments. It is the poor or desperate that we marvel at. They seem to leap up out of nowhere, passing us by with unexpected success. They are not satisfied. They hope for more. Too much success limits our hope. It covers up our greater need. Our riches blind us to what we need to be doing. Our desire for more product or packaging, another clever ad campaign, or instant web site messaging is only a fraction of our long-term existence and influence. Hold on and hope for the future.

In the 2002 Hollywood movie *Legally Blonde*, Reese Witherspoon plays Elle Wood, a Beverly Hills sorority princess turned serious Harvard law student. She voices our fears and frustrations of building our true brand on our true story. About to give up, feeling betrayed and abandoned by her friends and professors, she cries to the one person who believes in her, "I'm tired of panty hose and business suits. I'm going home to L.A. I'm tired of trying to be something that I'm not!" Emmett, her hero and the associate law professor, responds: "What if you're trying to be something that you are?"

It is hard to be who you really are. Being *you* isn't easy. It takes even more strength and determination than pretending to be someone else. It may cause ridicule. It may be awkward. Fitting in can be easier. Elle was a little bit fashion model and a little bit brain. In her Los Angeles sorority she denied her brains, while at Harvard Law School she denied her natural beauty and joy. It wasn't until she combined her brains and beauty into a complete package that she truly represented her whole self and created her true brand identity—which just happened to be incredibly successful. Lucky? No. Coincidence? No. The result of building a brand based on true stories? Exactly.

Brands can awaken us to the grand fact that humans are capable of much more than concrete service and productivity. Brands remind us of our promise to bring each other beauty and equality, courage, freedom, greatness, and human rights.

Go be your best brand and get the attention you're worthy of. Get the attention you need, in order to give back to everyone you come in contact with the attention they deserve. Your brand occupies the most important real estate that exists: the mind. Mind your business and it will build your business, whether it is professional or personal, for success of every kind.

Be Yourself and You Will Be the Best Brand

If you've never come to the point of being yourself, come now. No one else can label you good or bad. There's just you. There's no complicated pathway to follow. There's just the commitment to make to be you. Be thankful for you, now. The more grateful you are for you, the brighter you'll shine. The brighter your light shines inside, the farther it can be seen.

This branding process works on the principle that each of us, and our corresponding brand identity, is complete and whole. Know that this wholeness already exists inside of you. Give your brand time to be.

Brand Building Belief X

My brand already exists inside of me and my business. I will discover it, define it, and share it for the kind of success I need and want.

The Final Big 10 Brand Builders

1. Recognize that you already have a brand whether you know it or not. It's time to take control of it to build an authentic powerful brand destined for great success.

2. Identify and examine your own story, experiences, and life-changing moments in your personal and professional life.

3. Attach importance to your story because it is real, unique, and the only thing that can't be copied.

4. Connect your experiences to the things that are important to you—your values and beliefs.

5. Express these values as your brand values with corresponding elements that are visual and audial, as well as those characteristics that can be felt and make people feel.

6. Share these values in a way that incorporates as many of the human senses as possible.

7. Communicate these brand values so that they relate to your audience and can be easily remembered.

8. Reveal your authentic brand in a way that involves your audience, listens, responds, and maneuvers as you anticipate your audience's changing needs and wants.

9. Write down a specific plan for your brand development and the results you will achieve.

10. In the fullness of believing you are worthy and valuable, turn the attention your brand receives back to the world to meet and exceed their wants, needs, hopes, and dreams.

Notes

My sources for the ideas, stories, and quotes have been many and have come from a wide variety of people and places: radio talk shows, television, music, books, newspapers, films, magazine articles, Broadway plays, and conversations with friends and colleagues.

In my research I have tried to be as complete and accurate as possible. Any omissions of credit are entirely my own and are unintentional.

CHAPTER 1 Everyone Needs a Little Attention, Brands Need a Lot

1. Dr. Norman Vincent Peale, *The Power of Positive Thinking*, Random House, Prentice Hall, 1952.
2. Interview with Stan Mitchell, preacher, minister, national speaker, author, Nashville, Tennessee, August 2004, gracepoint.com.
3. NBC, Channel 4 Special Feature Report on Chris Hilicki by anchorwoman and reporter Terry Merryman, September 2003.
4. Bill Cosby, American comedian, author, movie star, television personality, and philanthropist. Brainyquote.com.

CHAPTER 2   True Confession: Good for the Soul, Great for the Brand

1. Henry David Thoreau, American essayist, poet, and philosopher, renowned for living the doctrines of Transcendentalism as recorded in his masterwork, *Walden*. QuoteDB.com.
2. *Inc.* magazine, January 2003.
3. Coca-Cola.com.
4. Dotson Rader, "My Goals Have Changed," *Parade* magazine, November 30, 2003.
5. Jill Lawrence, "Candidates Draw from the Painful and the Private," *USA Today*, December 3, 2003.
6. Eleanor Roosevelt became First Lady in 1933. www.whitehouse.gov /firstladys.
7. Rudyard Kipling, born in Bombay, India, English short-story writer, novelist, and poet. Quoteland.com.
8. Suzanne Vranica and Brian Steinberg, "McDonald's Seeks Spicier Tagline," *Wall Street Journal*, June 12, 2003.
9. Kevin Dunn, president, Dunn Enterprises, former U.S. president of Mc-Donald's, interviewed summer 2003 and August 2004.
10. Maya Angelou, internationally respected poet, writer, and educator. QuoteDB.com.

CHAPTER 3   Brand-Stand: Your Platform for Success

1. Brainyquote.com.
2. *Southwest Airlines Spirit*, August 2003, ORC International.
3. "Melissa Etheridge, Just Jeans and a T-Shirt, Thank You," *Self*, June 2003.
4. Conversation with Stephen Schutz, coowner, Blue Mountain Arts greeting card company and bluemountain.com, June 4, 2004, Chicago, Illinois, Book Expo Association trade show.
5. *Larry King Live*, guest Pamela Peele, May 4, 2003.
6. Brainyquote.com.

CHAPTER 4   Bring On the Brand

1. Walt Disney, Disney.com.
2. Lyriks.com, Janis Ian, pop singer and performer.
3. Neal E. Boudette, "BMW's CEO Just Says 'No' to Protect Brand," *Wall Street Journal*, November 26, 2003.
4. Brainyquote.com.
5. Joan Duncan Oliver, "Kindness: The Ripple Effect," *O* magazine, December 2002.

6. "Home Depot Bernie Marcus," *Southwest Airlines Spirit,* August 2003.
7. Interview with Julia Burney, founder, Cops 'N' Kids, October 2003, Maryland literacy campaign with Cops 'N' Kids.
8. Interview with "Van" Cronkhite, February 2004, Milwaukee, Wisconsin.

CHAPTER 5 Making a Brand Impression

1. Ralph Waldo Emerson, American poet, philosopher, and center of the American transcendental movement. Brainyquote.com.
2. Anthony Robbins, authority on peak performance, motivation, and the creator of Personal Power. Unleash the Power Within conference, March 2003.
3. *Inc.* magazine, interview with Barbara Corcoran, January 2003.
4. Tim McGraw, multi-platinum recording artist, "She's My Kind of Rain," Lyriks.com.
5. Greatquotations.com.
6. Marc Gobé, *Emotional Branding,* Allworth Press, 2001, from the Introduction, page xxiv.
7. Jeff Resnick, "Does Your Brand Walk the Walk?" in *Marketing Review,* 1966. Marketingprofs.com.
8. "US Teens Take Hard Line," *USA Today,* Spring 2003.
9. Bruce Orwall, "Wishing upon a Logo," *Wall Street Journal,* February 28, 2003.

CHAPTER 6 Brand Relativity

1. Anaïs Nin, *The Diary of Anaïs Nin* (Harcourt Brace).
2. "The New Establishment 2002," *Vanity Fair,* October 2002.
3. CMAWorld.com. 2002 MRI country listener analysis, 2002 analysis highlights.
4. Televised CMT biography of Garth Brooks, *Inside Fame,* 2003.
5. "Melissa Etheridge, Just Jeans and a T-Shirt, Thank You," *Self,* June 2003.
6. Research International Observer (RIO), "Branding: The Third Wave Is Here," 2003.
7. Bruce Orwall, "Wishing upon a Logo," *Wall Street Journal,* February 28, 2003.
8. Lorry Grant, "Retailers Try New Venues to Boost Sales," *USA Today,* May 13, 2003.
9. Bernard Condon, "Banking on Brashness," *Forbes,* August 16, 2004.
10. Peter Montoya and Tim Vandehey, *The Brand Called You,* ©2004.
11. Effective Seminar/Conference Marketing, Ralph D. Elliot, PhD, vice Provost for Off-Campus Distance and Continuing Education, Clemson University, South Carolina, http://odce.clemson.edu/esm/inhouse.htm.

CHAPTER 7 Planning for Your Brand

1. QuoteDB.com and ThomasEdison.com.
2. Interview with Tim Sheehy, president of Milwaukee Metropolitan Association of Commerce, Fox Point, Wisconsin, March 2004.
3. Interview with Phil Vischer, creator and founder of VeggieTales, July 2004.
4. C. S. Lewis, *The Inspirational Writings of C. S. Lewis*, Inspirational Press, 1987.

CHAPTER 8 Getting Results from Your Brand

1. BrainyQuote.com.
2. Interview with "Van"Cronkhite, author, in Milwaukee, Wisconsin, February 2004.
3. Interview with Pete Fisher, businessman, brand expert, and general manager of the Grand Ole Opry, spring of 2003.
4. Brian Tracy, *Victory! Applying the Proven Principles of Military Strategy to Achieve Greater Success in Your Business and Personal Life.*
5. Liz Murray Garrigan, "800-Pound Gorilla Rattles the Cage," *City Limits*, February 20, 2003.
6. Charles Darwin, Darwin.com.
7. Michael Meyer, "Recipe for Success," *USA Weekend*, July 18–20, 2003.
8. QuoteDB.com and ThomasEdison.com.
9. Brainyquotes.com.

CHAPTER 9 Sustaining the Results You Get from Your Brand

1. QuoteDB.com.
2. www.itsjustlunch.com, *Southwest Airlines Spirit*, August 2003.
3. Quoteland.com.
4. John Bloom, UPI, National Review Online, *Forbes*, March 31, 2003.
5. Robert S. Greenberger, "Victoria's Secret Loses Court Case on Use of Name," *Wall Street Journal*, March 6, 2003.
6. Ibid.

CHAPTER 10 Conclusion—Back to You

1. Norman Vincent Peale, *The Power of Positive Thinking*, Random House, Prentice Hall, 1952.
2. BrainyQuote.com.

3. "LeAnn Rhymes, Standing Up to the Spotlight," *Self*, June 2003.
4. Rudyard Kipling speech, February 14, 1923.
5. Quoteland.com.
6. Brainyquote.com.

Internet Reference Sources

anthonyrobbins.com

baseball-almanac.com

buildingbrands.com

cmaworld.com

crosswalk.com

dga.com

fastcompany.com

forbes.com

fsb.com

grokdotcom

hbsp.harvard.edu

history.org

inc.com

itsjustlunch.com

justdisney.com

MarketingProfs.com

opinionresearch.com

Petermontoya.com

scottjeffrey.com

self.com

sethgodin.com

wizardacademy.com

Index

About the Author

Chris Hilicki is an expert brand builder, founder of Dalmatian Press (one of the nation's largest children's publishers), national speaker, television personality, world traveler, and self-growth enthusiast, and author of *May I Have Your Attention, Please?*

As a scientist-turned-publisher she has helped to create patented products and best-selling children's titles. A survivor and conqueror of several life-threatening diseases and events, she inspires and motivates many people to persevere and succeed. Chris' most important mission is to affect lives so that people learn to like and love themselves, ultimately becoming more valuable and successful in the world.

Find out more about Chris and how you can build a better future at www.hilicki.com.